NIGHTMARE IN BARI

THE WORLD WAR II
LIBERTY SHIP
POISON GAS DISASTER
AND COVERUP

NIGHTMARE IN BARI

THE WORLD WAR II LIBERTY SHIP POISON GAS DISASTER AND COVERUP

by

Gerald Reminick

THE GLENCANNON PRESS

PALO ALTO
2001

Published by The Glencannon Press
P.O. Box 341, Palo Alto, CA 94302
Tel. 800-711-8985
www.glencannon.com

First Edition, first printing.

Library of Congress Cataloging-in-Publication Data

Reminick, Gerald, 1943-
    Nightmare in Bari : the World War II Liberty ship poison
gas disaster and coverup / by Gerald Reminick
        p. cm.
    Includes bibliographical references and index.
    ISBN 1-889901-21-0 (pbk. :alk. paper)
    1. Bombing, Aerial--Italy--Bari--History--20th century. 2. John Harvey
(Liberty ship) 3. Bari (Italy)--History, Military--20th century. 4. World
War, 1939-1945--Aerial operations, German. 5. World War, 1939-1945-
-Chemical warfare--Italy--Bari. 6. Mustard gas. 7. Chemical weapons dis-
posal. I. Title

    D763.I82 B377 2001
    970.54'215751--dc21
                                                      2001033483

ACKNOWLEDGEMENTS

There are many people who have helped me in my quest to write *Nightmare In Bari; the World War II Liberty Ship Poison Gas Disaster and Coverup.* A very special thank you is in order to the following people for their support: Professor Joyce Gabriele, who is my colleague and editor; Matthew Loughran, Historian of the North Atlantic Chapter of the American Merchant Marine Veterans and Leroy C. Heinse, whose survival at Bari was the inspiration for this book.

I would like to thank all the United States Merchant Marine and Naval Armed Guard Veterans who contributed their stories about Bari. Without their heroic experiences, this book couldn't be written.

A sincere note of appreciation is owed to the following people who contributed advice, stories, photographs, translation assistance, special documents, and interlibrary loan assistance: Edward Aho, Bernard Anderson, Thomas Basick, Myron Boluch, Thomas Bowerman, Warren Brandenstein, Teresa

Carlucci, Don Gritton, Jr., Juel Hansen, Jr., Dan and Toni Horodysky, Dominic Iannone, Charles Lloyd, Russell Krenciprock, Karel Margry, Capt. Arthur Moore, Dolores Perillo, James E. Smith, George Southern, Luca Ursini, John White, Jr., and John Whitley.

I would like to thank the following organizations for their assistance: The Caxton Press for allowing me to use a portion of *Kia-Kaha: Life At 3 New Zealand General Hospital 1940-1946*, written by E.M. Somers Cocks; Nimbus Publishing Ltd., and author, Gwladys M. Rees Aikens for permission to use a portion of *Nurses In Battledress: The World War II Story of a member of the Q.A. Reserves*; the Libraries of Suffolk County Community College; the United States Merchant Marine Academy Library; and the U.S. Military History Institute.

I would like to thank my family for their encouragement and support along with my colleagues at the Suffolk County Community College Library.

Finally, a special thanks for my editor, Bill Harris, for his skill and patience in bringing this book to fruition.

Dedicated to all the brave men and women
who died on December 2, 1943.
It is for those who survived
to tell the story of their escape from Hell.

Contents

1

BARI, ITALY
DECEMBER 2, 1943
7:30 PM

Bari lies along the relatively calm Adriatic Sea, at the top of the heel of the boot of Italy. Two hundred thousand people lived there during World War II. The city was comprised of an old medieval section with narrow streets and small houses and a newer section begun in the nineteenth century. Because of Bari's location and good climate, it has always been an important commercial shipping center.

On the evening of December 2, 1943, a baseball game was being played between two American service teams before a crowd at the "Bambino" Stadium in the Port of Bari. The stadium was named as a reward to the citizens of Bari for having the most male births in Italy. The war-weary populace was thankful that the Germans were retreating and the streets were crowded with people strolling, dining, greeting one another and enjoying the anticipation of the coming holidays.

Bari lies on the Adriatic, at the top of the heel of the boot of Italy.

Approximately fifty ships lay in the busy port, most of them waiting for their cargoes to be unloaded. These valuable supplies would support the final Allied thrust in Italy. So many ships were lined up along the sea wall, the piers and moored in the water that they almost touched each other. Some had unloaded and were waiting to depart through the breakwater entrance.

Late that afternoon, a convoy of American ships entered the harbor, their way lit by lights from shoreside cranes. Destroyers and mine sweepers darted in and out of the harbor protecting the ships and making sure the entrance was clear of mines. Security should have been tighter, but the British had become lackadaisical about defending the port. Germany was retreating and no longer considered an offensive threat. The primary concern of the Allies was to rid the port of mines left behind by the Nazis. These still created havoc with arriving freighters, their explosions causing many deaths and wrecked ships.

Suddenly, seeming to appear from thin air, the German Luftwaffe thundered down out of a clear evening sky, skimmed

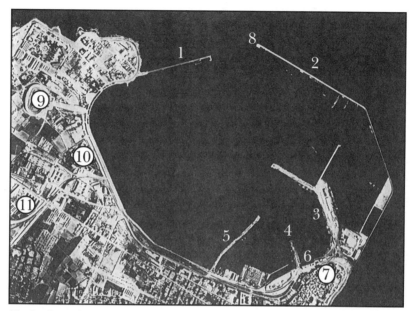

The harbor of Bari, a few months before the attack. 1. West Jetty. 2. East Jetty. 3. Vecchio Molo Foraneo. 4. Molo San Vito. 5. Molo Pizzoli. 6. The Stazione Marittima which housed the Allied War Shipping Administration Office. 7. Old Fort, the Port Director's Office. 8. Lighthouse. 9. "Bambino" Stadium. 10. U.S. 5th General Depot. 11. 4th Medical Supply Depot.

along just above the ships and laid waste to the busy port. It was 7:30 P.M. In the span of twenty minutes, the raid became the worst bombing of Allied shipping since Pearl Harbor two years earlier.

A total of seventeen Allied ships were destroyed. Five were U.S. Liberty ships: SS *John Bascom,* SS *John Harvey,* SS *John L. Motley,* SS *Joseph Wheeler,* and the SS *Samuel J. Tilden.* In addition, four British ships *(Devon Coast, Fort Athabaska, Lars Kruse, Testbank)* three Norwegian ships *(Bollsta, Lom, Norlom)* three Italian ships *(Barletta, Cassala, Frosinone)* and two Polish ships *(Puck, Lwow)* were demolished. Six other merchant ships were seriously damaged; the American *Lyman Abbott,* the British *Brittany Coast, Crista, Fort Lajoie,* the Dutch *Odysseus,* and the Norwegian *Vest.* Two smaller vessels, the Italian *Inaffondable* and the Yugoslavian *Yug* were also sent to the bottom.

Lungomare Nazario Sauro in Bari as it appeared before the war. The December 2 attack on the town turned it to rubble. Courtesy Karl Hamberger.

But the attack and subsequent destruction were only preludes of the horror to come. A U.S. Liberty ship laden with a top-secret cargo of mustard gas bombs received a direct hit and exploded, killing the entire crew and spreading the deadly toxic chemical across the water and through the air of Bari.

The success of the Luftwaffe attack was stunning. They destroyed or seriously damaged twenty-five out of approximately fifty ships in the crowded harbor. The first Allied invasion of Europe suffered a major setback. The loss of life was appalling. More than one thousand Allied servicemen and more than one thousand civilians were killed. The total number of deaths will never be known. In the horror and confusion records of treatment were poorly kept, if at all. In addition, many survivors of the initial bombing later died from toxic contamination but their deaths were not attributed to the attack.

Yet, to this day, few people know of the disaster at Bari.

2

THE ATTACK

Reports of possible German use of gas warfare reached President Franklin Roosevelt after Italian dictator Benito Mussolini's arrest in 1943. This, despite the fact that chemical warfare was looked on with revulsion after its use in the first World War and, in fact, was outlawed by the Geneva Gas Protocol of 1925.*

With the rest of the civilized world, FDR opposed chemical warfare, but knew the necessity of being prepared should the enemy use it.

> ... there have been reports that one or more of the Axis powers were seriously contemplating the use of poisonous or noxious gases or other inhumane devices of warfare. I have been loathe to believe that any nation, even our present enemies, could or would be willing to loose upon mankind such terrible and inhumane weapons.

---

* Although the United States did not sign the Protocol, it agreed to abide by it.

However, evidence that the Axis powers are making significant preparations indicative of such an intention is being reported with increasing frequency from a variety of sources. Use of such weapons have been outlawed by the general opinion of civilized mankind. This country has not used them, and I hope that we will never be compelled to use them. I state categorically that we shall under no circumstances resort to the use of such weapons unless they are first used by our enemies.

As President of the United States and Commander-in-Chief of the American armed forces, I want to make clear beyond all doubt to any of our enemies contemplating a resort to such desperate and barbarous methods that acts of this nature committed against any one of the United Nations will be regarded as having been committed against the United States itself and will be treated accordingly. We promise to any perpetrators of such crime full and swift retaliation in kind and I feel obliged now to warn the Axis armies and the Axis peoples in Europe and in Asia that the terrible consequence of any use of these inhumane methods on their part will be brought down swiftly and surely upon their own heads. Any use of poison gas by any Axis power, therefore, will immediately be followed by the fullest retaliation upon munition centers, seaports, and other military objectives throughout the whole extent of the territory of such Axis country.[1]

Retaliation meant having the weapons on hand in various theaters of battle. Chemical gas supplies were therefore necessary in the event Germany decided to initiate its use against the Allied thrust up the Italian peninsula and into Europe. Bari, now under Allied control, was the logical port of entry for the deadly chemicals. In addition, it was believed the nearby airfield of Foggia would provide air support.

The British, in charge of the port, defined their operational policy regarding poisonous gas in the following "minute dated 17 October 43" to G-4 (A) the Assistant Chief of Staff, G-3, AFHQ:

> Progressively build up over the next three months a stock of CW [Chemical Warfare] reserves on the Italian mainland equivalent to

approx 15 days supply, i.e., to complete approx 15 days supply by 1 Feb. Thereafter to conform to the general ammunition policy as it exists at that time.[2]

To conform with this policy, a memorandum was addressed on 29 Oct by NAASC to C-in-C AFHQ stating that the following tonnage was required by the [British] Air Force 'for maintenance of Italy' during the period 23 Nov to 2 Dec 43:

"For Bari Area:
Ordinance bombs and ammunition (US) 5500 tons Oran."[3]

President Roosevelt then authorized the confidential shipment of 2,000 (M47AZ) 100 lb. mustard gas bombs to Bari. The bombs, measuring four feet long by eighteen inches in diameter, were manufactured in the Edgewater Arsenal in Maryland. They were shipped through the Eastern Chemical Warfare Depot to Curtis Bay Depot of Baltimore by train and into the port of Baltimore for loading aboard ship.

First Lieutenant Howard D. Beckstrom was placed in charge of six enlisted men from the 701st Chemical Maintenance Company. His job was to shepherd the bombs to their final destination. Transporting these bombs was hazardous and required constant observation.

The maintenance, storage, and shipment of such toxics involved a number of special problems arising from the nature of the materials. Mustard itself required particular attention. In the form produced during World War II, the so-called Levinstein H mustard contained about 30 percent of unstable impurities which caused trouble when it was left in storage for any length of time. It evolved gases at a rate that sometimes built up dangerous amounts of pressure within the bomb casings where it was often kept. Handlers had to learn techniques for testing pressures in the containers, venting them when necessary, and cleaning them when drained.[4]

The men selected were: Sergeant Broadus J. Jamerson, Privates 1st Class Bennie G. Taylor, Charles N. Thompson, Frederick Wilson and Privates Wilson Bodie and William Tensley. Lieutenant Thomas A. Richardson was assigned the role of cargo officer in charge of security. All the men were well trained in the handling of bombs and toxic warfare chemicals.

According to Glenn B. Infield's definitive book, *Disaster At Bari,* the Liberty ship SS *John Harvey* was selected to carry the deadly cargo to Italy. This is at odds with a British Most Secret Document claiming that, "The mustard bombs were loaded on the *John Harvey* at Oran, originated in the USA, and had been discharged previously at Oran. The *John Harvey* did not bring any toxic ammunition from the USA to Oran."[5]

In direct contradiction to the British document is the fact that the *John Harvey's* manifest stating it had mustard gas bombs on board was sent from Oran via air to the British Transportation Officer in Bari.

The SS *John Harvey's* keel was laid in December of 1942. It took only forty-four days to build her and she was christened by Miss Margaret Grover on January 19, 1943. The ship's namesake had been a member of the Continental Congress and one of the signers of the Articles of Confederation.

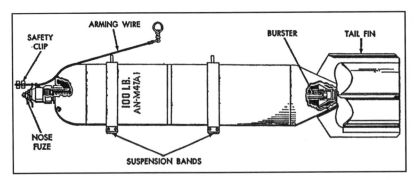

The M47A1 mustard bomb was filled with 68.5 lbs. of liquid mustard. The inside of the case of the A1 type was painted with black, acid-proof paint, that of the A2 was coated with oil. After the Battle *Magazine.*

The *John Harvey* was owned by the Agwilines Company of New York. Captain Elwin Foster Knowles, a well-seasoned master, was her only commanding officer. He received his baptism of battle on a previous mission to Murmansk, Russia as master of the SS *Ozark*. Captain Knowles was not told that he was carrying a top-secret cargo. However, it is unlikely that an experienced captain would not be aware what was taking place aboard his own ship.

The *John Harvey* sailed into Baltimore on September 30, 1943 and loaded the deadly cargo between that date and October 8, when she sailed to Norfolk, Virginia arriving the next day. She then sailed from Norfolk on October 15, 1943 and arrived in Oran, North Africa on November 2. While in Oran, most of her cargo was discharged and additional cargo consisting of ammunition was loaded.

However, not all of her cargo was discharged. The bombs containing the mustard gas remained on board. If one believes the British Most Secret Document it is possible that more mustard gas bombs were loaded at Oran. The *John Harvey* then departed Oran on November 19 in a convoy of forty ships. This convoy arrived in Port Augusta, Sicily, on November 25. The next day the ship departed in another convoy of thirty ships with half of this number sailing to Taranto. The *John Harvey* arrived in Bari, Italy on November 28 and was moored at Berth 29 on the East Jetty of the harbor.

During the next five days, Lieutenant Richardson made several attempts to have his cargo unloaded. Captain Knowles even accompanied Richardson on several visits to encourage the authorities at the War Shipping Administration Office to expedite the removal of the deadly cargo, but to no avail. Lieutenant Richardson had been sworn to secrecy and could not reveal his cargo's contents to the British who were in charge of the port. Lt. Richardson believed, "Apart from the military personnel aboard the *John Harvey*, no one else in Bari Harbour, not even the British Port Director, knew of the mustard bombs."[6]

Meanwhile, during the previous week, a German ME-210 reconnaissance plane flew over Bari repeatedly, taking photographs that were developed and rushed to Field Marshal Freiherr von Richthofen's headquarters. It had been decided that to halt the Allied build-up for the push northward into Italy, the Port of Bari must be destroyed. The photographs were for final target analysis.

Captain A.B. Jenks of the Office of Harbor Defense was worried about the spy plane, particularly because the Germans had recently increased their air attacks on the Allies. "For three days now a German reconnaissance plane had been over the city taking pictures. They're just waiting for the proper time to come over here and dump this place into the Adriatic."[7]

Captain Jenks' fear was magnified after hearing an arrogant statement made by the commanding officer of the British Air Force, Air Marshal Sir Arthur Coningham. It was his responsibility to support the British Eighth Army and its advance. In a press conference on the afternoon of December 2, Coningham tried to reassure the attendees that the German Air Force had been defeated, and would not be problematic again in the area. "I would regard it as a personal affront and insult if the Luftwaffe would attempt any significant action in this area."[8] His attitude was reflected in the complacency of those overseeing harbor operations and by the almost complete lack of defensive weaponry. There was only one British antiaircraft squadron operating one 40mm Bofors gun. Its guidance system had been erected on top of the Margherita Theatre at the waterfront of the Porto Vecchio. It was not working and on the night of the attack was still undergoing repairs.

The major problem was the lack of air support defending Bari. RAF fighters stationed at Foggia were occupied supporting Allied bombing runs into Germany.

Compounding the lack of harbor defense was the fact that Naval Armed Guard contingents aboard American Liberty ships were ordered not to fire at enemy aircraft. Ensign Kay Vesole, in

The radar installation which controlled Bari's antiaircraft gun was located on the roof of the Margherita Theater, on the waterfront of the Porto Vecchio. It was being repaired the night of the attack with the result that the gun crews had no warning until the bombers were overhead. After the Battle *Magazine.*

charge of the Armed Guard aboard the SS *John Bascom,* was told by a British officer, "in case of enemy air attack he was not to open fire until bombs were actually dropped. Then he was to co-ordinate his fire with a radar-controlled shore gun firing white tracers."[9]

This coordinating was to be done with the single gun whose guidance system was undergoing repair.

In the official accounts, the estimate of the number of German planes that attacked Bari range from thirty to over one-hundred JU-88s. The number is more likely around fifty. The mission began from several airfields in Northern Italy. Immediately before the attack the Germans dropped tin foil (Duppel), also known as Window, to jam radar facilities. The bombers then came in below the radar screens at about 200 mph and dropped their bombs in a horizontal arc. This technique was called the "Swedish Turnip System." It was based on the principle that it is easier to hit a ship when it is showing its beam, which naturally presents a larger target.

The following scene would be indelibly etched in one's mind had they been viewing Bari Harbor at 7:30 P.M. on the clear night of December 2: the faint but ever increasing sound of aircraft flying toward the harbor, tinfoil floating and landing like silver snowflakes and parachute flares suddenly lighting up the entire city and harbor. Then the piercing, whining screams as the JU-88s began their runs.

The American Liberty ships were lined up like dominoes. First hit was the *Joseph Wheeler*, then the *John L. Motley* and the *John Harvey*. All three were set on fire. The *John L. Motley*, carrying ammunition, was the first ship to explode, creating a giant tidal wave in the harbor.

Then came the horrific explosion of the *John Harvey*.

> The blast completely ripped apart the mass of inhabitants of the Old City that had crowded along the shore. Behind them, houses were folded up like cardboard dolls-houses and collapsed into heaps of rubble. Many died without knowing what happened. Farther away, the blast knocked down people in streets, unhinged doors and shutters and blew in the windows of almost every building in the city. The concussion was felt at some points 20 miles or more from the harbor.[10]
>
> From the depths of the harbor leaped a vast fountain of flame with multicolored jets streaming from its rim. It rose more than a thousand yards into the air. The blackness above it was slashed with streams of crimson, pink, rose, orange and green, and then in a terrible blast that succeeded this awful flash, everyone standing within a mile around was knocked flat and breathless.[11]
>
> Ray Bennet, a Royal Engineers captain, was standing with his sergeant in the small village of San Spirito when the explosion occurred. They were knocked off their feet and the bolted depot door behind them was blasted open. The village lies some five miles from Bari.[12]

In an action report filed after the bombing by the USS *Aroostock,* the explosion was described:

At about 2100 the ammunition ship at berth 28 or 29, exploded, sending flame debris, and smoke that appeared to be at least 6,000 to 8,000 feet into the air. This explosion was felt as far as sixty-two (62) miles away, and the damage to ships, harbour installations, and buildings throughout the city as a result of the explosion was great.[13]

Other ships were hit and caught fire. An oil line on a harbor quay was ruptured causing fires to spread. In addition to the bombs, flaming chunks of jagged metal and shrapnel rained down like confetti. While all this occurred the deadly mustard gas aboard the *John Harvey* mixed with the harbor water and vaporized in the air. The ship itself simply disappeared, along with her military contingent that could identify her cargo.

Soon thereafter the overcrowded hospitals, still not fully equipped because many of the supplies they needed were on the damaged or destroyed Liberty ships, began receiving casualties. Men were brought in with horrible burns, gaping wounds, many covered with toxic, oil-soaked water. The citizens of Bari were turned away. There was no time to record admitting information.

Questions abounded. Why had the attack occurred and why were the wounded showing symptoms of mysterious burns and sickness? No answers were forthcoming. The British, in charge of the port, denied they knew anything about mustard gas. In fact, Prime Minister Winston Churchill continued denying the fact even years after the war ended. The United States tried to cover up the incident.

Two weeks later, the *Washington Post* broke the story.

Secretary of War Stinson apparently had intended to release a few details at his weekly press conference. But after the *Post* story, newsmen found him sizzling. His anger seemed greater than it was justified by a mere premature news "leak." He was brusque, stiff, and cut the conference short. When a reporter wanted to know if the Allies had actually been napping, Stimson snapped: "No! I will not comment on this thing!"[14]

The doors of Hell were flung open on the night of December 2, 1943. The scene inside was surreal and horrible. The attack is known as "Little Pearl Harbor."

3

THE MEDITERRANEAN THEATER AND NORTH AFRICA 1941-1943:

A BRIEF OVERVIEW

Italy's Objectives

Benito Mussolini dreamed of restoring to Italy the grandeur that was Imperial Rome. He planned to conquer and expel the British from the Mediterranean. In October, 1935 he invaded Africa, thrusting that continent, an area which had remained fairly tranquil until then, into the Second World War.

Mussolini's attempt at colonial expansion was doomed from the beginning because the Italian army was neither properly trained nor equipped. Much of its equipment was obsolete and its armored units lacked heavy-duty vehicles. Italian armed forces were also handicapped by poor internal communication. The Italian navy was in better condition, possessing modern battleships, cruisers, destroyers and a flotilla of submarines. But, again, poorly trained commanders and seamen made for an inept fighting force. And, finally, Allied air superiority neutralized the

Italian navy when the British destroyed a large part of the Italian fleet in a surprise attack on the Taranto naval base.

Germany's Objectives

Germany's grand design was to make the African continent, especially the central part, subservient to her authority. Originally, this was to occur once she successfully conquered and controlled Europe. Hitler expected Mussolini to fight in the northern and northeast parts of Africa with a threefold objective: gain control of the Suez Canal, control the flow of oil from that region and control shipping in the Mediterranean. Once this was accomplished the assumption was that the Arab nations would come to the side of the Axis. But the decision on how to achieve this became one of the factors that turned the war against Germany.

Adolph Hitler did not necessarily expect to destroy the British empire. British possessions stretched from the Mediterranean to the Far East. Hitler's plan was to beat England into submission through bombing and submarine warfare, then impose a treaty which would give Germany access to the far-reaching British Empire. He did not have the resources to achieve German colonial aspirations while also conquering British possessions.

In 1940, Russia rejected Hitler's offer of a treaty. This forced him to invade the Balkans to ensure access to its rich oil reserves and raw materials, diverting manpower and machinery that might have been used in the Mediterranean.

Germany had two potential strategies in the Mediterranean, one was to attack Gibraltar, thus sealing off the mouth of the Mediterranean. Control of the Mediterranean would prevent the Allies from attacking Germany from the south. However, it also meant that Germany would have to protect and defend a large sea and the countries bordering thereon. Capture of Gibraltar required the cooperation of Spain's General Franco and Franco and Hitler never reached agreement on the point, even after Hitler offered part of French Morocco in exchange for Franco's aid.

The second strategy was to defend Germany only as far as the Northern Apennines in Italy, leaving the areas farther south to Mussolini, and to invade Russia. In the end, this is what Hitler did. But Mussolini forced him to divert his attention and resources when Italy began losing territory it had won in Africa.

Hitler did not want to forfeit Axis gains. In 1941 he sent Field Marshal Erwin Rommel to North Africa to rescue the Italian army.

> From a strategic point of view, Rommel's North African campaign was an operation simply hanging in the air, as neither his line of retreat nor his supply line was secure. The Afrika Korps could not be kept going by a few ships and inadequate transport by air ...[1]

Eventually, in 1943, Italy surrendered and the Allies gained a foothold on the ground and quickly gained air superiority over the region. More important, it made Germany vulnerable from the south.

> ... in the Mediterranean theatre, Luftwaffe losses had escalated from year to year against Allied air forces of ever growing strength; that finally the always inadequate resources allocated for the task had failed to protect the homeland against the strategic bombing offensive ...[2]

By diverting troops, planes and armor to North Africa, Hitler further weakened Germany's position in the European theater. This diversion, and the decision to march on Russia eventually proved to be catastrophic to the Third Reich. The Suez Canal remained in Allied control and badly needed supplies and war materials reached Russia through the Canal, providing Russia an avenue for materiel in addition to the treacherous Murmansk* run with which to resist Germany.

---

* The northern supply route to Russia went past Iceland, Norway and through the Barents Sea to Murmansk and Archangel. It was extremely hazardous in winter and the danger was compounded by constant attacks from U-boats and the Luftwaffe.

England's Objectives

At the Arcadia Conference held in Washington, D.C. in December 1941, following the attack on Pearl Harbor, Britain and the U.S. declared the wartime goals of the Western Allies. A joint resolution declaring total economic cooperation was adopted to ensure the defeat of Germany and Japan. Britain envisioned a calculated tightening around Germany that would eventually cause her collapse. As Allied bombers pounded the Nazis from the west, the east and the south, manpower and supplies would be built up by the U.S. for a final push in a cross-Channel invasion.

Britain viewed Italy as the

> 'ulcer' draining away Hitler's strength ... If the Axis began to falter, the Allied armies in the Mediterranean would be poised to throw open Germany's back door and should be able to forestall the Russians in Central Europe. There should be no need to repeat the unimaginative Western Front strategy of the First World War. No major landings would be needed in France until Germany showed signs of collapse.[3]

Britain's goal was to continue the conflict in the Mediterranean, isolate Italy, and continue controlling the Suez Canal and the oil fields in the Middle East.

The United States' Objectives

The American design for defeating Germany was in direct contrast to that of the British. According to the military leaders, the "events of the First World War had confirmed them in their dislike of the indirect strategy preferred by the British. The Kaiser's Germany had been defeated by direct assault."[4]

The United States had tremendous economic resources and a labor force that was working around the clock. The defeat of Germany in the fastest possible way was the main objective. Once this was accomplished, they could concentrate on the defeat of Japan. The shortest route to Germany's defeat would be a massive build up of forces and supplies via the Atlantic Ocean to Britain and then an all-out invasion crossing the English Channel.

The U.S. originally wanted this invasion to commence with an operation known as "Sledgehammer" in September 1942. A small force of British troops would be landed in the Fall followed by a cross-Channel invasion by the U.S., called "Bolero-Roundup," in the spring of 1943. However, an agreement between Britain and the U.S. could not be reached and the American Joint Chiefs of Staff asked Roosevelt to scuttle the plan.

The War In North Africa

In August 1940, Mussolini's troops moved eastward from Ethiopia and overran the British in British Somaliland in two weeks. On September 13, a second Italian army moved eastward through Libya and invaded Egypt, driving almost sixty miles into the interior toward the Suez Canal.

However, the British were able to take back the territory by the following summer. This enraged Hitler because he had offered Mussolini the assistance of German troops which Mussolini refused. Further compounding the situation, Mussolini took it upon himself to invade Greece in October. His motive was to show Hitler his indignation at not being included in Germany's war planning. But the Italian army was quickly repelled by Greece, further angering Hitler.

Meanwhile, Italy and then Germany, become involved in a seesaw battle with the Allies for the control of North Africa that lasted two years. The British army defeated and trapped the Italian army in Libya with more than 125,000 Italians captured in February 1941, causing Hitler to send Field Marshal Erwin Rommel into the area in March 1941 with his Afrika Korps.

In addition, Mussolini's naval fleet was nearly destroyed in two British air attacks. The first attack occurred at the naval base at Taranto and the second at Cape Matapan, Greece.

During the summer of 1942, the Afrika Korps under Rommel and the British Eighth Army under General Bernard 'Monty' Montgomery waged an all-out back and forth battle which lasted into September. The British held their position. Rommel ran out of fuel, was short on tanks; his men were exhausted, and his troops were constantly subjected to aerial attacks.

In July 1942 "Operation Torch" was agreed upon by Roosevelt and Churchill. Both leaders decided it was important to get the American ground forces into action and to invade North Africa. The invasion of North Africa was set for November 1942. This pleased the British and Stalin because another front would take pressure off the (Russian) Eastern front. The American military advisors, General Dwight D. Eisenhower in particular, were furious. They felt Operation Torch would siphon manpower and equipment from their main objective — the invasion of Europe across the English Channel. The diversionary plan was successful, however, pulling much-needed German manpower from the Russian front in Europe.

During 1942 the war against Germany reached its turning point. The U.S. economy was on a twenty-four hour, seven day-a-week production basis. A large part of the labor force was made up of women who took over the responsibility of making the wartime equipment, munitions, and supplies for the American fighting forces and merchant marine.

> Within a year after Pearl Harbor, U.S. War production equaled that of all the Axis nations together and by the beginning of 1943 was well ahead of that of the Axis powers. During the war the United States manufactured 296,000 planes, 87,000 tanks and 2.4 million trucks, as well as millions of rifles and millions of tons of artillery shells. From January 1, 1942, the nation produced 28 million U.S. tons of shipping, enabling the Allies to replace vessels lost to the enemy.[5]

Vital shipping across the Atlantic to Britain increased as the war against the U-boat turned in the Allies' favor. The German army was stalled at Stalingrad and put on a defensive retreat. And the Allies gained air superiority over Europe.

In September 1942, General Montgomery forced Rommel to retreat to Tripoli in Libya. As November 1942 unfolded "Operation Torch" was put into action. Over 100,000 Allied troops landed in Casablanca, Oran, and Algeria. The Allies had the opportunity to attack Rommel from the west as, in a pincer movement, he was pursued by the British Eighth Army from the east. The Allies captured these cities as well as the French Vichy naval fleet at Casablanca. The next step was to capture Tunis and Bizerte. Success meant the Allies would soon be at Italy's back door.

However, American tanks were not able to stand up to the more heavily armored German tanks and supplies ran out. As Winter approached, rather than slog it out in inclement weather, Eisenhower decided to wait until the rainy season was over.

In January 1943, Rommel defeated the Americans at Kasserine Pass and broke through into Algeria. However, Rommel retreated after General Dwight Eisenhower's troops set up a defensive action and was caught in yet another battle with the British Eighth Army. The British won, Rommel was recalled by Hitler.

Major General George Patton had molded the American 2nd Corps into a fierce fighting machine. The U.S. and British forces raced toward the retreating Afrika Korps in March 1943, capturing Tunisia. Although many Germans escaped via the ports of Bizerte and Tunis to Sicily, one quarter of a million Axis troops surrendered and the Axis occupation of North Africa ended on May 13, 1943.

4

THE MEDITERRANEAN THEATER: SICILY AND ITALY 1943

At the Casablanca conference in January 1943 Churchill and Roosevelt agreed that Germany was first to be defeated in North Africa. Sicily was designated as the next offensive in the Mediterranean theater and the cross-Channel invasion would be delayed until the spring of 1944.

Stalin refused to attend the conference because he wanted a southern assault against Germany in 1942 to relieve the pressure on Russia.

Roosevelt tried to assuage Stalin's concerns by declaring that Germany's surrender would be "unconditional." This appeased Stalin, who feared that Britain and the United States would arrange a bilateral peace agreement with Germany that would exclude Russian participation. In May 1943, Churchill and Roosevelt finalized plans for the invasion of Sicily at the Trident Conference. The cross-Channel invasion was tentatively planned to be in May 1944.

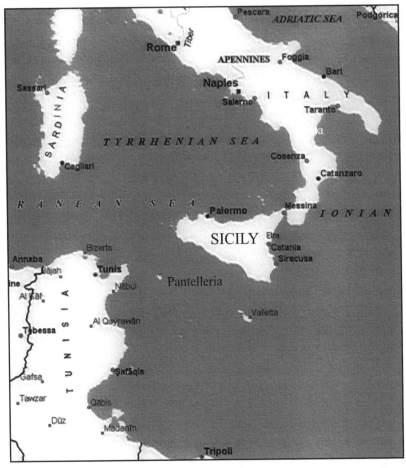

The invasion of Sicily was the beginning of the Allied thrust toward Southern Germany.

Sicily, the largest island in the Mediterranean, covers 10,000 square miles. It was a strategic objective because of its size and location. Capturing Sicily meant greater security for ships carrying supplies and war materials through the Mediterranean because the Luftwaffe's power could be controlled. Also, it was hoped that capture of the island might persuade Italy to surrender. If that happened, bombardment of both Germany and the strategic oil fields of the Balkans could be conducted from Italy. The attack on Sicily became known as "Operation Husky," under the command of British General Harold Alexander who served under General Eisenhower, the Supreme Allied Commander.

On May 18, 1943, the small island of Pantelleria was bombed to clear the way for the invasion of Sicily. By mid-June the Allies were in control of all the islands between Tunisia and Sicily. The airborne and seaborne invasions of Sicily occurred on July 9 and 10.

Field Marshal Kesselring moved four German units in to defend the island and Field Marshal von Richthofen took over command of the German Second Air Force in the Mediterranean. But von Richthofen's task proved too difficult; the theater was large and Germany no longer had Italian air support.

General Montgomery attacked the eastern part of Sicily with U.S. General Patton assigned to support the British attack. Patton, however, had other ideas. After landing at Gela and Licata his Seventh Army raced to the northwest and captured Palermo on July 22. Meanwhile, Montgomery was stalled in a stubborn German defense on the eastern coastal road. The two Allied armies eventually met in Messina on August 17, but most of the German army escaped across the Straits to the Italian mainland three miles away.

The Italian economy was in a shambles as industry crumbled and food was rationed. Popular support for Mussolini evaporated and the Fascist party turned on Il Duce. Arresting Mussolini, they removed him from office. Pietro Badoglio was made head of the Italian government and the Germans subsequently seized control of the Italian military sites.

After the fall of Sicily it was necessary to capture and control the ports of Augusta, Palermo, and Syracuse. Success there allowed for the creation of staging areas to assemble the war goods necessary for the invasion of the Italian mainland.

The Attack on Italy

Commander-in-Chief of the German army, Albert Kesselring, designed a three pronged plan to defend Italy. The southern part

(Toe and Heel) of Italy was to be defended by General Herr's LXXXVI Panzer Corps. This could prove hazardous if the Allies decided to invade farther north, cutting General Herr off from the remainder of the German defense. The middle section was to be defended by General Hube's XIV Panzer Corps. His responsibility was to hold the area from Naples to Foggia. The third and final section was the XI Para Corps, responsible for defending the area from Rome northward.

There were three objectives confronting Supreme Allied Commander Eisenhower after the fall of Sicily: to capture Corsica, Sardinia, and Italy. Once Italy fell, continued pressure would force German reinforcements to be pulled from the Russian front to defend Italy. It was also critically important to divert attention from the D-day preparations.

Pietro Badoglio signed an armistice with the Allies on September 3, but it was not announced until September 8. On that date the British Eighth Army crossed the Messina Strait and invaded the "Toe" at Reggio di Calabria, the Pizzo area, and Taranto, the "Heel." Their objective was to sever "the Boot" from Foggia to Salerno and move up the Italian mainland, securing the east coast from Brindisi to Bari. Once accomplished, the British Eighth Army could be supplied through the ports of Taranto, Brindisi, and Bari.

As these invasions took place, Italy's surrender was declared. The Allies were gratified, but the timing of the announcement was poor. Some of the determination and drive was lost in the Allies' offensive thrust; worse, it created greater determination on the part of the German army.

On the morning of September 9, 1943 the U.S. Fifth Army under General Mark Clark landed at Salerno, to capture Naples. This port was the key to supplying the American army on the west coast of Italy. As the Fifth was landing, so was the British Eighth. This was the Allies' first breach of "*Festung Europa.*"

The invasion of Naples was chaotic; over five hundred Allied ships were assembled off-shore loaded with supplies for Clark's army. The warships shelled the Germans, entrenched in their positions on the mainland. In turn, the Luftwaffe bombed the Allied ships and strafed the beaches. A furious battle ensued with the Germans counterattacking from September 11 through 17. The Germans were well-prepared and supported by tanks.

The Americans barely gained a foothold on the Salerno beach, the 2nd U.S. Battalion of the 143rd Infantry suffering staggering losses. Lieutenant Commander Frank C. Crismer USNR described the fierce fighting:

> As I stepped out onto the beach an armored car was hit and started to blaze. I turned, and stumbled over a soldier. I stopped to apologize, and saw that he was dead. One could barely move in any direction without stumbling over the American, British and German dead ... In the fields the cattle had been killed, by machine-gun crossfire and artillery. Where hand-to-hand fighting had taken place, the dead lay sprawled ...[1]

On September 13, the Germans broke through, but were repelled by the Allied ships' off-shore shelling. Eventually, on September 17, the Allies prevailed. As the Germans retreated from Salerno, Allied battle plans were made: a) close the Salerno-to-Bari connection, b) capture the Foggia Airfield complex and the Port of Naples, c) capture Rome and its connecting road, and d) try to attack behind the German lines to hasten their retreat.

The capture of the Port of Naples took three weeks. Before retreating, the Germans destroyed the harbor. They booby-trapped and sank ships, making navigation impossible. They demolished dockside facilities and loading equipment.

But victory in Naples was even more important to the Allies than they knew at the time. They were running out of ammunition, supplies, and fresh troops and needed harbors and ports to ship these vitally needed war goods.

The Threat of Gas Attack

During every campaign there was always the threat of the

German use of mustard gas [and not necessarily against the Allies].

> The possible use of gas by the Germans had been discussed by the Allies, for the first time since spring of that year, in August 1943 at the Quebec Conference, the Italians having reported during the armistice negotiations that Ribbentrop had threatened to use gas against them.[2]

Rumors of the Germans using gas against the Russians on the Eastern front as well as placing it in their new V weapons against Britain were common.

As the Allies advanced, captured German documents revealed they:

> had given instructions for the transport of Italian gas stock to Germany; the decrypt had added that if safe transport was in doubt the material was to be destroyed in such a way as to avoid arousing suspicions that Germany was initiating the use of gas. There was another decrypt in December 1943 about the safe custody in Italy of Italian gas stocks for which there was no storage capacity in Germany.[3]

According to a later decoded message, the "gas ammunition stored in Rome was to be sunk at sea at least six miles from the coast ... [4] In the Fall of 1944, "an Enigma decrypt had disclosed that the Germans were still sinking gas ammunition at sea off the Italian coast."[5]

Large quantities of Italian gas stock were found in St. Georgen Depot in southern Germany in May 1946, one of six chemical depots that the Germans used to store chemical munitions. "As the German armies met reverses in Italy and to the East in the Russian zone, thousands of rounds of toxic artillery shells and quantities of liquid toxics were shipped into St. Georgen for storage."[6] Field stocks of 75, 105, and 305mm artillery shells were found filled with mustard gas.

After these stocks were discovered, a German artillery captain, who was engaged by the Americans to convert munitions, stated he "personally directed the shipment of toxics from Italy into Southern Germany."[7] "The majority of these shells came to the depot from the Italian front in 1943 and 1944. Markings indicated that many of the shells were manufactured in 1937."[8] Other toxics included "Bulk toxics in drums were found at St. Georgen after the capitulation included: Italian mustard in 55 gallon drums, 4500 gallons, Italian Chlorpicrine, 6000 gallons."[9]

The Germans could have used gas against the Allies when they invaded North Africa but, for whatever reason, did not. And it may be assumed that they could also have used gas against the Allies when they made their landings on the Italian mainland because they had supplies stored. Nevertheless,

> Allied intelligence officers feared that toxics would be employed by the enemy, and as a result retaliatory stocks were brought in too soon. A tragic gassing of Allied forces in the harbor of Bari, Italy, occurred when enemy action breached a ship carrying Allied gas.[10]

While the Allies feared Axis usage of toxic gas, the Germans feared that the Allies might use it against German cities. A February 1944 decrypt, "expressed some anxiety about the possible use of gas by the Allies."[11]

The Aerial Campaign

The British Eighth Army encountered little resistance and captured Potenza, Gioia and the Foggia Airfield complex by September 27. The U.S. Fifth Army captured Naples on October 1.

> With the capture of Naples and the Foggia airfields, the primary missions of 'Avalanche and Baytown' had been accomplished. Italy had been eliminated from the war, and the Allies now held Naples,

Bari, and Taranto, three of the nation's best ports, and two of the most important air centers (Naples and Foggia).[12]

The aerial war was a crucial part of the Allied success in Italy, the continuous threat of air attack a major factor in Italy's surrender. The Allied air arm, known as the NAAF (North African Air Force),

> having seriously crippled the German Air Force, had brought the invasion convoys through with nominal losses, then had protected the assault forces as they poured ashore and set up their beachheads. Under air cover more than 200,000 troops, 100,000 tons of supplies, and 30,000 vehicles had come in over the beaches, with only five Allied ships sunk and nine damaged by the enemy air forces.[13]

The Foggia airfields were a strategic necessity because they were within range of Germany's communication, economic and industrial sites. "Within a 700-mile radius of the Fifteenth around Foggia, were twelve countries, enemy or enemy-occupied, containing a wide variety of economic, military, and political objectives."[14] As the aerial bombing from England over Germany intensified, it caused Germany to move more of its industrial plants farther inland, thus making them closer to the Foggia complex. "... 44 percent of the enemy's crude and synthetic oil, were less than 600 miles from Foggia ..."[15]

It was the intention of the Allies to occupy the air fields around Rome, but the German Army was firmly entrenched in the surrounding mountainous areas causing the Eighth and Fifth Armies to bog down. In October, the newly created Fifteenth Air Force was forced to stay in the crowded Foggia air complex because the Germans stubbornly defended the Winter, or Gustav, Line south of Rome. The severe rain and mud of November further stalled the Fifth Army.

In the first half of November the air war intensified as a combination of RAF and U.S. aircraft bombed and strafed German defensive positions, roads and rail lines. Occasional missions were flown behind the German lines north of Rome. The German Air Force countered by flying out of Rome and Viterbo, but had little success because of Allied fighter resistance.

During the last two weeks of November, the weather deteriorated rapidly. All operations and flights were reduced. However, the Fifth Army, with Allied support, was able to capture Monte Cassino in early December. The weather was better in the eastern sector and there was air support for the Eighth Army's attack on the Sangro River Line.

At the end of November, the Allies laid down a blistering attack.

> A German ground officer said that because of the air assault "counter attacks were impossible"; another remarked that "nothing can move"; and a third reported that his men, "at the mercy of the enemy air force," could no longer hold their positions "in the face of the bomb carpet." So severe were the air attacks that the enemy could never mass enough troops for heavy counterattacks, and the way was paved for the Eighth to drive through.[16]

General Eisenhower was confident of capturing Rome, providing the weather cooperated, with aerial support to cut the supply lines to the Germans. This was designated as the "primary responsibility of the new Fifteenth Air Force — the attainment of air supremacy through counter air force operations and the destruction of the enemy's aircraft production."[17]

In command of the Fifteenth was General James H. Doolittle. His command charge was:

1. To destroy the German air force in the air and on the ground, wherever it might be located within the range of our aircraft.
2. To participate in Operation Pointblank, the combined bomber offensive against aircraft plants, ball-bearing manufacturing sites, oil refineries, munitions factories, submarines pens, and airports.
3. To support the ground battle and attack communications facilities on the Italian mainland, along the route through the Brenner Pass, and in Austria.

4. To weaken the German positions in the Balkans.

In addition to these goals, ... targets that would pave the way for the invasion of southern France.[18]

In the II ASAC (Air Service Area Command), the Adriatic Base Depot was responsible for setting up and supplying the needs of the Fifteenth Air Force. The Adriatic Base depot

> was a unique organization. It was a USAAF (United States Army Air Force) installation in an area controlled by the British army, an air force agency doing the work normally done by a ground force base section. The depot's principal job was to procure, store, and issue common items of supply to the American air units in eastern Italy ...[19]

The Adriatic Base Depot was also responsible for construction. "It sped up the construction of a 650-mile pipe line system for the delivery of 100 octane gasoline direct from ports to the bomber and fighter fields around Foggia, Bari, and in the Heel; it smoothed out the operation at the port of Bari ..."[20] Unfortunately, the Adriatic Base Depot's operations received a setback in December 1943 and early January 1944 because vital supplies were stalled in Bari when the German attack on that port took place.

By November 1943 supplies were beginning to run low. Both the Fifth and Eighth Armies were over-extended. Not only were food supplies short, but vital armaments such as the ammunition for the new 4.2-inch mortar were needed as well. It was imperative that lines of supply continue to flow in support of the Allied offensive thrust and the port of Bari was crucial to this supply line.

Field Marshal Albert Kesselring desperately needed to stop the northward advance of the Allied Army and suppress the Fifteenth Air Force at Foggia. The toll on German planes and pilots was devastating, especially since support from the Italian Air Force no longer existed.

In late November, Kesselring brought his commanders together for a strategy session. They included the Commander of the Luftwaffe Two, Field Marshal Freiherr von Richthofen, Major General Dietrich Pelz, and General Werner Baumbach, General of the Bombers. The three officers were brilliant military strategists. General Pelz's expertise was in bombing. He had developed what was known as the "Pelz Doctrine," in which a large number of planes collectively bombed one strategic target.

Pelz was of the opinion that southern Italy was lost to the Allies. He eventually agreed with Kesselring that the Allies could be stalled by bringing more German troops to the front and that Foggia could possibly be won back. General Baumbach believed that the remainder of Europe was the major battle ahead and that Italy was a diversionary ploy by the Allies.

The four leaders agreed that the Allied Fifteenth Air Force must not become entrenched in Foggia. If they gained a firm hold, the long-range bombing of Germany and the oil fields in the Baltic would continue. It also meant that German fighter planes would have to be diverted to fight over Italy instead of defending Germany.

They disagreed, however, on the objectives of the plan. There were three choices of attack: bombing and destroying the Fifteenth on the ground at Foggia, bombing the advancing Fifth Army, or bombing the harbors to destroy the supply lines going to the Fifth and Eighth Armies. Bari was the key to stalling the Allied advance. Richthofen sent a ME-210 reconnaissance plane over Bari on a spying mission every day for a week to check on Allied activities.

With the fall of Italy the Allies had become complacent. On December 2, 1943, the night of the attack,

> Around thirty aircraft made the attack … but this time the enemy enjoyed a freak success. His bombs hit two ammunition ships which blew up in a ship-crammed harbor … and so damaged the port facilities that Bari's capacity was not back to normal for three weeks … the extraordinarily heavy damage occurred because the Allies had unwisely crowded their ships in the harbor.[21]

5

THE
U.S. MERCHANT
MARINE

Capturing Italy and harassing Germany from the south required a massive logistical effort. The armies and navies of the Allied forces needed enormous amounts of ammunition, food, rolling stock and supplies.

A census of dry cargo ships and tankers in the eastern Mediterranean during the fourth week of October 1943 indicates how enormous the supply task was, even though the Italian campaign was now north of Naples and Bari: fifty-nine merchantmen sailed into Oran; Algiers 75; Augusta 9; Bizerte 39; Bone 26; Bougie 4; Brindisi 16; Catania 7; Malta 41; Naples 52; Philippeville 6; Sousse 2; Syracuse 4; Taranto 18, and Tunis 5 (a total of 363 merchantmen).[1]

Reaching the staging areas of Italy meant convoys of merchantmen crossing the perilous Atlantic, then into the equally hazardous Mediterranean. The peril in the Atlantic — from fierce storms on the surface and lurking U-boats in the depths. In the Mediterranean it was due to the narrow, shallow waters. Ships could not zig-zag, as they did in the broad reaches of the Atlantic. Axis planes were within short distance of German-controlled air fields throughout the region and the ships were clearly visible targets in the long, narrow sea. Hundreds of air attacks were made on Allied shipping, often with the same aircraft repeatedly hitting the same convoys.

Samuel J. Pitittieri was a Naval Armed Guard gunner aboard the Liberty ship *James Ford Rhodes* that left Gibraltar in a convoy in early November 1943. His was the fifth ship in the fifth column.

> On the afternoon of November 11, the Commodore signaled us to change position to column one, fifth ship and a Dutch ammunition ship took our place. That evening, all ships were ordered to start a smoke screen. It was a partly cloudy sky and the escort on the starboard side flashed a yellow caution light. We were all ready at our battle stations while the smoke screen was on. The D.E. flashed a red light. I saw three German planes fly by the moon when all ships started firing. I was on the port side on my 20mm gun and firing toward the bow, when I saw the "Dutch ammo ship" go up. It just blew up from bow to stern and sank within minutes. When I looked around, I could see tankers on fire on the starboard side toward the shore. Other ships were being hit and falling back. We had to avoid hitting them. The attack lasted 10 to 15 minutes. We later heard that the planes were on a bombing run to Philipville, North Africa. We were lucky that they didn't drop all their bombs on the convoy.[2]

But the narrow Med did offer one advantage — it restricted the use of Axis submarines. Although German and Italian submarines operated in the Med, there were few places to hide and they did not achieve nearly the success the Germans had in the Atlantic.

Nevertheless, the Axis scored many aerial and some submarine successes, and were also successful in laying mines and sabotaging Allied shipping using frogmen.

These units operated almost under the noses of the British defenders, one group operating from an innocent-appearing villa on the Spanish coast just two miles from the roadstead. All frogmen, of necessity, were superb swimmers, and they swam regularly across the bay to attach explosives to Allied ships. Another group operated from an old Italian merchant ship docked across the bay from Gibraltar. The ship had an underwater door so that the frogmen and their torpedoes would be undetected, and it has been reported that the British never did learn where they had come from or where they had gone.[3]

In preparation for the North Africa landings, an enormous convoy of over one hundred Allied ships formed up on the East Coast and sailed to Africa in mid-October 1942. This convoy was

... a sight never before witnessed by seamen: 102 merchant and naval vessels had formed into nine columns and five lines that covered an area twenty by thirty miles. This was 'Operation Torch,' the WSA's first big convoy ... was bound out for the invasion of Africa. The secret of the long-planned operation had been so well kept that German U-boats knew as little as the thirty-five thousand head-shaved troops of the armada.[4]

Convoys consisting of dozens of ships crossed the Atlantic to bring the needed supplies to the fighting troops. Russ Krenciprock.

Heavily-laden Liberty ships often had difficulty staying afloat in the rugged weather of the wintertime Atlantic. This ship in distress was photographed in 1944 but is in a situation typical of those found throughout the war. Russ Krenciprock.

As the convoy crossed the Atlantic, the U-boat threat was on everyone's mind. Germany had scored stunning successes, almost severing Britain's supply of food and oil. Russia needed machinery, supplies, tanks and locomotive engines to continue fighting but much of it landed on the bottom of the Atlantic Ocean. German submarines had attacked the eastern seaboard of the United States. The fear of being torpedoed was ever-present.

> The men in the convoy — Army, Navy and Merchant Marine — were practically all untried in actual combat and the nervousness of it spread through every ship. Scuttlebutt told of ships seen at night that were trailing the fourteen knot convoy and reporting to U-boats so that a slaughter was imminent.[5]

Sinkings by U-boats reached an all-time high during the previous six months.

> In the first seven months of 1942, German submarines sank an appalling total of 681 Allied ships at small cost to them. One convoy, SC-42 (New York to England) was hit by U-boats off Cape Farewell, Greenland, and lost 22 out of its 63 ships before fog blew in, saving the rest from annihilation.[6]

It was part of what became known as the Battle of the Atlantic and it would be early 1943 before it turned in the Allies' favor. By then the U-boat force racked up almost eight million tons of Allied shipping.

Liberty Ships

The seagoing draft horse that carried all the supplies to the fighting forces was the Liberty ship. "Ugly Ducklings" they were called, or, as President Roosevelt described them, "Dreadful Looking Objects."

The United States let its merchant marine decline after World War I, but in 1936 Congress passed the Merchant Marine Act which became the cornerstone of its shipbuilding program. America developed a merchant marine capable of global trade and in wartime, the capacity to carry troops and war materials. Before the United States entered the war, the Act called for five-hundred ships to be built over a ten-year period. The U.S. Maritime Commission was created to coordinate this new ship building venture.

Within a year and a half after the United States entered the war in 1941 the shipyards were building ships faster than the enemy could sink them. From 1942 through 1945 United States shipyards built 5,592 merchant ships, of which 2,701 were Liberty ships, 414 were the fast Victory type, 651 were tankers, 417 were standard cargo ships, and the remaining 1,409 were military or minor types.[7]

One Liberty ship, the *Robert E. Peary*, was built and launched in a record time of four and a half days.

The mission of the Liberty ship was simple — get the goods delivered.

The Liberty Ship was an emergency product built primarily for war use to carry supplies of war to the Allied fighting forces and to keep world trade alive. They were built in abundance to replace the

THE ENIGMA MACHINE

Even before the war, Germany had developed an electrical machine which created coded messages. Set up similar to a typewriter, it contained a keyboard and three internal wheels that rotated when activated by electrical impulses transmitted by the typewriter keys. Each wheel contained twenty-six contact points, one for each letter of the alphabet, arranged in a scrambled sequence. Pushing a lettered key caused the first wheel to engage a specific letter. That wheel would then activate the two accompanying wheels, which in turn lighted up still another letter on a board visible to the operator. The operator then typed out his message on the keyboard and recorded the letters that appeared on the board. The letters he saw were the cipher which was then sent by morse code to a distant receiver. The receiving operator used an enigma machine and code book of wheel settings and went through the process in reverse to decipher the message.

The three wheels were interchangeable giving six possible combinations. Each new positioning of the wheels gave a different scrambling of the alphabet. All together there were three times 10^{18} possible settings for the machine. By the time the war started spare wheels were manufactured: with five spares, the number of possible wheel arrangements was now 336 and the number of settings 209 billion. Later the number of electrical circuits was increased and a series of plugs and jacks added that brought the possible number of settings up to 150 million million million.

As can be imagined, cracking the enigma settings was almost impossible. It was only when the British captured the *U-110* in 1941 with a complete enigma machine, settings for three months and code books, that they were able to read German messages. Then everything in the life of German U-boats was revealed — location, targets, fuel on board, torpedoes remaining, etc.

The Enigma machine. Courtesy CRYPTO AG,Zug.

many ships sunk each day by the enemy. They were built to be expendable in hopes that many would get through to their destination without being sunk, thereby keeping the flow of war material to the Allied fighting forces. If a ship got through and was then sunk, it was declared a success and worthwhile.[8]

A typical Liberty had a complement of approximately forty merchant mariners: the captain (master), the deck department consisting of chief officer, deck cadet, first, second and third officers, boatswain, carpenter, able-bodied and ordinary seamen; radio operator; steward's department consisting of chief steward, cooks, galley and messmen; purser; and the engine room department which consisted of chief engineer, engine room cadet, first, second and third engineers, watertender, firemen, oilers, and wipers.

Merchant ships faced danger from submarines, mines, armed raiders and destroyers, aircraft, "kamikaze," and the elements. Nearly 7,300 mariners were killed at sea, 12,000 wounded of whom at least 1,100 died from their wounds, and 663 men and women were taken prisoner. (Total killed estimated 8,380) Some were blown to death, some incinerated, some drowned, some froze, and some starved. Sixty-six died in prison camps or aboard Japanese ships while being transported to other camps. Thirty-one ships vanished without a trace to a watery grave.

One in twenty-six mariners serving aboard merchant ships in World War II **died in the line of duty,** suffering a **greater percentage** of war-related deaths than all other U.S. services. Casualties were kept secret during the War to keep information about their success from the enemy and to attract and keep mariners at sea. Newspapers carried essentially the same story each week: "Two medium-sized Allied ships sunk in the Atlantic." In reality, the average for 1942 was thirty-three Allied ships each week.[9]

How successful was the U.S. Merchant Marine in World War II? The Commander in Chief of the United States Navy and Chief of Naval Operations, Fleet Admiral Ernest J. King wrote, "During the past 3 ½ years, the Navy has been dependant upon the Merchant Marine to supply our far-flung fleet and bases. Without this support, the Navy could not have accomplished its mission …[10]

Emory Land, Administrator of the WSA (War Shipping Administration) wrote about the fighting team after the war, "There were three major players who represented the United States on that team: Our fighting forces overseas, the production army here at home, and the link between them — the United States Merchant Marine."[11]

Supreme Allied Commander General Dwight D. Eisenhower said, "Every man in the Allied command is quick to express his admiration for the loyalty, courage, and fortitude of the officers and men of the Merchant Marine … they have never failed us … When final victory is ours there is no organization that will share its credit more deservedly than the Merchant Marine."

And General Douglas MacArthur: "… they have shared the heaviest enemy fire … they have suffered in bloodshed and in death … They have contributed tremendously to our success. I hold no branch in higher esteem than the Merchant Marine Services."

The Armed Guard

Assigned to protect each of the U.S. merchant ships was a contingent of approximately twenty-eight men of the United States Naval Armed Guard. This total consisted of an officer, radioman, signalman, gunner's mate, and gunners. The Armed Guard became active in World War I to protect ships that were being torpedoed by the Germans. "In World War I, German U-boats had taken a fearful toll of Allied shipping: More than 5,000 ships, totaling more than 11 million tons, were sunk. One German captain alone sank 194 Allied ships."[12] Guns were placed aboard ships as a defensive measure to counter submarine and air attacks. The responsibility of the Armed Guard was to protect the ship, crew and cargo.

During World War I, the Armed Guard served on board a total

of 384 ships compared to 6,236 ships in World War II.[13]

At the start of World War II, the Naval Armed Guard were not aboard U.S. merchant ships despite several sinkings. The Neutrality Act of 1939 prevented the U. S. from arming these ships even though they sailed into the war zone. A total of six unprotected ships were sunk before the U.S. entered the war. The Act was repealed in November of 1941.

The plaque on the following page was erected in 1986 at Little Creek, (Norfolk) Virginia. It defines the contribution of the U.S. Naval Armed Guard to the war effort in World War II.

The Armed Guard suffered many casualties in carrying out their part of the war. "It has been said that 'If it were not for the U.S. Navy Armed Guard crews and other Armed Guard personnel, the ships and men of the Maritime would have been lost and so would the war.'"[14]

Subsequently, eleven U.S. naval vessels were named for the valiant and heroic Armed Guard members who lost their lives in the service of their country. Among these was Ensign Kay K. Vesole who was aboard the S.S. *John Bascom* when she was attacked at Bari harbor. The U.S. Navy named a destroyer, the U.S.S. *Vesole* (DD-878) after him.

The Merchant Marine and the Navy Armed Guard were present in Bari harbor on the night of December 2, 1943, suffering terrible casualties.

DEDICATED
To
U.S.N. ARMED GUARD OF WORLD WAR II

THE ARMED GUARD OF WWII CAME INTO EXISTENCE ON APRIL 15, 1941 AS USN NAVAL RESERVES BEGAN SPECIAL GUNNERY TRAINING. ON SEPTEMBER 25, 1941, ORDERS WERE GIVEN TO TRAIN 200 OFFICERS AND 1000 MEN BY JANUARY 16, 1942. THE BASE WAS OFFICIALLY ESTAB-LISHED ON OCTOBER 15,1941. THE FIRST CLASS OF 23 OFFICERS AND 184 MEN BEGAN TRAINING 300 YARDS EAST OF THIS POINT, KNOWN AS NAVAL SECTION BASE, WITH A STAFF OF FOUR GUNNER'S MATES. U.S.S. PUDUCAH, U.S.S. DUBUQUE, AND THE U.S.S. EAGLE 19 WERE THE GUNSHIPS USED FOR TRAINING.

ARMED GUARD CREWS CONSISTED OF OFFICERS, GUNNERS, SIGNALMEN, RADIOMEN, MEDICS, WAVES AND SHIP'S COMPANY, WITH A TOTAL OF 144,970 PERSONNEL SERVING ON 6,236 SHIPS. OF THESE SHIPS, 710 WERE SUNK AND MANY DAMAGED, WITH 1810 KILLED IN ACTION AND UNKNOWN INJURIES. ARMED GUARD P.O.W. TOTAL 27 WITH 14 SURVIVORS. 86,198 ARMED GUARDS WERE TRANSFERRED TO THE FLEET AS NEEDED ON LST, LCI, PT BOATS, SUBS AND LARGER SHIPS.

TO THE 1810 ARMED GUARDS WHO GAVE THEIR LIVES, TO THEIR FAMILIES AND FRIENDS, THE ARMY AND MERCHANT CREW THAT ASSISTED US SO WELL, THIS MEMORIAL IS DEDICATED BY THEIR SURVIVING SHIP-MATES.

OUR MOTTO "WE AIM - TO DELIVER" AND WE DID!

6

Bari Harbor
2 December 1943

Bari was a city of two hundred thousand people. It is the
capital of the Puglia region of Italy encompassing Bari,
Brindisi, and Taranto (the heel of the "boot"). It faces
eastward on the Adriatic Sea, enjoying a mild climate and flat
terrain.

The long history of Bari is one of conquest, destruction, and
reconstruction. It is a melting pot of architectural, cultural, and
literary history. Due to its location Bari has been a strategic pawn
in game of chess between warring nations. The Greeks and
Romans conquered Bari and their architecture remains. The
Romans made Bari into a first-rate seaport and its significance as
a center for commerce continues to the present.

Goths, Byzantines, Lombards, Saracens, Normans and
crusaders all left their imprint on the city.

The old section of Bari is a labyrinth of small streets and
medieval houses built in narrow alleyways. Surrounded by water

The Basilica San Nicola as it appeared before the war. J.R. Willig.

on three sides, the houses belong primarily to fishermen. There are several architectural treasures in this section. The Romanesque Church of San Gregorio was built in the eleventh century. The most important church is Basilica San Nicola. Construction began in 1087 and consecration took place in 1197. The church contains the remains of St. Nicholas (Santa Claus), stolen by sailors from Asia Minor. Another Romanesque church was the Cathedral of San Sabino built in 1292.

The Normans built a castle in Bari in the eleventh century. Norman occupation brought a period of economic prosperity which was lacking under the previous invaders, the Byzantines. The castle was destroyed in 1156 by William the Wicked, Norman king of Sicily, who also set fire to the city. The Holy Roman Emperor, Frederick II, rebuilt the castle (Castello Svevo) in the 13th century and re-fortified the city. As the centuries passed, Austria, France, and Spain would battle for possession of Bari.

The new section of the city, begun in the early nineteenth century, is connected to the old by two promenades. This district contains businesses, offices, hotels, movie theaters and an opera house. The main thoroughfare is Corso Cavour. The center of the

Corso Cavour from a pre-war postcard. J.R. Willig.

new district is located between Corso Vittorio Emmanuel, Corso Cavour and the railroad station at Piazza Roma.

Bari fared extremely well up to 1943. There was little bombing damage and few casualties. The city was captured by the Allies on September 11, 1943 and placed under British control. It was designated as the major port to supply the Allies' northern

Corso della Vittoria, part of Bari's new district before the war. J.R. Willig.

advance in Italy. Ammunition, food, parts, and other supplies were shipped to Bari to support the American Fifth Army, General Doolittle's Fifteenth Air Force, and the British Eighth Army. General Doolittle arrived on December 1 and was in the process of setting up his headquarters when the attack occurred. Most of the supplies for the Fifteenth Air Force were in the holds of Liberty ships in the crowded harbor waiting to unload. Equally important was the fact that these ships contained medical supplies for the hospital units that were being set up to support the northern advance.

There was a high degree of activity going on in Bari that evening despite the fact that it was a weekday night. The theaters were full, evening mass had just begun and the baseball game at Bambino Stadium had just ended before several thousand fans. At the dock alongside the East Jetty fourteen Allied ships were in various stages of unloading.

SS *Joseph Wheeler*

At berth 28 was the SS *Joseph Wheeler,* loaded with ammunition. She was a Liberty ship named for the only Confederate General to attain that rank fighting for the United States Army in the Spanish-American War. The *Wheeler* had her share of adventure before December 1943. Donald H. Gritton Jr., son of a Naval Armed Guard member, researched her history. His father and another Armed Guard member were aboard on her maiden voyage. In August 1943 their complement was replaced with the crew that took the ship to Bari.

"It seems that ship was cursed from the beginning."[1] While departing Guantanamo Bay on December 2, 1942 the *Wheeler* was rammed by the M.S. *Oldham* who severed her bow. After being repaired and sailing into the Pacific Ocean, she survived stormy weather lasting twelve days. According to Petty Officer "Cox" Meier, "the ship was nearly torn apart. They arrived in Fremantle, West Australia on February 20, 1943, forty-five days after leaving the Canal Zone. The ship damage could not be repaired.[2]

"The *Wheeler* left Australia February 24, according to the Armed Guard Report signed by a CTM William Stevenson, and headed on a zig-zag course for Bombay, India. On March 8, 1943, the *Wheeler* was about 200 miles south of the island of Ceylon (now Sri Lanka) when a Japanese submarine began to surface alongside the ship. Cox Meier recalled that he had been sitting on a hatch smoking cigarettes and shooting craps with some of the guys, when a submarine began to surface. He said that he and the other men manned their 5-inch/51 BS 50 gun. Meier was the gun Captain and said that they fired two armor piercing rounds into the conning tower before it began to sink out of sight. He recalled that the submarine had been so close to the ship that they could not lower the muzzle of the gun further."[3]

Sailing west from Bombay, the ship travelled down the east coast of Africa to Port Elizabeth. There several of the crew were hospitalized with malaria. "After leaving Port Elizabeth, the ship sailed to Rio de Janeiro, in South America, then on to Santos where it was loaded with tires. In Santos, the *Wheeler* joined in convoy with three other ships and started north. They had no sooner left Santos when the convoy was attacked by a German submarine. One of the other ships, which had overtaken and passed them, was torpedoed. That ship ran aground to save its cargo. The *Wheeler* and the other ships returned to Santos and subsequently returned to New York, via Trinidad, on August 8, 1943."[4]

The *Joseph Wheeler* "sailed from New York on November 11, 1943 in Convoy UGS-23, arriving in Bari on December 1, 1943 via Augusta, Sicily and Taranto, Italy."[5]

SS *John L. Motley*

The Liberty ship *John L. Motley* was named after an historian, writer and diplomat who served as the American minister to Austria and Great Britain in the 19th century. Completed in May 1943, the "*John L. Motley* loaded in Philadelphia, Pennsylvania and departed Lynnhaven Roads,

Chief Engineer John White, Sr. as drawn by Walter Honder, a German POW. John White, Jr.

Virginia on October 25 in convoy UGS-22, arriving in Bari, Italy on November 28 via Oran, Algeria and Augusta, Sicily."[6] Perhaps an omen predicting the *Motley's* future occurred on a prior trip when on August 8, 1943 calcium carbide caused a fire and explosion.

Joseph Oliver will always remember the *John L. Motley*. Oliver joined the Navy with his friend Patrick (Bobie) Alterice in July 1942. Alterice "had just graduated from California, Pennsylvania H.S. and both of them went to sea early in 1943, after graduating from the Navy Signal School at Champaign-Urbana, Illinois. I remember signaling to Bob while in convoy in November 1943. I wished him well. His destination was Bari. Mine was Palermo, but we heard of the Bari raid, I believe, the next day."[7]

SS *John Harvey*

The Liberty Ship *John Harvey* was named after one of the signers of the Articles of Confederation who was also a member of the Continental Congress in 1777. Launched on January 9, 1943, the *John Harvey* made her first trip from Wilmington, North Carolina to Moorehead, North Carolina on January 21, 1943.

While loading at Wilmington, it was discovered the ship was short of the turnbuckles used to secure cargo. "The Bosun asked Paul Washburn, while he was on the night shift, if he could locate some. He did; 108 of them during a midnight requisition. Due to the feat, he (Washburn) obtained the nickname 'turnbuckles,' later shortened to 'Buckles.'"[8]

On the second trip from Norfolk to New York, to North Africa and back to Baltimore, additional facilities were installed in order to carry troops over and prisoners of war back. The *John Harvey*'s third trip was from Norfolk to Casablanca back to Norfolk and Baltimore. It was on this trip "that a German prisoner of war, Walter Honder, who was an accomplished artist, sketched a pencil portrait of the *Harvey's* Chief Engineer, John White, Sr."[9] The *John Harvey* ended this voyage in Norfolk on September 23, 1943.

On the *Harvey's* fourth and final voyage she departed for Baltimore where she loaded a secret cargo of mustard gas. Two thousand M47A1-100 lb. bombs were loaded after being secretly shipped from the Eastern Chemical Warfare Depot to Curtis Bay Depot and finally to the Baltimore Cargo Port. The shipment had its own safety crew of seven men to ensure its proper handling. This crew checked for leaks and corrosion and monitored pressure levels within the bomb casings. A cargo security officer, Lieutenant Thomas H. Richardson, was placed in charge of the shipment. The cargo was so secret that the master of the *John Harvey,* Elwin F. Knowles, was not told what his ship carried. But Captain Knowles was a seasoned skipper and knew better. After loading the lethal shipment, the *Harvey* sailed for Norfolk on October 15 and arrived in Oran on November 2 in Convoy UGS 21.

Cadet Midshipman James L. Cahill wrote, "At this port (Oran) the cargo was discharged and another consisting of ammunition was taken on."[10] Relative to this part of the voyage, there is some confusion as to whether the *John Harvey* brought mustard gas over on this trip. Among various kinds of bombs and ammunition, the following was listed: 100 HS Bombs [included in the] 27,075 packages with a total tonnage of 5500 (HS is the code description for mustard) were loaded at Oran.

On November 27 the *Harvey* departed Augusta bound for Bari in Convoy AH 10. "There were nine merchant ships in this convoy carrying petrol, ammunition and supplies. The convoy arrived at Bari on 28 Nov and the *John Harvey* was ordered the same day to No. 29 Berth on the outer mole. It will be seen that some 15 ships were moored close together along the outer mole. The reason for this, it is understood, was that the unloading berths in the inner harbour were full or not ready for unloading, and it is unsafe to leave ships outside the harbour on account of U and [sic] boat activities."[11]

A mariner's view of the scene in the harbor was: "... It was a beehive of activity. Seemed like all the ships were being unloaded together. Shore leave was restricted so the crew could help with the unloading or other duties. When twilight came and we normally batten down the hatches, closed the port holes and cover them, secured the smoking lamp, but Orders came through to turn on all workable lights. The unloading could continue throughout the night. As I looked out over the harbor it was bright as daylight.

"The unloading seemed to be going rather slow and most of the crew were very uneasy. After all, we had came this far through U-boat infested waters and air craft attacks. We didn't appreciate being sitting ducks in a small harbor.

"Despite the knowledge that the German Air Force in Italy was still active and effective, air raid precautions were overthrown as darkness fell. Every light in port was turned on to speed the unloading of our vital cargo. We wanted our cargo delivered ashore above ground not on the ocean floor..."[12]

Meanwhile, "copies of the [*Harvey's*] manifest were received and signed for by the Docks Superintendent at Bari on 25 Nov. What happened to those documents is obscure; there is no trace of them now and no evidence that they were distributed to anyone. There was a manifest received from the Master after the arrival of the ship. The 'breakdown' was received by the Ordnance Officer XII AFSC (ADV) on 28 Nov. It was distributed by the US Transport Officer, Adriatic Base, to his branches and to the Acting Port Commandant and the Docks Superintendent, who received their copies on 30 Nov."[13]

According to a *British Most Secret Report*:
On the 26 [*should read* 28] or 29 Nov. a representative of the US

Port Officer went on board the *John Harvey* and was told by the Security Officer that he had a cargo of mustard gas.

There is some evidence that the presence of a cargo of mustard was discussed between the Docks Superintendent, the Acting Port Commandant, and the Sea Transport Officer, and it was considered, in view of her low priority and the berthing space available, that she was in as safe a place as could be found.

Neither NOIC nor Comd. No. 6 Base Sub area were aware before the raid that the *John Harvey* contained toxic ammunition.[14]

SS *John Bascom*

The Liberty ship *John Bascom* was named after a 19th century educator, philosopher, sociologist, and college president. She departed New York on November 1, 1943, arriving in Norfolk, Virginia on November 3 and departed November 4, arriving in Augusta, Sicily on November 27. The Atlantic passage was stormy. Warren Brandenstein, a member of the Naval Armed Guard said, "we experienced very heavy seas and lifelines had to be used on deck to reach the gun stations."[15] The *John Bascom*'s cargo consisted of 8300 tons of badly needed foodstuff, Army hospital equipment, high test gasoline in 50-gallon drums, and acid.

Cadet-Midshipman Leroy C. Heinse remembered that "coming into Gibraltar ships were hounded by submarines. Planes were also flying overhead and dropping depth charges ahead of the convoy. Ultimately, we came into a little port called Augusta, Sicily. This is where our convoy and other ships were laying to be broken up into other convoys. We left Augusta (28 November) and went up around the boot into the Adriatic Sea and came into the port of Bari. I had no idea of our destination. It was afternoon when we arrived and soon thereafter we heard anti-aircraft guns firing. They were firing at German reconnaissance planes that were flying over the port and looking at a target which ultimately was going to be theirs the following evening. That was the tip-off, so to speak, that something was going to happen ..."[16]

SS *Samuel J. Tilden*

The *Samuel J. Tilden* was a Liberty ship named after a 19th century governor, politician, publisher, and unsuccessful presidential candidate. The *Tilden* sailed from New York on July 14, 1943 in Convoy UGS 15 and anchored in Gibraltar for twenty days. John F. Whitley boarded the *Tilden* in June and was a naval gunner assigned to an old World War I 4-inch/50 surface gun. He remembered, "while we anchored there we had our first 'Liberty' on foreign soil. Watching the girls sunbathing and walking along the beach of Spain through our gun sights was a daylight pastime for our crew."[17] For the remainder of the summer, the *Tilden* shuttled back and forth carrying troops and war materials from North Africa to Sicily and Italy.

The SS *Samuel J. Tilden* arrived in Bari late on December 2 in the company of three other ships and an armed British trawler. One of these ships, *Puck*, was a Polish merchant ship that would be destroyed later that evening. The *Tilden*'s Captain, Joseph Blair, was annoyed because the ship had to wait in the harbor entrance for a pilot to direct her inside the harbor. On board the *Tilden* were 209 military passengers; 186 U.S. Army personnel and 23 British Army personnel. Her cargo consisted of "Army supplies, including 5 hospital units, trucks with full gasoline tanks in No. 4 and No. 5 holds and on deck, 2 tractor-trailer units containing 6,000 gallons of high octane gasoline stowed in No. 2 hold, 100 tons of ammunition stowed in No. 4 and No. 5 holds and a deck cargo of gasoline in drums."[18] One of the Naval Armed Guards recalled that the *Samuel J. Tilden* "had a deck load of mustard gas. This gas was in metal containers and very plainly printed, MUSTARD GAS, on the sides of the containers."[19] This was the second Liberty ship to bring mustard gas into Bari harbor. It would not be the last.

SS *Lyman Abbott*

The Liberty ship *Lyman Abbott* was named after a 19th

century editor, writer and minister. Naval Armed Guard member Donald Meissner boarded her in Providence, Rhode Island in June 1943. After one of the first voyages and unloading at Casablanca, Meissner stated, "after two weeks we headed back to the States. I did not realize that my next trip would tax me beyond my endurance ... We arrived in the States and entered port at night. It always made me happy to see lights in homes, on cars, and hear noises of free people. They didn't know how lucky they were.

"Our next cargo was that of a very grave nature. Our hatches on each side of the ship were loaded with wooden boxes labeled 'Chemicals,' which I believe was mustard gas. Sandwiched between the boxes were explosives. To live and fight on a deck covering this type of cargo drastically cut our chances of survival. One direct hit and there would be nothing left of the ship or us. Some of the longshoremen were complaining that they weren't being paid enough for handling all those explosives. I was thinking that we were going to transport and run the gauntlet with that stuff for two bucks a day. Army trucks were loaded and secured to our deck. Runways were built over the trucks. This would give us a quick way to get to our guns ..."[20]

Another Armed Guard member, Stanley Wisniewski, was assigned to the *Lyman Abbott* in May of 1943. On the return from Casablanca, Wisniewski said, "On 20 October, we returned to the States to Baltimore, Maryland and Newport News, Virginia, where we picked up our cargo of bombs and mustard gas. I myself and the crew assumed we were picking up general cargo. We then left Newport News, for Bari, Italy. Our convoy was rather large ... about 7 or 8 rows across; 10 rows deep. I'd say in the vicinity of about 60 to 80 ships."[21]

Donald Meissner continues: "We crossed the Pond in good time and went by the "Rock" and were in the Mediterranean. Italy was our destination. Going by the "Rock" always gave me an eerie feeling, as I felt from this point on, the Germans knew we were coming. We had smooth sailing all the way to the Adriatic. The Mediterranean was always a "hot spot" for German planes, and I was surprised that none came after us.

"On December 2, 1943, we entered Bari harbor. We anchored in the middle of the harbor. We were disappointed that other ships got to the docks first. All of us wanted to get rid of our cargo as fast as possible. I counted about twenty-four ships in the harbor. I was on watch on the stern of the ship and had my foul-weather gear on. It was quite cold, the sky was clear, and there was no wind. Off our port bow were the docks and I could see several ships secured to them. Dead ahead were some tankers and off the starboard bow were some more Liberty ships. Directly to my starboard was an Italian warship. It was larger than a Destroyer and smaller than a Battleship. It must have been some type of a cruiser. The sailors were leisurely walking her decks, and I noticed the bow was pointed out of the harbor. When I was relieved from my watch it was dark out. I went below to my quarters and took my foul-weather gear off. All I had on was a skivvy-shirt, a pair of dungarees, and some light shoes …"[22]

SS *Grace Abbott*

The S.S. *Grace Abbott* was a Liberty ship built in 1942 and named after an author, professor, teacher and sociologist. She sailed from Baltimore on October 22, 1943 in a convoy of approximately sixty-six ships and arrived in Augusta, Sicily on November 19. From there the vessel sailed for Bari arriving on the 22nd where she anchored on the port side of the quay jutting out into the middle of the harbor. It was a long stay for the *Abbott*. She was in the harbor for nine days prior to the attack while other ships streamed in and waited to unload. The port was overcrowded and chaotic. Being under British port command was also irritating to the Naval Armed Guard gunners.

SS *John Schofield*

After an attack-filled journey involving German submarines and bombers off the coast of Spain, the American Liberty *John Schofield* arrived in Bari on November 30, 1943. According to the late Cadet-Midshipman Theodore Schober, who died in April 1996, "Our cargo included 500 lb. Bombs, black powder, high octane airplane gas, personal foods for General Montgomery (including brandy), and many crated items which were marked 'Red Cross,' but which many of the ship's personnel were skeptical of."[23]

"While outside the breakwater, an English Port Officer boarded us and proceeded to the bridge. During the conversation between our Captain, Karl V. Katlas, and the British Port Officer, our Captain asked for procedures to be followed in the event of air attack. The British officer's reply was; 'We don't have air attacks in Bari.'

"We were told that we were in a British convoy and it appeared therefore that we would be given preference in unloading our cargo. We were ordered to dock at 'Pier 15' and did so ... Unloading was tediously slow or so it seemed at the time."

SS *Smith Thompson*

One lucky ship, the SS *Smith Thompson,* had departed Bari before the raid started. According to Armed Guard member Bill Collett, "after the *Thompson* entered the harbor, she moored at the large breakwater wall. The next day, two ships arrived and moored near her. I was heading for the chow hall at noon when General Quarters sounded. I jumped to my battle station and saw a plane overhead. Someone on another ship fired a few rounds and then there was silence and they secured from their stations. The very same thing happened over the next two days. A few more days passed with no more alarms.

"By now two more ships had moored against the break wall. They were beginning to line up. I heard a few of the captains had visited some office wanting to know just how long before they could start unloading. They also asked just how safe the harbor was from any attack. They were assured by higher authority that the harbor was well protected.

"Finally, the *Thompson* received orders to dock at a pier for unloading. Our ship was docked between two ships, one machine gun nest away from our bow, and another one to our stern, manned by two British soldiers in each. We began putting our cargo of 500 lb. bombs on the dock. There were at least fifteen Italian prisoners rolling the bombs along the dock. One British soldier was in charge to keep them working. I walked down the gangway and talked with the soldier for about twenty minutes. He mentioned that he had not had a good smoke for a long time because he had been in North Africa chasing Rommel. He had been wounded in the stomach by a Nazi bayonet but managed to kill his attacker. He thought he would be sent back to England, but instead landed in Italy. I gave him four packages of smokes. He insisted I take his bayonet as a remembrance of him and for the smokes. To this day I periodically lift the bayonet from my closet to examine it and I always wonder if he made it home.

"Once more the alarm went off and I proceeded to my gun tub. This time I saw the plane with its Nazi emblem on the tail and wing as he sped away. We gunners on the *Thompson* knew he was taking pictures. We knew something was going to happen, just when was on our minds.

"On the afternoon of Dec. 1st with our decks all secured for sea, we moved away from the dock. The sea watches were set and we headed out of the harbor. As we did so I looked back along the dock at all the bombs as well as eight or nine ships that were all lined up. We sailed all that night and day around the southern point of Italy and headed for the Strait of Gibraltar. Morning came and our Signalman walked into the chow hall and said, 'Hey guys, guess what happened, the Germans blew Bari harbor apart last night!' You could hear a pin drop …"[24]

S.S. *Louis Hennepin*

The American Liberty ship *Louis Hennepin* was tied up to the dock next to the *John Schofield*. A week before the attack, on November 22, a British mine sweeper had hit a mine and blown up in the harbor. A whaleboat from the *Hennepin* helped rescue the survivors. Bernard L. Anderson wrote in his diary to his wife,

Darling what an exciting day I had today. This morning at about 11:00 I had to lay down as I had a headache when all of a sudden a depth charge or mine went off right at the entrance to harbor … Well, when I heard this big boom that shook the ship from one end to the other I jumped up and grabbed my hat and coat and ran to the bridge, and there right near the entrance to the harbor was a mine sweeper that had been hit by a mine … There are 4 mine sweepers always at work and sometimes more outside the harbor as German planes and subs are always dropping mines. There was Mannie Maloney and 3 or 4 other fellows on the bridge when I got there. The Chief mate was there and he said, "Let's go," so we all ran and got our life jackets and jumped into the lifeboat that we have been using to get to the dock so we can walk to town. We started out for the wreck as we could see the fellows jumping into the water. One of the mine sweepers was blowing a siren for ships to come out. We were about the first boat to get outside the break water and behind us came about 6 or 8 torpedo boats and big motor launches. They passed us going like heck. We got out to the wreck about 5 minutes later and the mine sweeper had already sunk it and it went down in 12 minutes. The torpedo boats wouldn't go in to where it had sunk because the water was covered with an inch of oil and they were afraid their propellers would get fouled up in the wreckage that was floating around everywhere. There were 3 other small boats besides us and we went right in where it went down. The oil and steam was coming up in a gusher and my knees were really shaking by then. We picked up 6 fellows and were they ever greasy. You could hardly get a hold of them as they would keep slipping. We finally got them in the boat and pulled to where one of the torpedo boats was and we put them on board. The water was pretty rough and it was a job as the fellows were pretty banged up. One fellow's leg was broke in two places and he sure was bleeding bad. The other fellows had cuts all over them. They didn't have but shorts and undershirts on. They must have been sleeping at the time. They were all so shocked they couldn't talk ... We looked around for more survivors but we couldn't find any. By this time the oil was two inches

The Armed Guard gun crew from the Louis Hennepin. *Bernard L. Anderson is second from the left in the second row back. Bernard L. Anderson.*

thick on the water and it was so rough the water was breaking over the side and we were getting soaking wet with water and oil. There were 8 of us fellows in the lifeboat. We circled around poking at every piece of wreckage to see if there were any more fellows in the water, but we didn't find anymore. We headed back to the ship covered with oil and plenty scared from what we saw. I was covered with oil and I still stink from the smell of it. Tonight our officer came back to the ship and said that out of 125 fellows on the mine sweeper, only 18 were saved. It sure was awful and everyone was thanking us for picking up those 6 fellows that were just about ready to sink. They were just like an oil soaked rag. They were so shocked they couldn't hold a cigarette in their mouth. They sure have a dangerous job. The mines are magnetic and only go off when a ship doesn't have a degaussing machine on board. The machine makes a ship repel a magnetic mine. They explode about 9 or more every day since we have been here. About an hour after we had tied up the day we got in they exploded two right where we had passed over to enter the harbor. It sure makes a fellow realize that we are in a war.[25]

A commendation letter to GM3/c Bernard L. Anderson and nine others said:

While anchored inside the net at Bari, Italy, the men listed below went to the rescue of survivors of a British mine sweeper that had been blown up by an enemy mine.

Although there were larger launches at the scene, the small whaleboat used by the chief mate and Navy gunners drove through the frothing oil covered water and rescued six British sailors. Without regard for personal safety, the men continued through the heavily mined waters to a large rescue ship and the injured survivors were put aboard ...[26]

USS *Aroostock*

The USS *Aroostock* (AOG-14) was the third American naval ship to take the name of a river in Northern Maine. She was launched in December 1937 as a tanker for the Esso Corporation and then became a U.S. Navy ship in April 1943.

As she sat in Bari harbor, *Aroostock*'s cargo consisted of 19,000 barrels of highly volatile 100-octane gasoline. This fuel was vital to General Doolittle's Fifteenth Air Force. The gasoline would be unloaded then pumped through pipelines to the Foggia Air Fields. Captain W.R. Hays was anxious because he couldn't unload his cargo. The *Aroostock* was anchored off the San Cataldo Mole about 300-350 yards from the heavily congested area of merchant ships along the East Jetty.

7

"LITTLE PEARL HARBOR"
1920-1950 HRS.
2 DECEMBER 1943

The attack began with the JU-88's flying in low; the first bombs hitting the city of Bari itself. Fires broke out as explosions thundered through the old section of the city. A wind fanned the flames. Concussions rolled through the town toppling centuries-old houses.

From a British *Most Secret Report*:

> The air raid started at 1920 hours on 2 Dec. Owing to a number of circumstances … practically no advance warning was given. The attacking force consisted of 30 plus aircraft and the raid was severe.
>
> In the early stages, the oil pipe on the petrol quay was hit by a bomb and the consequent flow of petrol ignited. Ammunition and petrol ships in the harbour were hit and blew up setting fire to several other vessels and covering a large expanse of water with burning oil and petrol.
>
> The *John Harvey* was hit early and it is almost certain that the ammunition on board exploded. The gas bombs were not fused, but

their casings were very thin and the explosion threw some thirty casings on to the mole where a large patch of mustard was subsequently found. It is clear that many more bombs must have been cracked and broken and their contents thrown into the air and scattered on the sea and neighboring ships, in the form, partly, of a mixed spray of mustard, oil and water. Most of the mustard sank to the bottom of the sea, but some was dissolved in the oil, and thus the persons who were rescued from the sea, and their rescuers, were contaminated. What is described as a "tidal wave" followed the explosion of one ship and doubtless many persons were drenched.

The raid was over by 1950 hours. Numerous fires were left burning; many ships were hit and sank, in several cases after they had drifted away from their moorings. It was therefore very difficult at the time to identify particular vessels...

The Port Commandant saw NOIC [Naval Operations Intelligence Center] about 2000 hours on 2 Dec. and informed him that certain ships were dangerous and that one had mustard on board and should be scuttled. Comd No. 6 Base Sub Area was informed by the Port Commandant between 2030 hrs and 2215 hrs of a possible risk from gas. A naval officer took instructions to the HMS *Bicester* to sink the *John Harvey*; but the *Bicester* was herself damaged and unable to carry out this instruction. There is very little doubt that in fact the *John Harvey* sank of her own accord almost immediately after she exploded.[1]

SS *Joseph Wheeler*

The *Joseph Wheeler* was the first ship hit. "The freighter lay berthed at a jetty when German aircraft attacked the anchorage. During this attack a bomb pierced the deck near the No. 3 hatch and ignited the cargo of ammunition. With a tremendous roar the ship exploded, leaving only a burned out hulk."[2]

Ensign Eugene J. Kuhn, USNR, was the commanding Officer of the Armed Guard unit. He filed the following confidential report to Captain H.W. Zirolli, U.S. Naval Liaison Officer in Taranto, Italy, on December 6, 1943.

Subject: Report of Bombing Attack at Bari, Italy, on 2 December, 1943.

1. The SS *Joseph Wheeler*, according to all available information, suffered direct hits by enemy bombers which attacked the harbor of Bari, Italy, between approximately 1920 and 1940, 2 December, 1943, with the loss of all hands who were aboard at the time. Fifteen members of the Armed Guard Unit, who were aboard, are either missing or killed, and in addition about twenty-nine members of the ship's crew are also missing or killed. No trace of either crew could be found at the hospitals in Bari on 3 December, the day following the bombing.

2. Thirteen of the Armed Guard Unit had been granted shore liberty for the day (1300-2100), although one man declined. I was ashore making arrangements at the Army Disbursing Office to have the Armed Guard crew paid, intending to take the ship's liberty party boat at 2100, when the bombing occurred. Apparently the attack came as a complete surprise, since the alarm sounded almost simultaneously with the dropping of the first bombs.

3. Every effort was made to return to the ship. At the dock area, nine of the returning Navy crew were ordered to go back to the city. In company with the ship's first mate, Mr. Roy Newkirk, and the U.S. Army Security Officer, 2nd Lt. Glen Yates, C.W.S., I managed to go as far as berth #26 before we were forced back by flames from the burning ships (the SS *Joseph Wheeler* was at berth #29). With three members of the Armed Guard Unit who had apparently passed into the dock area before the British officers began ordering the men to return to the city, we did what we could along the breakwater. On one occasion we tended the stern lines of a small tanker in an effort to clear it from a ship burning alongside. However, the tanker swung into the blazing ship after we cleared its lines, and it is not known whether the ship's officers were able to take it out into the harbor and extinguish the fires. We also managed to free an ambulance which had become stuck in the debris on the road to the breakwater. Charles B. Milam, S2/c., USNR., received a slight shoulder sprain when he was knocked down by an explosion from one of the burning ships while we were freeing the ambulance.

4. After it became apparent that we could do little else of use, we returned to the city where we stopped at the headquarters of the 15th

United States Army Air Force. We were joined there by nine Navy gunners who had been turned back from the dock gates and by the remainder of the merchant crew. In all, there were twelve members of the Armed Guard Unit (enlisted men), Lt. Yates, Mr. Newkirk, and about fourteen members of the merchant crew who also had been on liberty. Lt. Col. P.R. Pattison, anti-aircraft officer for the 15th USAAF, made arrangements with other officers to bed all of us for the night.

5. The following day, hospitals were checked and survivors questioned in an effort to learn whether there were any survivors from the ship. None besides those of us who were ashore at the time of the attack could be located. That afternoon passage was arranged for the survivors and we went aboard the *Defender*, a British merchant ship, arriving at Taranto at 0900, 5 December, 1943.

6. Delay in transit was caused when the ship went aground during the night of 4 December, 1943.

7. As the *Defender* passed out of the harbor of Bari, we passed within three hundred yards of the SS *Joseph Wheeler*'s berth, and from what could be seen of the remains of the vessel, it appeared that the ship was on its port side and that its starboard side had been blown almost entirely away.

8. Following are the survivors of the Armed Guard Unit …

9. Following are the men who are either missing or dead (believed dead) …

10. Records of the next of kin of the above perished with the ship.

11. Aboard the *Defender*, which carried 135 survivors from four American, two Polish, one British and one Norwegian ship, were the following U.S. Navy personnel …"

Eugene J. Kuhn[3]

SS *John L. Motley*

The *John L. Motley* was the second ship to be hit by bombs from the dive-bombing JU-88s as they screamed overhead at 200 MPH. She was moored at berth No. 30 on the East Jetty between the U.S. Liberty ships, *John Harvey* and *John Bascom*, four ships north of the *Joseph Wheeler*. Her cargo consisted of high

CONFIDENTIAL
UNITED STATES COAST GUARD
REPORT ON U. S. MERCHANT VESSEL WAR ACTION CASUALTY

: Commandant, U. S. Coast Guard, Washington, D. C.

ip S/s _JOSEPH WHEELER_ Service _OCEAN FREIGHT_
ner _W.S.A_ Operator _SOUTH ATLANTIC SS Co_
formation furnished by _CHIEF MATE_ Date _28 OCTOBER, 1944_

QUESTIONS	ANSWERS
Year built and propulsion	Built _1942_ Propulsion _STEAM_
Tonnage	Gross _7126_ Net _4380_
Draft loaded (maximum allowed)	Fwd _28' (M)_ Aft _29'6_
Draft when attacked	Fwd _29 2'5"(M)_ Aft _30'0 2_
Cargo on board (any deck)	Nature _GENERAL AND AMMUNITION_ Tons _8000_
Voyage	From _NEW YORK_ To _BARI, ITALY_
Were routing orders followed	_YES_
Any criticism of orders	_NO_
Weather at time of attack	Weather _CLEAR_ Sea _CALM_
Was enemy sighted? When	_YES; DURING AND AFTER ATTACK_
Any friendly ships in sight	_YES_
Were navigation lights on	_NO_
Date and time of attack	Date _12/2/43_ Time _1930_
Position	Latitude _AT ANCHOR AT BARI Longitude ITALY_
Nature of attack (Give data)	_BOMBED_
Number of hits	_1_
Location of hits (Mark diagram)	_1- FOR'D. - 1 #3_
Effect of hits	_SANK SHIP_
Was ship armed? What type	_YES_
Was armament used? State result	_YES; UNKNOWN_
Any explosions or fires?	Ship _YES; EXPLOSION_ Cargo _YES; EXPLOSION_
Was deck ruptured	_YES_
Did ship break in two	_YES_
Was SOS sent	_NO_
Ship's speed	Normal _10.0_ When attacked _AT ANCHOR_ When abandoned _STOP_
Time abandoned, sunk	Abandoned _NO TIME TO ABANDON_ Sunk _2000 (30 min.)_
Was ship reboarded	By whom _NO_ When
Was ship brought in	How _NO_ Approximate damage _SUNK_

X

X

Fill in this diagram to show
attack hits, fires, etc.

The Confidential Coast Guard report documents the sinking of the Joseph
Wheeler as well as showing where she was hit. U.S. Coast Guard.

explosives, cyanide, and high octane gasoline. Like most of the other ships along the East Jetty, the *Motley* was moored with her stern to the jetty and her anchor down in the harbor.

Thomas Edward Harper, Coxswain, USN, was on the dock returning from liberty in the port of Bari on 2 December, 1943. At approximately 1950, he heard the roar of an airplane motor. Shortly after flares were seen dropping among the ships in the dock area. There were no alarms whatsoever, and bombs were dropped before the shore batteries commenced firing.

"Inasmuch as the undersigned, and all surviving members of the crew were ashore, what occurred on board ship is not known, but an Armed Guard, who was aboard the S.S. *John Bascom* during the attack, stated that the subject named vessel [*John L. Motley*] sustained three bomb hits, one in number five hold, the second in number three hold, and the third went down the stack. He further stated that after number five hold was hit, fire broke out immediately, but was brought under control very shortly. Later, however when number three hold caught fire, the crew was unable to extinguish it."[4]

Moored next to the *Motley* was the *John Bascom*. Her captain, Otto Heitmann, watched with horror as the *Motley* was hit. "Heitmann saw the crew of the *John L. Motley* begin dousing the burning cargo with water from the fire hoses."[5]

Coxswain Thomas Harper: "When the raid had been ten minutes old, it appeared that almost every ship in the harbor was burning. The raid lasted about twenty-five minutes, and shortly after its termination a ship probably subject named vessel exploded. [*Actually this was the* John Harvey, *not the* John L. Motley]

"Shortly after the all clear had been sounded the planes returned this time for only a few minutes. This time no bombs were dropped.

"The planes could not be distinguished because of the darkness but the undersigned was unofficially informed that planes were Stuka dive bombers, numbering thirty. It was estimated that the bombs weighed no more than one hundred pounds apiece.

"The undersigned had no idea of the outcome of the raid until the next morning when he was informed by the British Royal Naval officials that subject named vessel had gone down.

"The only naval personnel surviving the attack on subject named vessel were those who were ashore at the time ..."[6]

The *John L. Motley*'s demise came quickly. With her "deck cargo and cargo in the hold on fire, the flames burned through her mooring lines and the ship drifted down on the Jetty and exploded with a tremendous roar. She blew up when she was only about 50 feet from the S.S. *John Bascom*. The force of this explosion caved in the whole port side of the *Bascom*, sinking her immediately."[7]

The *John L. Motley* drifted toward the lighthouse at the end of the East Jetty and slammed into the seawall as she exploded. "The entire harbor seemed to empty as the tidal wave caused by the explosion of the *John L. Motley* washed over the breakwater."[8] The *John L. Motley*'s "complement was 45 Merchant crew and 28 Naval Armed Guard. Of this number, 39 crew members and 24 Navy men were killed.[9]

The radio operator, Melvin H. Bloomberg was severely injured and lying with the other wounded on the dock. He was found there by the Deck Engineer Carl Smith who took him to the hospital, but Bloomberg later died from his wounds.

Myron Boluch was in Section P-343 at the United States Merchant Marine Academy in the spring of 1943. One of his classmates was Edwin D. Howard. On the day assignments were given out, Boluch remembered that "I envied him because he drew the Liberty *John L. Motley* and I got the old (1917) Hog Islander *Exmouth*. He was a laughing kid (we were all kids). He died where only God could witness his charity toward his fellow man — an ammo ship was not easy to sail, but it would be painless. I did not sail with him and I only knew him during the few months we were together at Kings Point, Long Island. In my heart and mind, he was a young man, who gave his life for all of us."[10]

Two of the *Motley*'s Merchant Marine crew were ashore in Bari. Chester Filiwicz, utility man, and Osmond Jackson, cook, came back to the harbor, but saw no ship. There was only fire and

Myron Boluch, second row, right, was a classmate of Ed Howard, third row, left, at Kings Point. Here they undergo small boat training. Courtesy of Lt. Cdr.Myron Boluch, USNR (Ret.), taken while cadet-midshipman. Section P-343, U.S. Merchant Marine Academy, Kings Point, N.Y..

smoke. "The closest he could get to the site was approximately two city blocks, but that was close enough for Filiwicz to be convinced that he no longer had a ship."[11]

SS *John Harvey*

The *John Harvey*, according to the Italian Berthing Plan, was moored between berths 29 and 30. The *John L. Motley* was on her starboard side and the British merchants *Testbank* and *Fort Athabaska* as well as the American Liberty ship, *Joseph Wheeler*, were on her port side. "She caught fire when she was showered with flaming debris from a nearby ship which had been struck by bombs."[12]

Some of her crew were ashore on liberty during the attack. "Her complement was 40 crew members, 28 Naval Armed Guard, and 10 U.S. Army Chemical Warfare personnel."[13] "When the air raid occurred, however, only seven of the eight officers, forty-two men, twenty-eight armed guards, and nine passengers were aboard. The six merchant crew and a U.S. Merchant Marine cadet ashore were the only survivors"[14]

Cadet James L. Cahill was one of the survivors. His official report was submitted January 10, 1944:

… 2. On 2 December, 1943, at 1930, while subject vessel was anchored just inside the jetty with a full cargo of ammunition, the harbor and port were attacked by German bombers. Subject vessel was alongside two other vessels also loaded with ammunition. During the attack, one of the three ships was hit by a large aerial bomb, which exploded and the concussion caused the other two ships to explode.

3. The writer was ashore at the time of the attack and consequently does not know the exact details of the sinking. It was presumed that all hands aboard the ship at the time were lost.

4. The writer was taken from Bari to Taranto on the British ship, SS *Defender*, and spent one night at a transit camp in Taranto before being entrained for Naples where he was placed aboard the British transport, HMT *Cameronia*, and taken to Oran. At Oran, the writer was given passage on the SS *Marabeau B. Lamar* and arrived in the United States, 2 January, 1944.

5. To the best of the writer's knowledge the only survivors were the seven men ashore at the same time as the writer. The other three Cadet-Midshipmen assigned to subject vessel, namely; Cadet-Midshipman Richard B. Glauche, Cadet-Midshipman Alvin H. Justis, Cadet-Midshipman Marvin H. Brodie, were all aboard at the time of the attack, and it is presumed that all were lost. As far as the writer was able to learn, there was no trace found of the Cadet-Midshipmen and subject vessel was demolished.

Signed (James L. Cahill)

Cadet-Midshipman James L. Cahill,

Second Class, (D-1), USMMCC[15]

SS *John Bascom*

The *John Bascom* had been directed to moor in berth No. 31. There were three Allied ships to her starboard side and the *John L. Motley* was on her port side. The seawall had a bomb shelter built on it and it was patrolled by Italian personnel. Due to the threat of German U-boats, submarine nets were strung across the harbor entrance a short distance from the *John Bascom*. "[The] ship was moored to seawall stern to, blacked out, although port was lit up and the ships at dock were working cargo, the radio was silent, 4 Armed Guards were on lookout, 2 on the bow and 2 on the stern guns, and one merchant crew was on gangway watch."[16]

During the afternoon of December 2, "The Master (Otto Heitmann) and the Armed Guard Officer (Kay K. Vesole) and several members of the steward's department had left the ship since arrival although no liberty had been granted to crew or armed guard personnel."[17]

"At about 1930, the Master and Armed Guard Officer having returned aboard only a short while before, the Armed Guards sighted parachute flares descending from the moonlit skies and heard the motors of planes (presumably enemy aircraft) overhead. The general alarm was immediately sounded and battle stations were assumed although no planes could be sighted the gun crew opened fire laying down a barrage overhead."[18]

"As the attack began, the bright lights illuminating the piers and harbor were promptly extinguished, except for a spotlight (or searchlight) situated on a shore crane. This crane was abandoned by panicky Italian personnel and the light remained on for about 9 minutes until shot out by British Military Police."[19]

As the parachute flares were dropped, Cadet Leroy Heinse recalled, "they lit up the whole harbor. You could just sit there and read a book, so to speak, because of the brightness. My battle station was in the wheel house and I was supposed to reload these 20mm magazines which fitted into a Oerlikon gun. The gun jammed and went out of action and I proceeded to keep the other guns supplied with ammunition intended for his gun. We had ammunition for these reloading exercises in various parts of the ship, some of which were actually in the cadets' quarters. I was in the process of bringing those containers that had these into the wheel house where the first engineer was going to reload the canisters. Just about the time that I was arriving in the wheel house, a bomb hit our ship just forward of the wheelhouse and it went into the hold just forward of the wheelhouse. There was a tremendous explosion. It was so great that it blew off all my clothes. Shoes, everything. The only thing, to the best of my knowledge, was that I was left with my dogtag and silver identification bracelet on my left arm."[20]

"His entire right side, arms, legs, face and abdomen were seriously lacerated and a considerable amount of blood was lost.

Taken during the attack, this photo vividly shows tracer fire to and from a ship's antiaircraft gun position. Courtesy James Smith.

Semi-consciously, he tried to resume his duties but, on orders from the Master, retired to a settee in the chart room. Upon regaining consciousness, he found several officers working over him, preparatory to removing him from the ship."[21]

Seaman 1/c Warren Brandenstein, a gunner in the Naval Armed Guard, stated, "I had just returned to my quarters after showering when the general quarters alarm sounded. I quickly threw on some clothes and ran to my gun station on a 3.50 antiaircraft gun on the bow. The sky was filled with tracer fire and was lit up by flares dropped by the German Stukas. I reached my battle station, put on my helmet ear phones and proceeded to take orders from Ensign Vesole who was on the bridge. I was sight setter on the gun. All over the harbor bombs were creating havoc. The ship next to us took a hit and the next thing I did was to go to the magazine on deck to reset the explosive timer on the shells. At that time we were hit three times. Hold # 2, the bridge and after gun deck. My helmet and ear phones were blown off my head. I fell down and crawled on deck. All kinds of debris was showering down."[22]

Stanley Bishop, a Navy gunner gave his view of what happened to the *Associated Press*:

> I was sitting in the mess hall writing a letter home. All of a sudden the general alarm sounded, and the guns began to go off. I dropped my pen and tore up to my gun station on the bridge. The sky was full of tracers and flares and exploding shells, and it looked just like the Fourth of July.
>
> The first stick of bombs plunked about 100 yards away, striking a nearby vessel which exploded and sank.

There was a heavy jar and a wave of heat. Then there were explosions all around us. The ship next to us was burning.

I got out about 400 rounds of 20-millimeter gun before an erupted shell jammed it. Then two or three bombs hit our ship.

One bomb killed the man standing next to me, and blew me off my feet. The air was full of flying splinters and stuff, and a couple of German planes were strafing.

After the ship was hit, I went below to help bring up the wounded. Practically everybody in the crew was either dazed or hurt bad.

Ensign Vesole was shot all to pieces and hardly able to stand up, but he was in control all the time. Reeling all over the deck, he was giving orders and helping with the wounded.

… I was hit in the head by shrapnel so much that my helmet was cut to pieces.[23]

William Kreimer of the Armed Guard wrote that, "as the raid assumed proportions, lower flying planes came over and some strafing was experienced, a stick of bombs struck the *John Bascom* from stem to stern, three direct hits were scored. The bombs appeared to be powerful, striking the #5 hold, port side of the boat deck and #3 hold, the damage was extensive, the concussion of the explosions strong, knocking men around all over the ship, injuring practically every man aboard with shrapnel wounds. Hits were scored on ships on every side, and fire and disaster was present throughout the harbor. No aircraft warning was received from batteries ashore, nor was fire opened by them at the commencement of the attack. The 1st Engineer was killed outright by one of the bomb explosions, the only immediate casualty."[24]

Capt. Heitmann learned that the *John L. Motley*, loaded with ammunition and on the port side of the *Bascom* was a mass of flames and the fire was out of control. He gave the order to abandon ship at 2000. Unbeknownst to the men aboard the *Bascom* they had ten minutes before the *John L. Motley* would blow up. "Except for one lifeboat all life saving equipment was destroyed, the ship began to take water immediately and it is believed began to burn internally."[25]

During the abandon ship process, "The Armed Guard Officer (Kay Vesole) took charge of all preparations for abandoning ship, assembling the personnel and launching the remaining lifeboat, placing all badly wounded in the first boat and then loading it completely with merchant crew and armed guard personnel. It is not known definitely how many men were forced to swim (even though all were wounded and injured in some form), all hands managed to reach the jetty following the boat. Blankets, sheets and towels had been gathered before leaving the ship and efforts were made to aid the wounded with morphine shots. All able men proceeded under the direction of the Officer in Charge helping the wounded men out of the water, the wind was beginning to blow flames from burning oil over the jetty."[26]

Adding to the chaos was the fact that: "For several weeks before the attack it had been the practice of all ships when they finished discharging, to throw all their dunnage into the harbor; other ships had discharged a lot of fuel oil. This oil saturated wood was driven by a Southwesterly wind between the ships and the Mole and consequently caught fire. Upon abandoning the ships, survivors were met by this wall of fire, causing the death of many seamen and hampering the rescue of men in the water.[27]

"Escape over the jetty to the shore end was impossible due to the flaming mass, only a few minutes elapsed after arrival on the jetty until an ammunition loaded ship close aboard exploded and everyone again suffered from concussion and bruises, the blast was terrific and other ships began to burn, the *John Bascom* was then a mass of flame and slowly sinking."[28]

The ammunition ship, SS *John L. Motley*, was only about fifty feet away from the SS *John Bascom* when she blew up. The resultant concussion caved in the *Bascom*'s entire port side sinking her immediately.

Prior to abandoning the *Bascom*, "Captain Heitmann went through the ship looking for injured and took charge of giving them first aid bandaging most himself. He did not leave the boat until he had made sure all the crew had left or were in the lifeboat."[29] According to Gunner Stanley Bishop, "We wrapped up the injured, put 'em in the boat and lowered her into the water. All the men who had life jackets just went over the side. We rowed over to the seawall and then we found we were trapped there by fire between us and the shore."[30]

Warren Brandenstein was also there: "When we started to abandon ship I was the last one off the gun station after trying to find my wrist watch. Crazy as it sounds, one of my shipmates, the radio operator came to get me.

"Only one lifeboat was intact on the second deck and I finally got up there. Many of the Armed Guard crew went into the water and swam to the breakwater only a short distance away. I was ready to go into the water when Ensign Vesole said, 'Brandy get into the lifeboat, you're wounded.' I guess I didn't realize my face and hand was a mess.

"After getting to the breakwater in the lifeboat there were many other men from other ships there. We got into one of the shelters, closed the door and prayed. Suddenly a blast like nothing I ever heard before blew the door in. I believe it was one of the ammo ships going up.

"The harbor was aflame with burning oil on the surface of the water. Ships were aflame, blowing up, etc. The offshore wind was blowing the flaming surface oil toward us on the breakwater. Luckily the wind shifted, otherwise our only choice was to jump into the sea on the other side of the breakwater or get burned.

"About this time our signalman from the *Bascom* (Bob Kelly) somehow got hold of a signal lamp. He kept signaling to anyone on shore. Luckily, a U.S.N. destroyer had been lucky enough to escape the bombs and was headed out of the harbor. They must have seen our signal and the next thing we saw were small launches coming out to take us off the breakwater. As my boat left I can still remember thinking while looking at what was happening in the harbor that *this must be what Hell is like!*"[31]

Meanwhile, Captain Heitmann saw Cadet Midshipmen Heinse lying on the deck. "The twenty-three-year-old cadet was covered with blood and all his clothes had been blown off. His stomach was covered with lacerations. Heitmann washed the wounds with water from a nearby bucket and then tried to pull the worst wounds together with adhesive tape. As he did, he recalled a short time before the bombing he had seen Heinse at the starboard forward top bridge gun reloading the magazines and, apparently gotten there by walking. He wondered how he had gotten that far before he collapsed."[32]

Regarding the lifeboat, Heinse was told later, "There were people like myself that needed to be gotten ashore to receive medical attention. I can only speak of myself because I don't remember who else was in the boat with me. They put me in the lifeboat with the other people. They lowered it over the side and took me over to the wall of a breakwater. (There were fifty-two men in it and Captain Heitmann ordered even more over the side to climb into the lifeboat or get into the water and hang unto the seine floats.)"[33]

"The breakwater was a large structure that encompassed the docking area where all the ships were located. There were rooms (shelters) up on the breakwater for people to get out of the weather. The rooms had steel doors on them. However, there was a problem because the breakwater was quite high relative to the tide. The problem was how to get me and the other injured up onto the breakwater. The bottom line was that they had to establish a human chain of people leaning over the breakwater and getting hold of people like myself and pulling them up and placing them into the shelters. All the while, the whole area was heavily saturated with mustard gas, either in gas or liquid form, and was splashing onto various and sundry things that a person would come in contact with. I was awake and heard people saying, 'That ship over there is loaded with bombs. We've got to get into these shelters right away or we are going to be killed.' I remember them taking and dragging me into the shelter and laying me on the floor. Someone said, 'Get that door closed, that ship is going to blow anytime.' Some period of time after that it (the *John L. Motley*) blew. I remember the concussion that the thing caused. It blew off the door or slammed it open. The people that were standing around me were knocked on top of me and I was covered with people, so to speak. I found out later that it created a tidal wave in the harbor whereby all the mustard gas that was on the surface of the water splashed up on the breakwater and shelters. This is where I got clobbered with the mustard gas."[34]

Capt. Heitmann had high praise for his Armed Guard officer during the action. "When the attack came all hands were aboard and stayed at their stations under continuous fire until all the guns had been put out of action by the heavy bombing. There were at least three heavy bombs which hit the ship. It was a tribute to the discipline the officer (K.Vesole) maintained that all hands stayed at battle stations until the last possible minute.

"The gun crew as a whole, of whom I heard that nine had died as a result of the action, were a fine group of young boys and the gun crew and merchant crew got along well together. From the time we abandoned ship and were split up in different hospitals I hear that both gunners and merchantmen have kept in touch with each other and want to ship out together again.

"Despite the fact that two ammunition ships alongside were burning, the gunners and merchantmen went quietly and efficiently about rendering first aid and helping the wounded to get off the vessel. When we got on the seawall we went to the seaward end about 1600 ft. away from the ship. All the wounded were carried on make-shift stretchers and placed on the wall to be assisted by those still able to help. Most of the crew were taken by me and sheltered as much as possible. Mr. Vesole at that time, with a stretcher, assisted by members of the crew, on several of his missions from the end of the seawall went down into the fire. The whole harbor was ablaze and flames were encompassing the 80 foot sea wall. He took the wounded one by one to the sheltered end. From the time we left the ship he had a broken right arm and shoulder but kept going with the other arm …"[35]

In a United States Naval Armed Guard meritorious conduct letter filed in March of 1944, information was gathered by the surviving members. Concerning the action of Ensign Kay K. Vesole, 210513, D-V(S), USNR, Unit Commander:

While directing the fire of the guns, as a result of a bomb explosion on the ship, this officer having the majority of his clothing blown from his body, received a bad shrapnel wound in the right shoulder, and extensive wound over heart. His shoulder bled profusely and right arm was immobilized. Without regard to his personal injuries, Ensign Vesole collected himself and continued in complete control of the situation, going from gun station to gun station, directing action, inquiring of the safety of the personnel in his charge, rendering aid to the injured and wounded, constantly encouraging his men. As the raid passed over, despite the burning and sinking condition of the *John Bascom*, disregarding the painful nature of his wounds and resultant weakness from loss of blood, Ensign Vesole conducted a party of his men below decks and supervised the carrying of wounded personnel to the boat deck. He personally inspected the entire ship for wounded, and supervised loading of the only lifeboat not destroyed in the action. Ensign Vesole calmed members of the merchant crew who showed evidence of panic, saw that syrettes of morphine and medical supplies were procured, even bringing along several cartons of cigarettes for his men. Upon abandoning ship, Ensign Vesole insisted that, to make room in the boat for others whom he regarded worse wounded than himself, he would swim to the jetty or seawall approximately one hundred feet distant, his men having to use physical force to make him take a seat in the boat. In the boat, Ensign Vesole insisted upon rowing with his uninjured arm; upon reaching the jetty, Ensign Vesole immediately directed and assisted in disembarking the wounded again disregarding his own personal discomfort by manual exertion. Ignoring the constant present danger from a momentarily expected explosion of a burning ammunition ship close aboard, Ensign Vesole, although almost overcome by smoke and gas fumes, personally pulled three or four helpless wounded men from the water unassisted. Ensign Vesole, together with three members of the crew, then carried four or five wounded, unable to walk, on stretchers procured, to a bomb shelter near the end of the jetty. The nearby ammunition ship exploded about fifteen minutes after the boat reached the jetty, and Ensign Vesole, with his body already a mass of burns from the burning oil, started back into the flames which were being carried along the jetty by the wind and tide, and again had to be forcibly restrained by members of his crew from almost self sacrifice in his effort to aid and assist, as it was seen that it would have meant certain death due to the intensity of the fire, and the remainder of the wounded on the jetty were beyond help. As flames began to sweep over the jetty, Ensign Vesole had the presence of mind to despatch signalmen to the end of the jetty to signal with flashlights the predicament of the survivors to undamaged vessels nearby, and as boats were sent to evacuate, Ensign Vesole again attempted to make self sacrifices and remain until the last boat, although his condition was then pitiful, bordering upon complete collapse. It is evident that Ensign Vesole's actions throughout were responsible for the saving of countless lives.[36]

Ensign Kay Vesole was taken to the hospital where he later succumbed to his wounds and mustard gas burns. To the very end he was concerned about his crew. When the explosion took place on the jetty Vesole was thrown nearly thirty feet, "but he still tried to help others. During this time, was laughing, joking with the men to keep them calm. In the hospital, he was always courageous and cheerful until death … He treated every man alike; fairly, firmly, and with true leadership. Created mutual understanding, friendliness and cooperation between naval personnel and merchant crew, and this teamwork saved many lives, and caused less confusion and disorder during raid. In my estimation, and probably the opinion of every man that saw his action the night of the raid, he is unquestionably an outstanding hero."[37]

Ensign Kay Vesole's last words were "I've got a 3-month-old baby at home. I certainly would like to see my baby."[38]

SS *Samuel J. Tilden*

According to the Official Survivors Report:

The ship was anchored with her bow in an ESE direction, navigation lights dimmed and directly in beam of high-powered search light from the shore, radio sealed. There were 14 lookouts —

12 Armed Guard and 2 merchant crew in the bow, forward midships and aft gun tubs, top flying bridge, and bridge …[39]

Upon arrival at the entrance to the harbor of Bari, the ship was placed in the beam of a British Naval Control searchlight from the mole in the harbor awaiting boarding by a pilot. This took place just before the air raid began. The searchlight completely illuminated the ship and rendered it an easy target.

At 1810, 2 December, enemy planes appeared over the harbor and an air raid ensued. Several bombs were dropped but no hits were scored until approximately 1820 when a high explosive bomb crashed through skylight and exploded in engine room. Shortly thereafter aircraft dropped 3 flares and incendiary bombs, one of which hit the ship immediately forward of bridge.[40]

Cadet-Midshipman Robert F. Donnelly reported that,

Approximately five minutes after the first flares were dropped, a bomb was dropped through the fidley hatch, just aft of the stack. This bomb completely demolished the engine room where the writer was on duty. The concussion blew the writer up to the next deck where he lay for fifteen minutes. The rest of the men on duty in the engine room, including the First Assistant Engineer, Second Assistant, Third Assistant, two oilers and two fireman, are all believed to be lost. As the writer lay on the upper deck unconscious, another bomb hit on the starboard side amidships and the vessel began to burn fiercely.[41]

The Official Survivors statement continues:

Aircraft then returned and strafed deck from an approximate altitude of 200', damaging 1 lifeboat. No hull damage visible to survivors but a hole approximately 18" in diameter was reported left in deck. Explosion of the H.E. bomb destroyed all wooden bulkheads, bulged all metal bulk heads, buckled deck plates over the engine room and completely destroyed the engine room skylight. Fire broke out from the incendiary bomb and spread forward to bow and then aft. After the abandonment of the ship, the magazine on the poop deck exploded and ship was completely enveloped in flames. No distress signal sent. Alarm sounded and gun stations manned, but no counter-offensive offered.[42]

Naval Armed Guard S1/c, John Whitley remembered that "The Abandon Ship order was given as soon as we were hit. All of the boats were lowered immediately and life rafts were released. Some of the lifeboats were damaged from the strafing and shrapnel. Many men were in the water either blown overboard, or had jumped. I do remember tossing life rings to the soldiers in the water. I was able to get on a life raft and was picked up by the British launch. They gave us a drink of rum then put us out on the nearest jetty. We were told to walk ashore so they could return to the scene to search for other survivors, which they did. While walking along the jetty a ship in the harbor blew up and we fell down flat on the jetty, and we could feel the heat passing over us."[43]

Naval Armed Guard S1/c, William Waters said, "I got off the burning ship and got into a lifeboat and very shortly the bottom was blown out of it. The Second mate picked me up in another lifeboat and we rowed away from the burning ship. About an hour or so later the British picked us up in their motorboat and carried us to the end of the jetty."[44]

Naval Armed Guard S1/c, D.B. Queen recalled, "When the ship started sinking we were ordered to abandon ship. Army personnel first, Armed Guard, then Merchant Marine. The Merchant Marine did a great job in helping fill the lifeboats and life rafts. I have great respect for them. We were in the water several hours and a British patrol craft came out and started picking up survivors. It made several trips before completing its job."[45]

Regarding the searchlight, "It was not extinguished until 7 minutes after the raid began, although ship immediately extinguished her dimmed navigation lights. This was the first British controlled port entered by the ship where such practice was encountered.

"At the beginning of the air raid shore batteries of 40mm guns opened fire on attacking aircraft. Because of misdirected fire or unsuitability of the guns for AA defense (they were subsequently learned to be coastal batteries), the ship was subjected to continuous rain of shells from the shore batteries; destroying equipment, killing and wounding men, rendering the ship incapable of defending herself."[46]

Gunner William Waters said that the British shots "were mostly hitting the smoke stack so the bridge crew got behind the stack and stayed there."[47]

The Survivors Statement continues:

> Since it was impossible for the gun crew to serve the guns, they were ordered from their stations by the Armed Guard Commander. Both the 5-inch/51 and the 3-inch/50 caliber guns were rendered inoperative by hits from the coastal batteries. Master stated that more then half of the casualties were caused by the shore batteries; the unjudicious use of the searchlight materially aided the enemy in inflicting the remainder.[48]

D.B. Queen said that, "when the attack started spotlights from shore zeroed on the *Tilden*. The artillery from shore started strafing the ship. Our ship was lit up like a balloon with all them lights on us. We had several army casualties from the strafing, because they were all on the top deck. All the army personnel I saw that were killed or wounded was from the shore shelling."[49]

And finally, according to the Survivors Statement:

> No effort was made to maneuver the ship after attack started since chances of avoiding damage appeared better by remaining stationary, than by maneuvering in heavily phosphorescent, unfamiliar, crowded waters. Survivors commented on the general state of unpreparedness which existed at Bari."[50]

In a *World Telegram* article, Navy Lt. J.D. Anderson, who was the gun crew Commander, said,

> They just caught the Adriatic port "like a sitting duck." ... the Junkers 88's swooped in on the medium level. The second wave came

mast-high. They hit 17 ships so fast that it was a mammoth Fourth of July melee.

Because he learned at Algiers, Palermo, Naples and other places that a ship still "has more chance" of being missed in the outer harbor, Lt. Anderson said he and his gun crew sat tight for 20 minutes.

I was on the bridge. JUs were zooming under chandelier flares. Then they hit one of two ammunition ships, 8000 pounds of explosives. Shells, from block-busters to small arms, went up a half-mile. Green, red and purple lights danced in the heavens and then debris started to shower the harbor. The second ammunition ship went. I saw two JUs go down and by then the air was full of ack-ack.

The blow from the ammunition ship explosion knocked out Anderson's upper teeth and riddled him with shrapnel. Lt. Anderson, knocked 10 feet, blood streaming from his mouth and head, rallied his gun crew but realized the ship had received a death blow ... Only two of his battery of 20 mm., 3-in. and 5-in. guns were working. In two minutes the ship took a 20-degree list, settling five inches... "The Captain and I went over the ship from bow to stern — survivors were then in lifeboats or rafts — and I was last to leave..."[51]

The SS *Samuel J Tilden* was the fifth and final U.S. Liberty ship sunk in Bari harbor. After being bombed, strafed by enemy and friendly gunfire, and burning for almost seven hours, the *Tilden* was finally torpedoed twice and sunk by the British at 0200. This was done to prevent her from exploding and further blocking the harbor entrance. Of the complement of 278 men on board, only ten crew members and seventeen Army personnel were killed. After the Abandon Ship order was given, fifty-six men in lifeboats, eighty men on rafts, and fifty-six on floats made their way to safety after spending approximately one and-a-half hours in the water.

However, overshadowing all the saved lives is the horror of all those men killed by friendly fire. This tragedy will haunt the survivors for the rest of their lives.

SS *Lyman Abbott*

The second assistant engineer, George Maury said, "We

arrived in Bari on the morning of December 2, 1943 and anchored in the harbor to await our orders for unloading the next day. There were 37 ships in the harbor laying at the docks or anchored in the harbor. We were about in the middle of the harbor and about 300 yards from the nearest quay. Captain Dahlstrom and the Gunnery officer, Lt. Walker, went ashore to the Port Authority to receive their orders and to draw money and shore passes for the crew, etc. They returned in time for the evening meal, and then we went to the Purser's office to sign for our draw. The Purser's quarters was just on the other side of the alley from mine. I don't know how it happened, but they ended up in my Quarters, discussing the queer look of the script that we were to use as money in Italy. The Chief was standing there and said, 'Let me see that stuff.' I handed it to him and he said 'It really is funny,' and threw it in the air, and about that time, there was one hell of a big bang. With no warning, the bombing had started, and we were sitting in the middle of the harbor, with all our lights on, a perfect set-up for the German bombers. I bent over to pick up the money and was damn near stomped to death by everyone on their way to battle stations. I was assigned to the 20mm anti-aircraft gun on the port bridge. My job was to wind up the spring feed of the magazines and pass them to Lt. Browne who was the loader ...[52]

After arriving in port, Gunner's Mate 2nd Class Leo Krause, spent "the rest of the day just looking at ships in the harbor and checking the guns on the ship. We left them all uncovered and the ready boxes were full of ammo. We were quite uneasy and when it got dark that evening I was in the mess hall having a cup of coffee and talking with some of the gunners when all of a sudden there was a loud whomp-whomp. I was sure they were bombs. We all headed for our gun stations. My gun was the 3-inch on the stern of the ship. When we got in the turret we looked up and all we could see were parachute flares and it was bright as day. Bombs were falling all over the place and some ships were hit and on fire. Some were exploding. We pointed our gun up in the sky and started firing with the hopes of hitting some planes. It sounded like the end of the world was coming. All kinds of debris were flying all over the place. This lasted about 20 minutes. Then we stopped firing and I got down off the gun and looked around. I just couldn't believe what I saw. It seemed like the whole place was on fire and exploding when all of a sudden a bomb dropped close by and the concussion hit me. The next thing I knew I was lying on the deck. I was stunned pretty bad and all I could see was blood. I started feeling around then. I knew I was hurt pretty bad. My helmet was banged up and blood was getting in my eyes. Then I started feeling for my right leg. It was all bent and I felt the bone sticking out and it was all bloody. Right there, I said to myself, "I wonder if I'm ever going to see Pine Grove again."[53]

Donald Meissner said that when the attack began, "I think we all heard them at the same time, as you can't miss the sound of German bombers. I remember saying, 'The S.O.B.s are coming!' I stuffed cotton in my ears, put my helmet on, and ran to my gun. There were no planes to shoot at as they were staying above the flares which seemed to be staying in the sky illuminating the harbor. The ships in the harbor were an easy target for the bombers. We directed our fire directly over the ship hoping this would keep the planes from dropping a bomb directly on us.

"Three bombs hit the water off our bow. The fourth one hit off our stern. It hit so close the mud from the bottom of the harbor struck me in the face. I know the ship came out of the water because I felt it slap the surface when it came back down. There was no need for the planes to use flares now as the harbor was a blazing inferno. Suddenly, there was a brilliant flash as if night had turned into day. Then a thunderous explosion sent us sprawling to the deck whose massive steel was vibrating as if to fall apart. It then began to rain shrapnel on the deck and you could tell the different sizes of it by the sound of impact.

"When all the fury of the explosion subsided, there was a deathly silence except for the moans and cries of the wounded and the dying. A lot of blood was coming out of my nose and ears from the concussion, which also blew the shoes off my feet.

"One piece of shrapnel entered my mouth, went up through my upper left jaw, fracturing it, and came out under my left eye.

I had intense pain under my lower left rib and found that I couldn't put weight on my left leg. The Coxswain came to my gun tub and said the Captain gave orders to abandon ship.

"I looked out at the harbor which was on fire, and survival did not seem possible to me. When we headed for shore in the lifeboat, ships were exploding, bombs were still screaming down, and there was fire everywhere. One of the ships was riding high in the water and was coming right at us. We managed to get around it and I will never know how we got to shore.

"I found myself on the ground above the shoreline trying to figure out what that strange smell was. Two British soldiers picked me up and carried me to a Jeep. One of them looked at me and said, 'We had a bit of a bloody time didn't we sailor?' I didn't answer. ..."[54]

Third Assistant Engineer Frank Nicholls recalled, "I was in the engine room at the time of the air raid. A fireman and an oiler were also in the engine room. We heard all the sounds of the gun fire from our own ship and some of those around us but the big blast was when a nearby ship blew up. The concussion and noise was unbelievable and the vibration caused the steam pipes to shake so much that a gasket blew out and steam was hissing out of the joint. Everyone was afraid of being scalded and they all yelled, 'Get out of the engine room!' We all did as quickly as possible and ended up on the main deck."[55]

James Roark, gunner's mate, remembered, "We did not get a direct hit but did get a lot of debris from one of the ships. A deck plate from one of the ships landed on us. The Captain thought we were hit and gave the command to abandon ship. We were bouncing all around from the concussions of the bombs ..."[56]

Stanley Wisniewski, sight setter for the 3-inch/50 aft gun recalled, "At the time I was in the mess hall, which was also our swing room, getting ready for a friendly game of Pinochle. What got my attention first was the sound of the general alarm bell. We did not hear any air raid sirens nor did we hear any shore batteries firing. We were told much later that the search lights and shore batteries were sabotaged. We did not see any of the planes, but we did see the flares coming down that were dropped by the German planes to light up the harbor. We could not hear the planes because of the gun fire that our ship was sending up. When the alarm sounded there was a slight feeling of fear but then the training took over and we did what we had to do. We got our life jackets and helmets and went to our stations in a matter of seconds. To the best of my knowledge there was no confusion aboard the *Abbott* by either the Navy crew or the Merchant crew. The Merchant seamen that were assigned to our ammunition locker were doing their job. A very good job at that. We were never waiting for ammo.

"During the attack I was at my position on the gun setting the sights for the gunner. Of course we fired as soon as the gun was loaded but we had no idea where the planes were. It was pitch black and because the flares were coming down we could not see up. As previously stated, the search lights were not operating. We were hoping we could get lucky and shoot one down.

"The *John Bascom* was, to the best of my recollection, to the port side of us. One of the ships to the port side of us was hit and it exploded. That's when I was knocked unconscious from my position on the gun. I have no idea how long I lay there on the deck. When I awoke, I felt pain in my foot and buttocks. I also had a head wound and felt the blood running down my face. I did not realize how bad my arms were burned. I heard the blasts of the ship's whistle and I knew it was the abandon ship call. I saw a burning Polish ship that had lost anchor heading towards our ship. Being loaded with tons of bombs and ammo and gas, I believe our captain had no choice but to abandon ship.

"I limped forward where I found my very close buddy Paul Miller. There he was holding a fire hose into a forward hold. Only there was no water on deck. Until this day he doesn't know how or what he was doing there. I looked at him and saw a pool of blood coming out of his thigh. I knew he was hurt. He was also hit with a piece of shrapnel the size of an orange. I said to Paul, 'Let's get the hell out of here, the Captain has ordered the ship abandoned.' I helped him down into the life boat that was heading toward the burning freighter … As far as seeing what was happening to other ships around us all I can recall is seeing men running for their lives. Ships were on fire all over the harbor …"[57]

Lt. Michael Browne was a victim of the hazardous debris raining down throughout the harbor. He was acting as loader for the port bridge gun. George Maury saw what happened, "He was killed in the gun tub when a large piece of steel rolled up about the size of a ten quart pail landed in the tub, and bounced up and hit him in the back of the head, just under the rim of his helmet … This all happened when the ship that was close by, and loaded with munitions, was hit and blew up, showering us with debris. I remember that at the blast I dove down behind the ready box and my head was out over the coaming, and I was looking down at the hatches of the number three hold. I remember thinking that if that hold blew up, with my head out over the edge, it would take my head off. There was 2,300 tons of fragment bombs in that hold and if that had happened, it would have been more than my head taken off.

"When I was down behind the ready box, all the junk started to fall. Something hit me in what was stuck out from behind the box and it hurt like hell. I thought, brother you've had it. I felt around to where it hurt, but there were no holes or damage to my clothes or life jacket, so I checked some more. It appears that a case of 45 caliber bullets had hit the rail around the flying bridge and burst open and a package of bullets had hit my life jacket by my hips.

"I don't think the actual bombing exceeded twenty minutes, but ships that were hit and blowing up made a terrible din. Our ship was covered with junk from those ships. The blast from the ship beside us blew in the side of our smoke stack. It was a mess everywhere. The captain called a meeting on the boat deck to assess our damage. The third mate, Rex Grodevant, came forward and reported that we had taken a hit aft and it had blown up the deck all the way to the boat deck. He pointed to the spud locker and said it had come out of there because it looked like the deck had been torn up by the blast. What happened was that a huge piece of steel from one of the ships had landed on top of the spud locker. From the report of the mate, the Captain decided it was too dangerous to stay aboard, and ordered abandon ship. We gathered the wounded and dead and lowered the lifeboats and rafts ...

"The lifeboat I was in had holes punched in the bottom and filled with water up to the thwarts so we were sitting in water. We didn't know at the time that there was anything in the water that might be dangerous and a few of us got gas burns in sensitive places ..."[58]

The subsequent debris severely damaged the *Lyman Abbott*'s lifeboats and fire fighting equipment giving Captain Dahlstrom further reason to abandon ship. Cadet-Midshipman George H. Baist stated as part of his *Enemy Action Report*:

> The ships in the harbor were attacked by a fleet of 30 German bomber planes. The writer's vessel was anchored in the center of the harbor and during the attack, the Master gave the order to abandon her. The writer then descended down the Jacob's ladder to the motor lifeboat, but because the propeller was fouled by debris, it was necessary to row about a quarter mile to the dock. During the abandonment of the ship, the writer was severely burned, by what was later determined to be mustard gas, on the ankles, buttocks, elbows and hips.[59]

Concerning the lifeboats, Frank Nicholls said, "We all went to our assigned lifeboats, removed as much of the debris as we could, then lowered the lifeboats to the water. The boat immediately became filled with water because it had numerous holes in it that were caused by shrapnel from the bombs and exploding ships. Luckily the lifeboats were constructed with air tanks in them which kept them afloat.

"When we got into the lifeboat, several of the men picked up oars to row ashore. I was in the stern of the boat and there were no oar locks to put the oars in. I held the middle of the oar as tight as I could against the top edge of the lifeboat so the man next to me could row ..."[60]

Capt. Carl Dahlstrom made the decision to abandon ship after the explosion of the *John Harvey* and the ensuing debris rained down on the ships in the harbor. By then, the *John Bascom* was also adrift, having had her mooring lines burned away, and lay directly in front of the *Lyman Abbott*. The harbor was a blazing inferno.

SS *Grace Abbott*

Ensign Charles P. Lippert, Commanding Officer of the Armed Guard Unit, filed the following report:

> The first warning we had was the sighting of enemy planes over the port dropping flares and bombs at approximately 7:25 PM. The attack continued for thirty or forty minutes. During this time extremely heavy damage was inflicted upon the ships in the harbor. As near as could be observed the next morning about twenty ships had been completely destroyed and several others damaged; the destroyed ships included four or five American Liberty ships. Most of the ships lost were tied up at the "break-water" awaiting berths at the docks and were fully loaded. The ships that were lost for the most part blew-up and burned and the resultant loss of life on these ships must have been very high.
>
> No advance warning of the raid was given. The ship's general alarm was sounded when the first flares and bombs were dropped. The Navy gun crew and those of the merchant crew assigned gun stations manned the guns immediately. The (*British*) D.E.M.S. (*Defensively Equipped Merchant Ship*) Officer boarding our ship upon its arrival at Bari had instructed me verbally and through mimeographed instructions not to open fire with our large guns unless specifically directed to do so and in no event to continue with these guns over two minutes. [*Author's note: The command had been given to the other American Liberty ships that any commencement of fire was based on British orders.*] Our 20 MM fire was to be governed by white tracer of a "master" 20 MM gun on one of the piers, but being unable to find this "master" tracer, I opened fire with our eight 20 MM guns instructing the gunners to fire at any planes coming within our

range. Fire was opened by the petty officer in charge of the 5" 38 through misunderstanding, but after three rounds were fired I stopped the firing of this gun.

The attack was a medium or high level attack and the flares dropped at the start of the raid made it impossible to see the attacking planes. I never saw any of the attacking planes, although they could be heard overhead, of course.

Our own fire and, indeed, the defense of the entire port was pathetically ineffective. For the most part our gunners were firing at the flares dropped by the German planes. I am sure that no enemy planes came within range of our 20 MM's. Most of the firing being done was by the 20 MM's and 40 MM's, although some 3-inch/50 and 5-inch/38 fire was observed from the ships in port.

I do not believe any of the enemy planes were destroyed in the raid. Most of the fire I observed was low and in no way hampered the activities of the attacking planes. So far as could be observed or determined from the sounds overhead, no night-fighters were sent up to engage the enemy planes.

The instructions furnished me by the D.E.M.S. Officer listed as part of the harbor defense twenty searchlights. During the attack only one light was observed and that light remained stationary and was not directed against any of the attacking planes.

No direct hits were scored upon our ship. Considerable damage was done to the ship, however, by the concussion of a "near miss" and a nearby explosion and by flying shrapnel and wreckage.[61]

George Maury who abandoned the S.S. *Lyman Abbott* with his shipmates, rowed toward the quay. Maury stated, "We landed on a quay where there was another ship moored, strangely her name was the *Grace Abbott*. We went aboard her and she wasn't damaged, but she did have some junk on the deck. While we were there another ship blew up and a complete winch landed on her deck."[62] A bomb did land directly in the No. 1 hatch, but miraculously it didn't explode.

The Merchant and Naval Armed Guard crew aboard the *Grace Abbott* escaped injury and death. "The ship's Chief Engineer sustained a cut over his right eye when knocked down by the concussion of the 'near miss.' Except for very minor bruises and scratches among the gun crew, there were no other injuries sustained by members of our crew."[63]

SS *John Schofield*

Cadet Midshipman Theodore Schober: "On December 2, 1943, at about 1925 hours, we heard bombs exploding in the area near our ship. Since there was no doubt that we were undergoing an air attack, I immediately ran to the bridge. Since our ship was designated as the 'duty ship' we were equipped with a telephone. In accordance with instructions, I blew four blasts of the ship's whistle, then proceeded to my gun station on the flying bridge. Bright flares had been dropped by the German aircraft and the entire harbor was brighter than anything I had ever seen before. In addition, all the harbor unloading lights were on, for what seemed an eternity, after the first bombs were dropped. One of the Armed Guard gunners shot down many flares, thus giving us somewhat less brightness ...

"At some point in time, shortly after the bombing started, we were hit by a bomb which may have detonated on the dock, and which blew a substantial hole in our starboard bow. The odd fact is that we had just unloaded two large piles of 500-pound bombs from the #1 hold, and one pile of bombs had taken a direct hit where it lay about 30 feet from our starboard bow. Fortunately, the bombs had not been armed so not one of them exploded.

"The blast of the bomb exploding on the starboard bow blew our ship away from the dock, parting our forward lines, and causing the ship to roll at what seemed to be 45 degrees. The gangway dropped into the water, and was damaged by our rolling ship. Several Armed Guard and Merchant seamen were blown into the water between the ship and the concrete dock. Some sailors, returning from a few hours leave, helped pull some of our sailors from the water. I believe one Able-Bodied Seaman ... was crushed to death at that time."[64]

Schober may have been mistaken for, according to author Robert Browning, "None of the eight officers, thirty-six men, twenty-eight armed guards, and an undetermined number of British Army stevedores on board reported any injuries during the attack."[65]

Schober continued; "Our Engineer Cadet, Donald McAnulty, was on the bow manning a 20mm gun. He was blown from the bow into the water, along with several sailors. McAnulty's shoes were blown off. He managed to get onto the dock and pulled an Armed Guard sailor out of the water, but was so dazed that he was taken to a military hospital, where he was released and returned to his ship the next day, prior to his departure."[66] In a letter from Donald McAnulty's widow, Bette, she stated that Don had told her upon his arrival back to the ship that, "The Captain must have liked me because he cried when he saw me. The ship left port about fifteen minutes later."[67]

SS *Louis Hennepin*

On the day Bari was attacked Bernard L. Anderson wrote in his diary,

> Returned to ship about 5:15 and at chow was playing cribbage. At about 7:30, all of a sudden the guns on shore started firing. I went out and all the ships were opening up. I ran to my gun tub and was knocked down a couple of times by the concussion of bombs. We were having an air raid and bombs were hitting everywhere. They were over us before anyone knew it and dropping bombs before I even got to my gun. We were tied to the dock here and one bomb hit about 30 feet from the bow and my gun tub. It was about 500 lbs. The water and mud were thrown up and I got soaking wet. Another hit the dock about 50 ft. from the ship. The buildings were flattened. After I shot all my ammo I went over to Mannie's gun tub and helped him. Parachute flares were dropping all around us and everything was all lit up. The smoke and fumes from the guns were so bad you could hardly breathe. Ed Leahy and another fellow were hit by shrapnel. They took Leahy to the hospital. I believe he will be all right. In my gun tub I found a 40mm from one of the shore batteries and a bunch of shrapnel. I am bringing some home if I ever get home.[68]

The *Louis Hennepin*'s Radio Operator, James E. Smith, wrote the following in his *Remembrances.*

I was in the Radio Room monitoring BAMS and Port Watch circuits when the raid started. With split earphones I moved out onto the Bridge Wing and had first hand visual/audio observations of the action. Not certain how long the raid lasted ... don't believe more than 15 to 30 minutes, if that long. The resultant explosions with fire and smoke continued well into the early morning hours of 12/03/43. The dockside floodlights were on for most of the raid and some ships that had just arrived were firing their 20mms. With the aircraft engine sounds and explosions from bombs, ships blowing up, shore side gun fire and flames from ships on fire providing background noise and lighting, it was not **QUIET TIME.**

We were alongside one of the dock berths discharging cargo when the raid started. Probably about half empty. Initially we thought the ship had been hit with a bomb through the engine skylight and someone passed the word "We are sinking." Not true as the ship was rolling back and forth and smashing into the dock piles.

In this type of an affair, actions/reactions of people are somewhat disjointed. Two men attempting to leave or get back on board because of the reported 'sinking' got caught between the hull and the dock pilings. Others attempted to lower a lifeboat on the starboard side even with all the 'junk' flying around (Pieces of ships, dunnage, cargo, shrapnel and the smell of burning oil mixed with some other odors). I remember an oily sulfur odor although others said they smelled garlic. Some of the crew got hit with flying junk while trying to get into the Bridge. One piece of junk was about two feet by three feet in size. It looked like a piece of a ship's hull with a vertical weld intersecting with a horizontal weld almost as if you had punched your fist through a wet piece of cardboard. The weld intersection was in the middle of the piece of steel. One of the crew was trying to shoot out the dockside lights without a magazine for his 20mm. Two others were complaining they couldn't find their life jackets — They Had Them On.[69]

The American Tankers

The following is an excerpt from the Anti-Aircraft Action Summary report filed by Capt. Hays of the *Aroostock*:

> The Commanding Officer was, when the first flares were dropped and the subsequent engaging of the enemy aircraft by gunfire from the ship and shore batteries, just leaving the Psychological Warfare Board Headquarters, Bari, and was immediately driven to the port area, arriving there within eight (8) minutes. Every effort to obtain transportation to the ship in the harbor met failure. An effort was then made to proceed to the outer end of the fueling quay, which location was within 360 yards of the ship, but a direct bomb hit, about one-third of the way out on the quay, resulting in a large fire due to ruptured gasoline mains, prevented access to the outer quay for several minutes. Access was finally accomplished by crawling along the seaward side of the wall, past the fire, and then back onto the quay. Captain McCamey, U.S. Army, of the Adriatic Base Depot Group (Liaison Officer ...) accompanied the Commanding Officer to the outer end of the quay in this manner. Upon arrival at this point, about fifteen (15) minutes after the action had commenced, it was impossible to proceed to the ship because no boat or other conveyance was available. Thought was given to an attempt to swim, but it was feared the oil and petrol fires on the water would continue to spread rapidly, making it impossible to reach the ship in any case.
>
> The sky was lit up brighter, even, than day, and the Commanding Officer could clearly see the effort being exerted on his ship against the enemy. What appeared to be the most effective and most consistent barrage of any activity in the harbor area was maintained by the U.S.S. *Aroostock* until all firing ceased. The sky was filled with flying sparks, burning debris, with much schrapnel and other missiles being hurtled through the air and falling white-hot, into the water, on the ships, and on the quay. At least three bombs were seen to explode in the water close astern the U.S.S. *Aroostock,* throwing large geysers of water into the air and onto the ship.
>
> Two ships, [Polish registered *Lwow* and *Puck*] anchored within 260 yards and 400 yards, respectively, of the *Aroostock,* sustained

direct hits and immediately sank in about (4 ½) to (6) fathoms of water, the upper decks and superstructure still burning fiercely …

Approximately two hours after the action started, a large amunition ship exploded within 375 yards of the U.S.S. *Aroostock*, the impact of the explosion causing considerable superficial damage to the ship, and momentarily stunning everyone in exposed positions. The Commanding Officer, about 700 yards distant from the exploding ship, was nearly blown into the sea from the quay, and suffered partial deafness."[70]

From the quay, Capt. Hays witnessed the ensuing conflagration:

At about 2120 the ammunition ship, at berth 28 or 29, exploded, sending flame, debris, and smoke what appeared to be at least 6,000 to 8,000 feet into the air. The explosion was felt as far as sixty-two (62) miles away, and the damage to ships, harbor installations, and buildings throughout the city as a result of the explosion was great. Explosions of a lesser intensity occurred throughout the night and following day as the fires reached the magazines and explosive cargoes carried in the burning ships.[71]

It was later learned that from five (5) to seven (7) heavy caliber bombs were dropped at scattered points in the city, causing great damage to property and the loss of very much life.[72]

Frustrated at being unable to reach his ship, Capt. Hays could only watch:

Shortly after this explosion, the executive officer, Lt. (Jg) J. Umstead, Jr., U.S.N.R., got the ship underway and maneuvered through very dangerous waters to a safer anchorage farther away from the intense heat and fire of the adjacent burning ships. The Commanding Officer marveled at the manner and swiftness in which this maneuver was executed.

Since the ship was at all times very close by, excellent vantage was had of the entire action of the ship during all but the first eight (8) to twelve (12) minutes of action. Everything appeared to proceed in the manner of a well-organized drill …[73]

At 1927 the U.S.S. *Aroostock* opened fire with all guns, following the lead of the master gun on shore until that gun was silenced by a near-by explosion at about 1938.[74]

The U.S.S. *Pumper* (YO-56) carried 10,000 gallons of fuel destined for the Fifteenth Air Force. She was dangerously close to the *Aroostock* and her Captain, E.A. McCammond was upset over the crowded conditions of the harbor. A ship collision involving a tanker would be catastrophic, let alone a collision with another tanker. When the *Pumper* first arrived in Bari, she was assigned a berth alongside the other crowded Liberty ships on the East Jetty. The captain requested and received permission to move his ship to the outer harbor because off-loading wouldn't take that long. This act probably saved the ship and its crew from the attack.

During the attack, *Aroostock* and *Pumper* countered with as much firepower as possible against the German planes. They were practically the only ships capable of doing this as the German bombers concentrated on the East Jetty area. During the battle, Captain McCammond became increasingly concerned as he saw the burning *John Harvey* drifting toward his ship.

"One moment the *John Harvey* was a huge mass of flames moving across Bari harbor from east to north, the next she was gone. To the men of the U.S.S. *Pumper* the world seemed to stand still for several moments when the merchant ship blew up. There was a whispering sound as the air around the tanker was sucked toward the center of the blast and a fraction of a moment of silence. Suddenly the violence of the explosion ripped the area. The initial crack of the sound threatened the eardrums of every man in the vicinity and seemed to vibrate every bone in a person's body until even those who were not knocked off their feet found it difficult to keep their balance."[75]

Luckily U.S.S. *Pumper* sustained only minor damage. Most of what was left of the *Harvey* after the explosion passed over her and rained down on the surrounding ships. However, there was some damage: "The ship was literally showered with nose fuses and small fragments of the *John Harvey*. One piece of hull plating that was nine inches wide went through a port on the bridge breaking out the glass and lodging inside the superstructure."[76]

The British Ships

George Southern was an able-bodied seaman aboard the Hunt-class destroyer HMS *Zetland*. The *Zetland* and her sister ship, HMS *Bicester* were severely damaged and contaminated with mustard gas. "I was standing on *Zetland's* forecastle facing the *John Harvey* and the other ships when one of the vessels in the line blew up. Instantly I was hit by a gigantic blast of terrifically hot air which filled my lungs and body with excruciating burning sensations and at the same time I felt as though I were being crushed in a massive vice. Yet surprisingly, I can still remember my feet lifting from the deck. Some minutes later (though I have no way of knowing how long) I came to, lying on the deck under the bridge wing. Just afterwards *Zetland* lowered a boat and five men including myself manned it in order to carry out rescue work."[77]

Four British merchant ships were destroyed in the attack: *Devon Coast, Fort Athabaska, Testbank,* and *Lars Kruse*. The tanker *Devon Coast* had fifty tons of high octane gas on board. She caught fire and sank the next day. The following statement is from her survivors: "Ship was the southernmost in the harbor, moored on the breakwater, blacked out ... At 1830 the drone of low flying planes was heard; the next moment guns commenced firing. During the next 20 minutes bombs and flares were dropped continuously and planes were attacking from all directions. Ship ahead was struck by a bomb, and several bombs were near misses; the force of the explosions caused ship to pitch and roll. The captain thought the bombs were large. At 1850 a bomb struck in #2 hold causing a bright green flash which was followed by an explosion. Although the scene was brilliantly illuminated by flares and fires, the crew were unable to see anything for a while. The No.2 hold was completely wrecked and the crew, who were aft at the time were blown forward. The SS *Lom,* a [Norwegian] vessel moored alongside, had also been struck by a bomb and was on fire. Her bow moorings had parted and she was drifting perilously near, the wind blowing flames right across the fore part of the *Devon Coast.* It was not long before the ship caught fire and commenced burning furiously. Ship was last seen by survivors at 0600, 3 December and she was still burning fiercely. Fire eventually subsided and when only the shell remained, ship rolled over on her side and sank. Oerlikon guns were fired for about 20 minutes ... Survivors abandoned ship on a life raft and by jumping overboard. They made their way to shore as best they could. Total complement on board was 23, including 2 Army and 4 Navy gunners; exact number of casualties not known, but at least one is missing. The planes were not sighted before the attack."[78]

On board the freighter *Fort Athabaska* were two highly-prized 1,000 lb. German rocket bombs. Their presence was a closely-guarded secret. Bound for England to be analyzed, this type of bomb had caused fear and havoc with Allied shipping, notably the sinking of the British troop ship, HMT *Rohna* in the Mediterranean November 26. Over 1100 men, of which more than 1000 were American troops, perished from a direct hit by one of these rocket bombs. It was the greatest troop loss aboard ship in American history. As with the presence of mustard gas at Bari, a wall of secrecy shrouded the incident and it was only in the 1990s that the story began to emerge.

"The *Fort Athabaska* was damaged, probably from a bomb at 1830 GMT, while alongside the mole in Bari harbor with a cargo of 76 tons general cargo, 238 bags of ordinary mail for Algiers and two 1,000 lb. German Rocket bombs. Vessel was destroyed at 1850 when an ammunition ship that was tied up alongside blew up. The *Joseph Wheeler* was adjacent on the port side.

"At 1830 ships in the harbor were attacked by enemy aircraft. At 1850 there was a terrific explosion and a brilliant red flash. It was later learned that the ammunition ship SS *Joseph Wheeler* was struck by a bomb and blew up causing the *Athabaska* to catch fire and sink within 5 minutes. It is possible that the 2 German rocket bombs, stowed in #2 'tween deck, may have exploded at the same time. All ships moored to the mole were burning fiercely and frequent explosions of varying degrees of violence were taking place every few seconds. Fires continued burning throughout the next day, making a thick pall of smoke over the harbor. When survivors left the harbor 1600, 3 December, the remains of the *Athabaska* were seen. She was a burnt out wreck, resting on the bottom with only the blackened and charred stump of the mainmast visible. Survivors are sure this was their ship because the remnants of the ATN booms were seen and the ship was the only one in the harbor equipped with nets. Total complement aboard was 56, including 6 Navy and 4 Army gunners; 2 killed, 44 missing, 10 survived. The Chief Officer, senior survivor interviewed, could give very little information as he was ashore at the time of the attack.[79] According to George Southern, "only the bodies of the Master and the Carpenter were found."[80]

The SS *Testbank* arrived in Bari on 19 November, "loaded with military stores, moored alongside the mole and commenced discharging cargo that night, later shifted to another berth where discharging finished at 1500 29 November; from that time ship remained in harbor waiting for a convoy. On 2 December ship was moored stern to the mole (believed to be #18 berth) together with several other ships. Degaussing was on.

"At 1830 hours ships in the harbor were attacked by enemy aircraft. First bomb dropped on west side of wharf, quickly followed by numerous bombs all over the harbor. Within 15 minutes a number of ships were on fire. In the confusion it was impossible to tell exactly how many ships were hit, or how many caught fire due to blazing debris in the water. At 2030 a ship blew up with a terrific explosion lighting up the sky for miles around. The *Testbank* was destroyed without warning from this bombed ammunition ship. No information on how ship was abandoned. Total complement on board was 75, including 7 Naval and 3 Army gunners; about 70 are missing, several of whom were injured and died in the hospital, 5 survived. The third engineer, senior survivor interviewed, could give very little information as he was ashore at the time of the attack.[81] According to George Southern, "not one body was found."[82]

The British freighter SS *Fort Lajoie* escaped destruction, but was severely damaged. According to the survivors summary: "The *Fort Lajoie* was attacked by enemy aircraft at 1830 GCT while at anchor in Bari Harbor. Bombs exploded in the harbor, one of which near missed the ship on port side inflicting no damage. Flare dropped by planes fell into starboard amidship Oerlikon nest, setting it on fire. Fire party organized but flare burned through iron deck and set fire to gunners' accommodation below. At about 2100 two terrific explosions occurred from the direction of the outer end of the mole and ship was peppered with red hot splinters and several small fires started. Full force of blast appeared to pass over ship. Pieces of red hot metal blown into #4 hold setting fire to rubbish. Forepart of lower bridge was also alight which, together with fire in the Oerlikon nest, made 3 separate fires burning at the same time. All hatches, fore and aft, blown off and tarpaulins ripped to shreds. There were several large dents in the decks; one piece of plating 10' x 6' x 4' wrapped around one of the winches. A large anvil weighing about 6 cwt (Hundredweight) landed on deck and an ammunition box fell from about 200', cut through #4 derrick and fell into #4 hold. Decks were covered with unexploded ammunition apparently blown from other ships. Six 2 pounder shells found buried in the lagging of the boiler fronts — no damage to the boilers. Fires were fought and an attempt was made to shift ship out of danger of flames from oily waters, but it was impossible to knock steel pins out of cable shackles. Fires aboard ship under control by 2100. Oerlikons fired throughout the attack, also 2 rounds from the 12 pounder. The gunners stated that the Italian machine guns on shore which were supposed to fire white tracers to indicate position of the planes did not do so, consequently ship's firing was blind. Injured were taken ashore about midnight. Total ships complement 55, including 8 naval and 4 military gunners. There are 54 survivors, 1 killed and 8 injured. Ship did not sink and was not abandoned, but proceeded to Augusta under her own power, arriving 1600, 5 December.[83]

The Other Ships

The Dutch ship *Odysseus* carried a load of coal and was the last ship moored on the East Jetty. The Captain had been playing cards with some of his officers when the raid commenced. Although the dive bombers didn't hit the *Odysseus* directly, she received severe damage from bomb concussions. One bomb in particular blew up near her port side. George Glenton, (who served on *Odysseus*, and wrote a book about her journeys) recalled: "Most of her deck fittings had been crushed, ripped through by bomb splinters, or torn from their bolts and mountings and blown over the side. Heavy wooden doors had been ripped from their hinges and lay about like shattered matchwood. Cabins and bulkheads had been gashed open as if by some Titan with a colossal can-opener.

"Above all, where her funnel should have been was now only shocking space revealing the livid sky. All that remained of that once imposing and most important centerpiece was the crushed and jagged stump outlined against the background of leaping flames."

It was a crippling blow, for the *Odysseus* depended entirely on her tall smoke stack for the natural draught to maintain furnace heat which was the source of her steam power.[84]

The flames on top of the water were heading directly toward the ship and the tide was working against the men trying to get away in a life raft. They were forced to return to the ship where they put their ingenuity to work. George Glenton: "Already the engine room crew had hammered into some sort of shape the twisted and buckled steel which was all that remained of the original smoke stack. Using it as a base willing hands urgently and ingeniously raised above the gaping hole a multi-sided shaft, praying it would not catch whilst fervently hoping for the uplift of air.

Castello Normanno Svevo where hundreds of Bari citizens sought shelter from the attack. The castle walls saved many lives, protecting those inside from the bombing attack and the explosions of ships in the harbor. After the Battle *Magazine.*

"Braced inside with salvaged and commandeered metal bars, wedged and lashed around with chain and stayed with wire, its ludicrous appearance belied its immediate importance. Encouraging cries from below proclaimed that the fires were drawing again, not vigorously but heartily enough to add to the low head of steam on which all hopes of survival depended."[85]

Describing the flight of the *Odysseus,* Glenton wrote: "Painfully slowly through the narrowing channel between the leaping flames and the inhospitable wall she crept to the entrance and limped safely out into the Adriatic."[86]

In the city of Bari there was confusion and pandemonium as the residents, who only seconds before had been calmly savoring the quiet evening, struggled to comprehend the sudden disaster and decide what to do. Instinctively repeating their practice over the centuries, many panic-stricken citizens fled to the safety of the Castle Svevo.

The explosion of the *John Harvey* killed many Bari civilians who sought refuge in the harbor, trying to escape the fires caused by the bombs dropped in the city. Author Glenn B. Infield wrote,

> There was no time to run, no time to hide, no time for anything. One moment the inhabitants of the old section were rejoicing in their fortune for escaping from inside the wall, the next they were dead. The brilliant light of the blast clearly outlined the survivors as they lined the shore. It also attracted their attention and they turned to look out to sea just in time to face the unbearable concussion that swept out from the doomed ship in a 360-degree circle. For most of them it was their last look at anything on earth.[87]

Ambulances screamed throughout the night carrying Allied personnel to the hospitals. The citizens of Bari, for the most part, were disregarded. Medical care for military personnel came first. The old part of the city was in shambles as buildings crumbled from the bombs that missed the harbor. In *A History of The Twenty-Sixth General Hospital*, it was reported that, "Shattered glass littered the streets. Steel shutters covering shop windows were twisted and ripped off. Roofs and sides of buildings were caved in. Huge fragments of metal lay in the streets. It was no wonder that the civilian population were terrified!"[88] Panic and terror spread quickly through the populace. A mass exodus had begun. "Women carried bundles on their heads. Some refugees led a goat or a sheep on a leash. Everyone was frightened. Where they were going we do not know, but they were intent on leaving the city behind. No one seemed to know how many civilians were killed during the raid, but the number of casualties must have been high."[89]

As the explosions continued through the night and into the next day, the following eyewitness account was printed in the *Chicago Daily News*.

> Long before daylight the harried civilian population took to the roads in a panic resembling that of the last days of France. By noon little boys and girls on bicycles or scooters or afoot were slowly

Taken in September, 1944, this photo shows the effects of the attack on the downtown area of Bari. Russell Krenciprock

moving toward their aunts and uncles and other relatives who lived in greater security along the interior highways.

High-wheeled carts from the olive groves had been pressed into service and Bari's people in steadily increasing numbers, had started on one of those treks that never get anywhere. It was like making the retreat to Bordeaux all over again to watch them — serious-faced oldsters and clusters of little children, all mounted high on cartloads of pitiful household trash, sewing machines, pots and pans, chairs, tables, pitchforks, shovels and bedding — always sewing machines and bedding.[90]

On the docks that morning about 25 badly burned British and American sailors sat outside the navy house waiting for someone to take them somewhere else. They had been unable to get into any of the overcrowded hospitals and had been treated right where they were. They were foul with refuse of the harbor and streaked with the horrible purple dyes of burn unguents ...[91]

The initial bombardment severely damaged the Fifteenth Air Force's new headquarters as well as various hospital units which were being set up.

Bernard Anderson, who was on board the SS *Louis Hennepin*, wrote in his diary on December 4th,

> The town here which has a population of 60 to 80 thousand was bombed too and every window in the city is broken. The roads leading from the town are full of people moving out. We can see the buildings from the ship that were bombed and there isn't much left of them.[92]

The houses in the old section were toppled and blown over as if they were made of paper. For miles inland, windows in practically every building were blown out. Thousands of inhabitants were killed.

On December 6, Bernard Anderson and a Naval Armed Guard shipmate walked into the city of Bari. He wrote in his diary,

> Everyone is leaving town. Mannie and I walked up town today and every building in the town has nearly every window broken, even the window frames. About two bombs or more hit the city and they are still digging bodies out of the debris. The people here sure don't like the Americans. They blame the raid on us and they sure give us a dirty look … The ships that were sunk are still burning. They have been trying to put them out, but they are oil fires and are hard to put out.[93]

But this was not the end of the disaster. A deadly poison was in the air and in the water, which would kill many more in the days, months and years to come.

8

NIGHTMARE IN BARI

Most of the damage was caused by the explosion of two munitions ships, rather than the bombs themselves. U.S. Army Signal Corps, courtesy National Archives.

For those of us who were at the hospital, the first indication of trouble was the rumble of anti-aircraft fire. Then came the thunderous bursts of big guns, and the hospital lights went out. Outside, the sky was ablaze with streams of tracer shells cutting the darkness in every direction. Over the harbor, lighting it brilliantly with a dazzling bluish light floated the flares dropped by the enemy. Spent flak dropped on the roof and in the gardens.

Then came the roar of bombs, and the red glow of fires. Suddenly we saw a mushroom of flame, sparks, and smoke explode hundreds of feet into the air. A few seconds later the force of the explosion reached us, actually pushing against us with a powerful pressure. Glass shattered in hospital windows, and even casements were blown out. At the same time the sound of the explosion came with a crash so intense that it defied description. An ammunition ship had blown up.

Shattered glass and falling casements had injured some of our men, so the dispensary called for surgeons to attend them. Working by the light of flashlights, and with only the instruments and materials from the dispensary first aid kit, doctors dressed wounds and extricated glass fragments embedded in flesh.

A few minutes later a second ammunition ship blew up, with effects similar to the first. And more and more spots of the dull red glow of fires appeared in scattered positions.[1*]

The American 26th General Hospital was being set up at the Ospedale Militare in Bari. Most of the needed personnel were on hand, but "one officer and nineteen enlisted men were on board the Liberty ship, *Samuel J. Tilden*."[2] In addition, the ship carried the vitally needed supplies for the American 26th Hospital. The *Tilden* quickly became a blazing inferno and early the next morning was sunk by British torpedoes. The single death aboard the *Tilden* was Pfc. Leo S. Kaczmarczyk, one of the medical personnel. Several of the others were injured, but none seriously. But, with the torpedoing of the *Samuel J. Tilden*, the 26th Hospital's critical supplies were sent to the bottom of Bari harbor.

It was now crucial to commence care of the victims of the raid. Therefore, immediate action was taken to set up an emergency hospital to operate on a limited basis in order to provide an expansion of the existing medical facilities which were provided by a British and New Zealand hospital operating in the vicinity.

On December 3, 1943, one hundred hospital beds, bedding, pajamas, bedside tables, and two dressing carts were obtained from the Air Force General Depot 5, and the Adriatic Medical depot. Later, additional supplies were obtained from Naples.

---

[*] From a description of the attack recorded by the American 26th General Hospital

The U.S. General Hospital in the Sanatorio Cortugno received many of the mustard gas victims after the attack. Shown is the gate on the Viale Orazio Flacco as it appears today. After the Battle *Magazine.*

On December 4, 1943 the first patients were admitted to the hospital. Most of the patients were mustard gas casualties. Before the end of December, 218 patients had been admitted … [3]

The 26th was involved in myriad other activities after the raid. Among them was finding lost casualties.

In addition to operating the hastily assembled emergency hospital, the organization made other contributions to the care of victims of the disaster. Anesthetists, technicians, and nurses were sent on detached service to assist in the care of patients at the Ninety-eighth British General Hospital. That service was continued for sixteen days, covering the critical period following the attack.

Furthermore, officers and Red Cross workers of the Twenty-sixth General Hospital made a search for missing American Army, Navy, and Merchant Marine personnel. The search covered the entire surrounding district as far as Brindisi and Taranto, and it resulted in the prompt location of sixty-four United States Army men, and one hundred and seventeen members of the United States Navy and Merchant Marine. At the same time we located our own personnel who had been injured on board the *Samuel J. Tilden*, In the meantime the facilities of the hospital were expanded as rapidly as possible, and as they were expanded, American military personnel were transferred to our care from the British and New Zealand Hospitals.[4]

Gwladys May Rees Aikens served as a nurse in Q.A. Reserve — Queen Alexandra's Imperial Military Nursing Service/ Reserve. The Reserves were formed in wartime to provide nursing care to soldiers in hospitals. Aikens was part of the 98th General Bari Hospital at the Polyclinic which, according to her, had about 5,000 people working there when she arrived. Her experiences were compelling: "It was late afternoon. I was scheduled for night duty later on, but as I had promised to write a letter from one of my patients to his girlfriend, I went to see him before my shift began. The navy chap for whom I had begun writing the letter had a tiny anteroom to himself because of eye injuries. We never knew what sort of buildings we would find to put our patients in, but private rooms were rare.

"I was sitting by my patient, writing as he dictated to me. Everything seemed to have quieted down. We were not busy, but we were expecting a train convoy at 5:00 the next morning and had finished all preparations for it. There was also an air evacuation from the hospital to take place about the same time. This young man had lost his sight in a mine disaster and should have been on the morning flight to the U.K., but due to another injury, the medical officers didn't think he was quite ready to travel. I believe he was Canadian, and I recall he had a package of lifesavers. The patients often received care packages from home via the Red Cross and this chap had found lifesavers in his box of goodies. I think he could sense that I was curious about the candy with the hole in the middle, so he offered me one. I thought it delicious.

"About 6:00 p.m., while I was writing, I could hear gunfire in the distance, which was strange, as the war had supposedly moved up the coast. Curious, another Q.A. and I decided to try to see where the gunfire was coming from. I told my patient I would be back shortly, and the other Sister and I donned tin helmets and cloaks and ventured stealthily, like a couple of spies, up to the flat roof. There was definitely something happening; the barrage was becoming intense over the harbour, and within an hour the whole place was a blazing inferno. Some of our staff were down by the waterfront seeing to evacuation arrangements for patients going to the U.K. by ship the next day, and we hoped they were alright.

"As we lay flat on our stomachs, peering over the sight below us, a powerful explosion suddenly shattered what we thought must have been every window in the building. It was, we decided, time to get back downstairs. Brushing off shards of glass that had landed on us, we gingerly descended the steps, crunching glass. The power was off. No one seemed to have been injured by the flying glass and it didn't appear to be sharp to walk on. The scraping of glass particles being swept away from the main thoroughfare by the orderlies brought on a flood of apprehension, because we knew that with the disaster would come the patients.

"It wasn't long before the influx of wounded began and I never did finish that letter for my patient. The rumours circulating were all the same — a lone bomber had managed to score a direct hit. Seventeen ships of the Allied forces had been hit. The terrific vibration of the ammunition ships exploding was what had turned our hospital into glass shambles, but at least it was still standing.

"We supposed that the ships could not have been too heavily loaded with ammunition, or else we wouldn't have been alive to think about it.

"We worked by the dim glow of hurricane lamps. I can remember at one point fixing an intravenous by the light of a single match held by the orderly in front of a heavy screen to prevent the draughts from blowing out the light.

"While the bitter December wind forced its way through our makeshift window coverings, we found we had hot running water for the first time. Nothing short of a miracle.

"We worked long and hard into the night and early morning. Intravenous bottles were dripping from every third bed and

Entrance to the Bari Polyclinic on the Piazza Giulio Cesare. After the Battle *Magazine.*

corridors were crammed with patients for whom we could find no accommodation. We were soon receiving patients via the operating theatre, patients with bilateral amputation of legs still wearing their life belts.

"The work of the often-overlooked Royal Army Medical Corps orderlies and stretcher-bearers was admirable. They were marvelous, carrying patients in, transferring them to different wards, making hot drinks and keeping us in cups of tea for the next two days and nights. They worked along side of us nonstop, keeping up a cheerful banter, helping us to maintain our sanity.

"The whole staff worked in complete harmony and cooperation, even though each ward had, for two days, double its usual number of patients. The ward I was on had 160, but with many orderlies working and extra nurses on shift, we handled the workload.

"The aftermath of the explosion was almost too pathetic and grim to describe.

This was the building used by the British 98th General Hospital on the grounds of the Polyclinic. After the Battle *Magazine.*

"Only a few hours after dawn following the raid we began to realize that most of our patients had been contaminated by something beyond all imagination.

"I first noticed it when one or two of my patients went to the sink looking for a drink of water. This was odd, because the drinks had already been taken around as usual after supper. Suddenly there were more looking for water and we could hardly control them. They were complaining of intense heat and began stripping their clothes off. Patients confined to bed were trying desperately to rip their dressings and bandages off.

"With what little knowledge we had, our first thought was that these boys were suffering from mustard gas burns. There were blisters as big as balloons and heavy with fluid on these young bodies. We were not sure whether the staff was at risk as we did not know what that fluid contained. Although we tried to get tests done, we were never informed of the results. We did everything humanely possible — draining the blisters, constant intravenous and eventually mild sedatives, but it was no good. It was horrible

The next day most of those ships which weren't sunk were still burning. "No smoking" sign in English and Italian can be seen to right of soldier. U.S. Army Signal Corps, courtesy National Archives.

to see these boys, so young and in so much obvious pain. We couldn't even give them strong sedatives, since we weren't quite sure how they would react with whatever had poisoned them.

"The medical officers tried to get through to the War Office in London for information, advice and an antidote, but none was forthcoming. We were all furious. And yet, if the War Office couldn't release the information, it must be a military secret, and if that was the case, we were certain we were witnessing the effects of a poisonous gas. Although we didn't know it at the time, there was indeed the very worst kind of poison involved.

"Both day and night staff now were on duty. Despite our ministrations, we were at a loss to battle this poison and we couldn't save the majority of the wounded; almost 1000 men died in one night and just as many in the aftermath. I think they knew we were doing our best to save them. We tried to make their last hours as painless as possible. Most of them were conscious

By the next day official U.S. military estimates were that sixteen ships were destroyed. Most of those afloat continued burning. U.S. Army Signal Corps, courtesy National Archives.

throughout their ordeal and were so confused about their injuries. Their eyes asked us questions we couldn't answer."[5]

George Southern, in a letter to this author, wrote about Bob Willis' graphic experience as a medic in the 98th British General Hospital.

> Bob Willis was a medic who was knocked unconscious by a blast when meeting the ambulance train which had arrived from the northern war zone. Hundreds of survivors overwhelmed the staff. They had to be placed on the floor of wards and corridors, some on camp beds others on blankets and coats and others just left to die in one room as there was no hope for them. Bob recalls a dying man crying out in pain, and against orders holding his hand to comfort him. Bob said, 'I would have been in serious trouble if I had been found out.' Surgeons operated with streaming eyes unaware that the patients were contaminated. Many patients were covered with blankets which unfortunately facilitated the absorption of mustard gas through the skin. Had the medical staff been aware of the true facts, many men

A ship's 20mm antiaircraft gun frames burning ships the day after the German attack. Unseen and unknown at the time was the presence of mustard gas in the harbor water and surrounding atmosphere. U.S. Army Signal Corps, courtesy National Archives.

could have been saved. Willis afterwards spent many days and weeks in the makeshift morgue in the cellars of the hospital where an Italian carpenter made wooden box-like coffins ...[6]

E.M. Somers Cocks wrote a history of the New Zealand Hospital contingent titled, *Kia Kaha: Life At 3 New Zealand General Hospital 1940-1946* (3NZGH). She and the 3NZGH arrived in Bari on the afternoon of October 31 aboard the H.M.S. *Dorsetshire*. 3NZGH was established in a wing emanating from the center of the horseshoe complex at the Polyclinic. Unfortunately, the hospital's anti-aircraft gun was nearby and whenever it was fired, the noise was deafening. She recorded her experiences:

It took days to extinguish the fires and was three weeks before the harbor could be opened again. U.S. Army Signal Corps, courtesy National Archives.

At half-past seven on the evening of December 2nd, just one month after our arrival at the Polyclinic, we were admitting a convoy of 100 battle casualties, when suddenly, a terrific barrage opened up, and the air-alert siren wailed its dire warning. The German planes were over in full strength, it appeared, and the harbour was full of ships.

The ships shrouded themselves with an artificial fog; enemy planes dropped flares, lighting up the night with an eerie whiteness, then a string of bombs was loosed. There was a great explosion, and an immense wall of flame seemed to leap out of the harbour. A few seconds later, there came another gigantic explosion — the hospital rocked, doors were wrenched off hinges, windows were shattered, and the bricked up windows scattered their bricks like hail.

Explosion after explosion occurred, with more flames each time, shooting high into the air, a thousand feet or so, with side shoots, like sky-rockets, darting off on tangents.

The barrage barked and growled; the noise was deafening, and with every fresh explosion, the building creaked and rattled, rocking like a ship in a storm. The scene at the harbour now was an angry glow with billowing smoke rising from it, and every now and then, a hideous flame would shoot up into the darkened skies. Still the hum

An antiaircraft gunmount on the SS Louis Hennepin *frames the pall of smoke from burning ships in the background. James Smith.*

of enemy planes roared overhead, the whine of dropping bombs, and the intensity of the ground fire provided a hellish accompaniment to the flames and the smoke.

At the hospital, the lights were switched off at the main, and those not on duty dived for cover. In the wards, all was well fortunately, none of the patients being struck by glass or falling debris. The beds were dragged hastily into the centre of the wards, and in only one smaller room were bricks dislodged and blown inwards by the blast. Patients who had been there, had, by the mercy of Providence, been moved out a few hours before.

All work came to a standstill, and the convoy of battle casualties lay on the floor of the Reception room for two hours till the raid was over.

Among these battle casualties were some German POWs. They looked as pleased as punch listening to the explosions, and gabbed away excitedly to one another. They were lucky we didn't knock their blocks off, but I suppose we would have felt the same had the boot been on the other foot!

Those two hours of the raid seemed to last a lifetime. The shattering din and the inferno of smoke and flames was appalling.

As soon as peace returned, we set to work dispatching the battle casualties to the wards. We'd just managed to get them safely into bed

Fires and explosions continued well into the next day as shown in this photo taken on December 3. James Smith.

when casualties from the harbor raid began pouring in. Most of them were from the docks, seamen and workers on the wharves. They were all nationalities. Besides English, there were Americans, Poles, Indians, Norwegians, and Italians. They came in covered with oil, grim spectacles of a grim disaster. Most were badly burned and all were severely shocked, and some suffered from exposure, having been in the sea for a couple of hours before being rescued. They were thoroughly exhausted. We waived all Army regulations for admitting these poor wretches, and sent them straight to the wards and bed, without bothering to take particulars.

A few who came in were so badly injured, they died soon after they were admitted, and before we had time to find out who they were.

All night we worked, getting these casualties in bed. We hadn't nearly enough room for them in the wards already functioning, and had to put up stretchers, hastily, in the unfinished building where there was no light, or water or any sanitary arrangements — but where, at least, they could have our care.

In the morning, the place was a shambles. The whole of the Polyclinic buildings showed signs of having suffered. There was broken glass lying all over the place; doors looking as though someone had been at them with an axe, leaned drunkenly in odd corners or cluttered up passage-ways where they had been flung. There were bricks everywhere, broken pieces of timber, and shattered tiles from the roofs.

As the smoke (some of it laden with mustard gas) cleared, sunken ships were seen throughout the harbor. James Smith.

At the harbour, a thick pall of smoke hung over the devastated area, and a strong acrid smell of diesel oil floated into the air. Stricken ships lay topsy turvy; some still burned and continued to burn for a couple of days; others were blackened hulks projecting starkly above the water, and others, still, had sunk from sight. Altogether about 17 ships were lost, and over 1000 people were killed or injured.

As well as the disasters in the harbour, there were at least five direct hits on buildings in the old and new parts of the city. One stick of bombs fell on a large block of flats only about 500 yards away from the hospital.

We were told to expect even larger explosions than any we had had, as one of the ships in the harbour, still burning, was filled with TNT. We waited for it — but nothing happened, owing to some cold-blooded bravery on the part of the Royal Navy!

Of course, the civilian population got the breeze up after the harbour bombing and fled into the country for safety, but although we had plenty more air-raid alarms, that was the only full scale raid made by the Germans on our area.

We were fortunate none of our patients was hurt during the raid, but the staff suffered some minor casualties …

We have been at Bari under two months (*By Christmas 1943*), but in that short time we had admitted 1554 patients, discharged 1165, and had 18 deaths — 14 as the result of the raid.[7]

Taken during happier days, this photo shows part of the SS Louis Hennepin's *Naval Armed Guard gun crew. Only the officer in charge, Ensign Upson, is identified. Bernard L. Anderson.*

After the raid, the British Port Commandant informed higher command that there was a possible risk of mustard gas in the harbor and that the Liberty ship *John Harvey* should be scuttled. There was no need to carry out this order because at this point the *John Harvey* no longer existed. When she exploded, her perilous cargo spread throughout the air and water, while an undetermined number of unspent mustard gas shells went to the bottom of the harbor.

In the meantime, word was passed to the 98th General Hospital of possible gas in the harbor. "The Naval Duty Operations Officer said that he passed a telephone message to 98 General Hospital about midnight that there was a possibility of gas casualties, and asked them to warn their casualty stations to be ready to deal with them."[8] Early on the morning of 3 December, "The PAD Officer No.6 Base Sub area visited the docks and reported to his HQ at about 0900 hrs. that mustard had been smelled in the dock area. About 0930 hrs., HQ No. 2 District telephoned and confirmed that some gas was in the dock area."[9] One hour later, the British Base Military Officer stated, "the first definite knowledge he had about gas was on 3 Dec about 1030 hrs. He went around with the Port Defence Officer to sites suspected of contamination. He boarded the HMS *Vienna* where he found that sick bay personnel had their eyes affected and the doctor, a blister on one foot. He also inspected the French tanker *Ladrone*, which he thought might have been affected, but found no signs of contamination. The quay was closed and sentries posted to forbid anyone from going there for unessential purposes."[10]

Ten hours earlier, at midnight, casualties began arriving from the harbor area.

> The hospitals were puzzled by the nature of some of the casualties they were receiving and their subsequent development. Such warnings as they may have received (if any) about the possible presence of gas certainly did not reach the appropriate quarters, and there is some evidence that, on a telephone inquiry being made by 98 Gen. Hospital (where the majority of casualties were) to Navy House on the morning of 3 Dec., no confirmation of the presence of mustard in the harbour could be obtained. Whether the alleged informant was ignorant of the facts or was impressed with a supposed desirability of secrecy is not clear.[11]

The Harbor

Gunner's Mate Gene Dorsey was aboard the S.S. *Houston Volunteers*. They carried a load of bombs for the American Fifteenth Air Force and arrived in Bari shortly after the raid. Dorsey stated, "I witnessed war torn cities in North Africa, but nothing was like this. As we entered the breakwater, bodies were floating in the harbor. Seems like more popped to the surface as a result of the ship's wake. I also remember there were British and American grave registration battalions there doing their obvious duty. They sort of used our mess hall for coffee breaks. I remember one comment, 'at least it's cool here, not like North Africa.'"[12]

James E. Smith of the *Louis Hennepin* said, "The view of the harbor in daylight on 12/03/43 was not pretty. Ship's masts and funnels were sticking up out of the water and some had disappeared completely. The harbor surface was covered with up to a foot thick layer of oil and debris. A pall of smoke, soot and odors covered the whole area. Bodies had begun to surface through the scum and their skin coloring was yellow."[13]

9

THE TRUTH

The 2nd District was a huge complex being set up at the Bari Polyclinic, fifteen minutes from the harbor. Shaped like a horseshoe, the Polyclinic was the brainchild of Benito Mussolini. It was to be *the* medical center offering complete care for Southern Italy.

While the Allies moved northward the Polyclinic housed the following hospital groups: 3rd New Zealand General, 98th British, 14th Combined General, 30th Indian General, 34th Field Hygiene Section, and the 4th Base Depot Medical Stores. Nearby was the American 26th General Hospital. In addition, other hospital units were nearby in Taranto. Unfortunately, at the time of the attack, most of the personnel, medical equipment and supplies had yet to arrive.

Almost all the casualties were covered with oil, burned, and in various degrees of shock and/or exposure depending on whether or not they had been immersed in the water. There was no time in most cases to properly interview, admit a patient, or bed them with a hospital gown. In most cases the oily wet clothing was left on the patient and he was wrapped in a blanket for twelve to twenty-four hours and given a hot cup of tea. They were never properly washed or cleaned. "Many of the cases were not admitted to the hospital the first night. As they appeared in good condition, they were sent to an Auxiliary Seaman's Home (still clothed in their oil contaminated clothing). These men were admitted to the hospitals the next morning when symptoms developed."[1] Little did the medical authorities know, but this treatment only hastened the absorption rate of mustard into the body. It was exactly the wrong treatment for a mustard gas victim. "The first indication of an unusual type of casualty that evening was noted in the resuscitation wards. Casualties that supposedly were suffering from shock following immersion and exposure did not appear to fit the usual clinical picture and did not respond in a typical manner."[2] Patients didn't respond to plasma, pain-killing drugs, and were generally apathetic.

Approximately six hours after the attack patients began having problems with their eyes. Many were practically blinded as their eyes teared and became more painful as if they had sand in them. Eventually their eyes were swollen shut. Over 800 Allied casualties would be hospitalized and more than 650 of these had mustard burns. The burns and subsequent blisters were hideous looking and occurred wherever the person came in contact with harbor water, whether from swimming, sitting in a lifeboat or using a life raft to get to safety. The genital areas were particularly vulnerable and swelled to many times their normal size.

Besides military casualties, the citizens of Bari also needed vital medical attention. Unfortunately, they were last in order for treatment. No records were kept of casualties or deaths involving the people of Bari. It was estimated that more than 1000 Bari citizens were killed in the attack. How many people went untreated for mustard gas inhalation and burns, or would eventually develop complications, will never be known.

Lt. Col. Stewart F. Alexander was instrumental in forcing authorities to recognize the presence of mustard gas. After the Battle *Magazine.*

For a time military casualties from mustard gas burns were diagnosed as "Dermatitis NYD," NYD indicating "Not Yet Diagnosed." Among those treating the wounded, however, a growing suspicion that chemical warfare was used became stronger. Even so, the question remained: What type of chemical and which side used it?

As the first glimmer of dawn lightened the sky on December 4, it was decided to bring in a higher authority to witness the peculiarities taking place in the hospital wards, since nothing seemed to be helping the victims. Panic was setting in among many of the patients as they concluded they were permanently blind or their reproductive organs were being destroyed.

A call went out to General Fred Blesse, Deputy Chief Surgeon of the Allied Headquarters in Algiers. General Blesse despatched Lieutenant Colonel Stewart F. Alexander, a chemical warfare expert. Alexander had worked specifically on mustard gas warfare at the Edgewood Arsenal in Maryland and knew that gas might be present at Bari.

Lt. Colonel Alexander flew directly to Bari and immediately began a tour of the hospitals. The first thing he noticed was the tell-tale garlic smell. After examining blisters and sputum samples and viewing chest x-rays, Lt. Colonel Alexander concluded the problem was definitely caused by mustard gas. However, he was not sure whether it was liquid or vaporized mustard, nor could he determine the method of delivery since the harbor water had diluted it.

The next step for Alexander was to analyze tissue from deceased patients and conduct an analysis of the harbor water. Meanwhile, rumors ran wild, predominant among them was that the Germans had used the gas in their attack. This was put to rest when the British recovered a shell fragment from the harbor bottom with traces of mustard on it. The bomb fragment was from an American M47A1 bomb.

How the bomb got there was the next puzzle to be solved. The British offered no explanation because, according to them, no mustard gas was shipped to Bari.

In *Disaster At Bari,* Glenn Infield wrote,

> The British, from top-level politicians and high ranking officers down to the Bari port authorities, refused to concede that the victims were suffering from mustard exposure for a long time. Much too long. This complicated the treatment of patients and caused unneeded delay in communications to medical facilities regarding the true condition of the casualties.[3]

Lt. Colonel Alexander, frustrated because no explanations were forthcoming, took it upon himself to resolve which Allied ship might have contained mustard. He drew up a harbor berthing plan based upon what ships were in the harbor during the attack. By the process of elimination and comparing the number of deaths on each ship in the harbor, he discovered that the *John Harvey* was at the center of the problem. Alexander pressured the British authorities further with his findings. Finally, the British conceded that the *John Harvey* had a shipment of mustard gas aboard.

Now that the toxic element had been established, the proper medical treatments could be applied:

> With mustard now established beyond doubt, Alexander advised the hospitals of the proper treatment. The blisters were punctured and drained, with the skin left intact as a protection under the sterile dressing. Prophylactic sulfaniomide therapy was prescribed for all

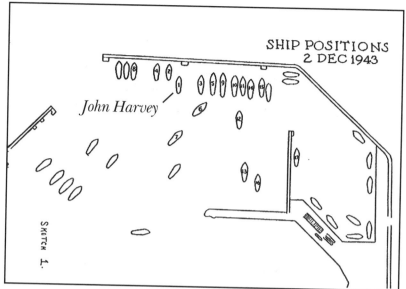

Lt. Col. Alexander's drawing of ship locations revealed that the Liberty ship John Harvey *was at the epicenter of the explosion. This caused British authorities to finally admit that the ship carried gas bombs. After the Battle Magazine.*

the victims with irritated respiratory tracts, together with nose drops, gargles, mouthwashes, and steam inhalations. Unfortunately, in many cases this treatment came too late and, to the desperation of doctors and nurses, the number of deaths increased. By December 17, 69 patients had died from the effects of mustard, either because of body surface burns, or through intoxication of internal organ systems. In many cases, blast damage to the lungs or bacterial infections that would not otherwise have been lethal, when combined with the mustard effects, produced death. In all, some 84 servicemen died from mustard-related causes in the Bari area. However, the true number was much greater, as many of the American patients were transferred to hospitals in other parts of Italy, North Africa, Britain and the United States, and died without it ever being recognized or recorded that they were victims of mustard poisoning.[4]

Toward the end of December, Alexander filed his preliminary official Secret report. The British also filed their Most Secret Report and in it they stated,

> The position with regard to casualties from the raid was as follows: On the night of the 2/3 Dec. about 300 to 400 persons were admitted to hospitals in Bari, some badly wounded, some burnt, some suffering from shock and the effects of immersion and many covered with fuel oil. The hospitals were already working at high pressure with battle casualties evacuated from the forward areas … The outstanding fact that emerges from our inquiry is that a number of persons suffered from mustard burns which might have been allayed and possibly prevented if the true nature of their injuries had been appreciated from the beginning … It is probable that had the appropriate medical authorities received definite information that a ship carrying mustard had exploded in the harbour they would have been able to make a true diagnosis a good deal earlier …[5]

Lt. Colonel Alexander's report was circulated amongst the hospitals in Italy, to the Edgewood Arsenal, and to Porton Down in England. Porton Down was the British chemical warfare counterpart to Edgewood Arsenal.

In January 1944 Lt. Colonel Alexander received a commendation letter from the Medical Division Chief, Colonel Cornelius Rhoads. It stated:

15 January 1944

Dear Colonel Alexander:

I would like to let you know of the high praise that has been given your report on the Bari Disaster. It provides us with such complete information as to represent almost a landmark in the history of mustard poisoning.

We plan to use this report as a model in the plants where industrial accidents may occur. I am sure it will be most useful.

Sincerely yours,

Cornelius P. Rhoads

10

... BUT FOR THE GRACE OF GOD ...

In the days following the attack ships and people regrouped, assessed what happened and renewed their efforts get supplies to the fighting troops.

SS *Joseph Wheeler*

John Willig was a Navy radioman who shared duties with his merchant marine counterpart. According to Willig, "The officer in charge of the USN Gun crew, aboard the armed merchant vessel, S.S. *Joseph Wheeler,* had divided the crew into two groups, Port and Starboard. Each group would take their turn standing watch, for approximately 8 hours or so. During early afternoon, the USN officer announced that one of the groups was entitled to liberty, and that the members could go ashore, if they so desired. I don't recall which group I was attached to, but several of us realized that the officer had named the wrong group to remain on board. We decided to take our chances and go to the officer and tell him that he had made a mistake.

"After listening to us and checking his records, he agreed with us and changed his instructions to the entire crew. I and the rest of my group were now entitled to go on liberty, and to avail ourselves of the opportunity to go ashore and visit the city of Bari. Had this not happened, I would not be alive today to tell this story, because all on board that night were killed.

"I and one of my shipmates decided to go ashore and visit Bari. That evening, my friend and I heard planes overhead as we were walking in downtown Bari. We noticed that the planes were not Allies as we knew them, and about that time they started dropping parachute flares that lit up the harbor and parts of Bari. The next thing we witnessed was a second wave of planes coming in from the Adriatic Sea (Albania), and at that point we heard explosions.

"It was obvious to us what was taking place. The Luftwaffe was bombing the Allied ships tied up in Bari harbor. The first few bombs overshot their target and landed in downtown Bari not far

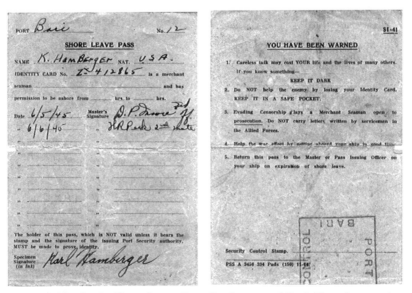

Front and back of a Shore Leave Pass for the port of Bari. Note the warning on the back. Karl Hamberger.

from where we were standing. We ducked inside the nearest building to escape the flying shrapnel and other flying objects.

"In situations like this, our officer had instructed us to return to the ship immediately. We headed back to the harbor where the ship was tied up, and when we arrived we were met by British soldiers on guard duty, who would not let us pass. They said it was useless, the ships were all burning and exploding, the oil on the water was burning, and that rescue efforts were already underway. They suggested that we report to the 12th and 15th U.S. Army Air Corps Headquarters, located in one of the hotels in downtown Bari. This we did.

"Just think, if we had not challenged the officer's word on which group was entitled to liberty that day, I would have been aboard the S.S. *Joseph Wheeler* when it took a direct hit and exploded.

"I experienced another eye opener when I was standing in the lobby of the hotel headquarters of the 12th and 15th Army Air Corps. In walked none other then my childhood neighbor, Ralph Wilderman, who was a copilot on a bomber flying between England and Italy. We had quite a visit. Ralph and I lived across the from one another in Weehawken, New Jersey. It's a small world.

"I eventually arrived back in the U.S. at the U.S.N. Armed Guard Center in South Brooklyn, New York. We were asked to write letters to the survivors of the deceased. I was given the name of the wife of my former roommate aboard the *Joseph Wheeler*, Lyndahl Miller, Boatswain, and I gave her an account of the last hours that Lyndahl spent on earth. This was rather difficult, because I was not aboard the ship in the hours prior to the air raid. I wrote her anyway."[1]

SS *John Harvey*

Juel Hansen, Jr. described the quirk of fate that put his fellow Cadet-Midshipman, Richard B. Glauche in Bari on the night of the attack: "My basic training was coming to an end. As our date to go to war came closer, the excitement in Section P363 grew. The men of section P363 were in the 18th Company of the third battalion. The first platoon of the 18th Company was composed of first classmen, the second platoon of second classmen and the third platoon of the prelims of Section P363. Most of the 17 companies were organized in the same fashion, a mix of three different classmen. We heard many sea stories and war stories from our upper classmen company mates and we were all anxious to go to sea and become part of the big picture.

"My last weekend liberty before shipping out I went home alone. I visited the parents of my pals and generally just goofed off and took it easy. Liberty was over for all the cadets at 2200 (10 PM) on Sunday nights and I was back in plenty of time. My sea bag and foot locker was already packed and secured to move out.

"Monday morning after breakfast, section P363 started to load gear into the bus we were assigned to. Other sections were doing the same. Several prelim sections were now ready to be bussed, with gear, to 45 Broadway, New York City, for ship assignments. Those cadets not assigned to ships that Monday would return to the Academy and return to 45 Broadway the following day and so on until all had been assigned a ship. We were all pretty excited and were talking about the kind of ship and type of run we hoped to get as we rode in the bus to New York. It was a beautiful sunny warm summer day in July and we all had recently been patriotically fired up by the recent past 4th of July celebrations. Dick Glauche was having some stomach cramps and discomfort and just not feeling well. All the rest of us were raring to go.

"We unloaded our gear and reported to a large room that had a counter along the street side of the room, several oaken desks and rows of fold up camping style chairs for the cadets to sit on. Roll call was taken periodically. Once immediately upon arrival, and again after lunch and coffee breaks. Names were being called alphabetically for both deck and engine cadets as ship assignments became available. There were lots of hand shakes, pats on the backs, and shouted congratulations and other remarks as friends and classmates left for their ships. The head (toilet) was down the hall from this assignment room, a good 40 or 50 feet away. There was a steady stream of cadets making the trip to the head in answer to Nature's response to our eating, drinking and general excitement. Dick Glauche's stomach pains had him making this trip often with a mild but persistent case of the runs.

"After lunch, Dick's name was called. I reported him in the head and volunteered to go and get him. This was denied and the next name was called: Hansen, Juel Jr. I reported PRESENT and was assigned to the S.S. *James Lykes* of the Lykes Bros. Steamship Co. The ship was tied up at the old wine piers in Brooklyn, N.Y. and was a 'C-1' type cargo ship. The 'C' ships were Maritime Commission designs and the slowest and smallest was the 'C1' with a top speed downhill of near 15 knots. I was briefed and signed off to leave my ship as Dick returned from the head. I told him what had happened, we said goodbye and good luck to each other and shook hands and the name Glauche; Richard was called out as I left the room.

Dick was assigned to the S.S. *John Harvey*, an 'EC2' Liberty ship. The 'EC2' designation was also a Maritime Commission designation for 'Emergency Cargo No.2 size' ship. I did not know the ship Dick got at that time. I only learned of the ship's name and demise much later when I returned to the Academy after my sea training on the SS *James Lykes* was over. So, but for the finger of fate and Dick's runs, I would have been assigned to the S.S. *John Harvey* and Dick would have been assigned the S.S. *James Lykes*."[2]

Anthony Pellegrini was a messman in World War II aboard the S.S. *Deborah Gannett*. He was well-liked by the Naval Armed Guard aboard the ship for his culinary skills. In 1945, Anthony read an article in the *Boston Daily Post* about Mrs. Mary Gawlak who was trying to find information about her son, Joseph F., who was killed at Bari along with the other two Naval gunners seen in the photograph accompanying the article. Pellegrini remembered he saved the clipping in his seaman's wallet, which he stored away during the attack and wrote to Mrs. Gawlak. "I wrote to the mother of the sailor in the center of the photograph and I told her about the sailor, his name was John Gentile and lived on the next street over from me. We went to school together and we were childhood chums. The sailor on the right of the photo was Domenic Gianetti, who lived in Newton Center, a village of Newton, whom I did not know. Mrs. Gawlak, the mother of Joe in the center of the photo, wrote to me and thanked me for the information."[3]

Chief Engineer John White was an extraordinary mariner. He was thirty-eight years old at the time of his death and the father of five children. He had made the sea his career since the age of seventeen. One of his prior shipmates told his son John, Jr.: "Not being a seaman you probably do not know that very many Chiefs are so arrogant that they will not even speak to anyone but the Captain and First Engineer, but let me tell you about the kind of man Jack White was. Merchant ships had no medical people at all so when Leroy Hopkins, the Second Engineer, came up with unbearable pain from infected teeth, the captain contacted a destroyer in the convoy and they took Leroy aboard and kept him over 2 days while the Navy dentist worked on his teeth. Rather than having the other two engineers double up to cover Hopkins your father took his watches. I do not know another Chief that would do this. To top it off he allowed them to put in for overtime for the hours he actually worked. You had a great father, the best I ever sailed for or I would not have made so many trips in her. I can still see him clearly and it was with great sorrow that I heard about him and Captain Knowles. Again thank you, the *John Harvey* has been in my thoughts all these many years ..."[4]

"Captain Knowles and your father were the two best officers anyone would ever want to sail with ..."[5]

John White, Jr., wrote the following in his father's biography: "When it was getting close to Christmas there was a story of a loss of ships at Bari, Italy. I paid no attention to the story and sweated out Dad to be home with us again. The sad news arrived in January 1944, that Commander John J. White was missing in action. Shipmates and friends of Dad's called looking for him, but we had to say he was missing in action. A shipmate called Mother and asked if he could come by. He was with Jack and said that he would not becoming home and that he could not discuss any of the details. Then two gentlemen in shirts and ties came by the house and they said that we were not to talk about where he had sailed or any information about the ship. They even asked for and took anything that mentioned the name *Harvey*. Reality finally came to me when I attended a Requiem Mass at Our Lady of Perpetual Help Church in Lindenhurst, L.I., New York."[6]

John White, Jr., eventually enlisted in the Air Force and while waiting in Nouasseur, Casablanca, Morocco for new orders he discovered how his father died. "They scheduled me for base charge-of-quarters the night of the 1960 presidential election between Kennedy and Nixon. This meant we had to monitor incoming messages and stay awake. There was a senior officer, a junior officer of the day (he was my squadron Adjutant) and myself. Everyone bought a magazine and coffee to stay awake. It was early morning and I was down to the last article when the name S.S. *John Harvey* appeared, my Father's ship. After 17 years it revealed the details of the horrible disaster that took place at Bari, Italy. Tears were in my eyes and my Adjutant asked me what was wrong. When I told him, he read the article, and tears came to his eyes. I told my family about it and after all those years we finally knew the facts about Dad's death."[7]

SS *John Bascom*

On board the *John Bascom,* Cadet-Midshipman Leroy Heinse was wounded and brought to the breakwater when the *John Motley* blew up. His ensuing hospital experience was typical of many of the casualties. The explosion was the last thing that Heinse remembered about the harbor and the bombing. He subsequently was brought to the British 98th General Hospital.

"Anything that I later learned was in some sort of makeshift hospital. It was operated by the British. I was sort of startled when I found somebody saying to me that I'd have to be taken to the theatre and I said to myself, 'I'm obviously all banged up here. What would somebody want to take me to a theatre for? Did they want to get my mind off my problems or what was going on?' I later found out that the British called the operating room a theatre and their nurses were called sisters.

"I have no recollection of ever going to an operating room. I don't remember what the bed was like until another time when we were told that we were under another bombing attack. I kept saying to somebody, 'Is this building marked with a red cross?' They assured me that there was a red cross on the building and it was illuminated for night vision. They had been feeding us at the time and I do remember that I was on a cot with the food right below my chin. When the sirens went off they moved all the beds to the center of the ward, away from any flying glass, so they could cover our faces and be protected. A funny thing happened during this situation. They just took the plate of food which I think was spaghetti and meatballs and turned it right over on my face.

"A little about my treatment. The Navy authorities came from Palermo, Sicily, where they had a hospital. They found that the care we were getting, particularly those exposed to mustard gas, was not in accordance with the treatment appropriate for handling casualties that were exposed to mustard gas. Mustard gets on your skin and it produces a tremendous burn. In my case, I had a burn scar from the middle of the calf of my leg, all the way up to the next section of my leg which goes up toward the hip. I have about two feet of burn area that varies anywhere from six inches to maybe eight or ten inches.

"They flew us out to Palermo, Sicily. The main thing there was that the Navy had all these injured Armed Guard that they were immediately responsible for. The Merchant Seamen like myself were sort of secondary, but they did oversee that we were getting the same treatment that the Navy injured were. They also had the moral responsibility of treating us in the same manner that we were treated in the British hospital. I don't know how many days I was in the Bari hospital. One of the first things they did to me was to tend to my badly burned right leg which had been put in a plaster cast. It began to smell pretty bad. Later I found out that what the British had done in good intentions was incorrect. I was in great pain and I tended to bring my leg up to loosen the skin under my knee. If I had healed with the cast on, I wouldn't have been able to stretch my leg out. So, their first order of attack was to get the cast off. They took me to the operating room and began to peel off my cast. My flesh had become embedded in the gauze. I remember the horrible pain and just screaming while they were doing the procedure. Ultimately they put me into some sort of restraining device whereby I couldn't retract the leg anymore and put me laying face down in a bed. They treated the wound with hot saline dressings made up of saline pads soaked in salt water and on top of that they'd keep hot water bottles. This was the procedure that they used to treat people that were subject to the mustard gas material. I found out at a later date that on the right and front side of my body, I had many shrapnel and glass wounds; some of them were an inch to an inch and a half long. When they got me to the hospital in Bari, all they probably did was to put on butterflies because I've got these scars on my body without stitch markings.

"It was Christmas in Palermo and I had absolutely no personal possessions in the way of toothbrushes, razors, or anything like that. When my ship went down I lost all my possessions. While you're at sea, you perform what is known as a sea project. You have all these textbooks, outlined courses of study. All of these materials were lost. All I was left with was my dogtag and identification bracelet. I am indebted to and will always wave the flag for the Red Cross because they came to my rescue. They supplied me with a little ditty bag that had a razor, toothpaste, brushes, and numerous other things that you would need in the hospital. I'll never forget that. I hear a lot of people bad-mouthing the Red Cross, and what they did and so on and so forth, but that wasn't my experience.

"I'll always remember a Roman Catholic Priest named Redmond. He would come by and ask if there was anything he could do for me. I said to him, "Well, you could write my folks and tell them of my relative condition. I'm sure they were notified that I was injured, but didn't know my condition." After that day, that gentleman would religiously come by and would always say, 'Would you like me to write a letter to your folks?' and I'd say 'yes.'

"In late January, I was flown to a U.S. Army Hospital in Algeria and spent the next month there. I was next moved to the U.S. Naval hospital in Casablanca. On 4 March, 1944 I was put aboard the USS *General Butmer*, bound for Norfolk, Virginia. I'll never forget the ship voyage because we had German POW's on board. The expression on their faces was that of self-defiance. Like how dare we put them in prison. When I reached the States I developed some respiratory problems and was soon transferred to the U.S. Public Health Hospital in Baltimore. I met a wonderful student nurse at this hospital and eventually we were married. While at the hospital, I underwent many operations to repair nerve damage in my fingers and arms. To this day, I still periodically develop fish-like scales on my leg where I was burned from the mustard gas."[8]

(*Author's note: Today, Leroy has little feeling in his hands and left leg because of nerve damage. In January of 1998 his right leg was amputated below the knee as a result of neurological complications caused by the mustard gas burns. He wears a special leg brace to prevent his left leg from becoming deformed like the right one.*)

Also on board the *John Bascom* was Naval Armed Guard Warren Brandenstein. He was sent to the British 98th Hospital. When Brandenstein regained consciousness in the hospital, he thought it strange that a party of people was going around collecting clothing, including his own. He was lying between two German prisoners and other survivors were all over the floor. His Royal Army Medical card read, "Fracture Compound, proximal Phalanx, Head lesion, shaved scalp dusted sulphanilamide. Dermatitis of scalp, sulphanilamide: 10 days later scalp burning; profuse purulent discharge. Dressed, dusted with Ensol. Saline irrigation for conjunctivitis, left eye. Ruptured drum, left ear: Sulphanilamide powder inserted."[9] Brandenstein's scalp was infected and oozing pus from mustard gas burns. His back was black and blue and his fingers and nose were shredded by shrapnel. He was blinded by the mustard gas for two weeks before regaining his sight. Brandenstein spent four months recovering in hospitals. Today, Warren Brandenstein still has tintinitis in one ear and the other is scarred.

SS *Samuel J. Tilden*

Gunner John F. Whitley was on board the *Samuel J. Tilden*. After being picked up by a British launch and given a drink of rum he was put out on the nearest jetty. As soon as he got to the dock area he was taken to the nearest hospital. "We got as far as the lobby entrance and the halls were already full with injured civilians and military personnel. There was a German pilot in the lobby, still wearing his sidearm. It was obvious that this hospital did not need any more patients because they could not take care of their own. We were taken to a British field tent hospital, 'Mash Style,' Our quarters for the next several days was the floor of a large gymnasuim in the city. During our stay in the gym, a doctor kept going from man to man asking, 'Are your eyes bothering you?' Seems that the next day, some men began having trouble seeing.

"During our stay in Bari, German reconnaissance planes would fly over to observe the damage they had done. This would cause an air raid alert each time and sharing an underground air raid shelter, with the local men, women, and children crying and praying while standing in water was an experience in itself, and one I will never forget.

"One of the Armed Guard gun crew had left the ship without taking his shoes for he was taking a shower when the General Quarters was sounded and he did not wait to put his shoes on before going to his battle station. I lost my shoes while sleeping in the gym. I made the mistake of taking them off! We walked down to the dock where the British had piles of supplies. A British soldier on guard gave us both a pair of British combat boots.

"Gunners Mate Humphries convinced the British doctor to release us from the "walking wounded," and we would take care of his men. The U.S. Army Air Force from Foggia, Italy, furnished us a truck and driver and they moved us to Taranto, Italy. Our quarters in Taranto were a public school building.

"Here, I had my first experience with a toilet-hopper that was shaped like a bowl, a couple of inches above the floor. You squatted over the bowl in the floor and pulled a chain overhead. Crude, but it worked (almost). Before conquering this Italian lavatory, we were put on LST #359 which was bound for Bizerte, North Africa. We arrived in Bizerte on December 9. We spent four days in an olive orchard in a small masonry building.

"On the fourth day we were loaded onto a C-46 to be flown to Catania, Sicily. When we asked for information on how to use our parachute, the Air Force officer advised us to use them to sit on because it was much safer to ride the plane down. The Catania air strip seemed to have been an old Nazi air field because all the hangers and buildings nearby had been shot up. From here we were taken to Augusta, Sicily and went aboard the S.S. *Lyman Abbott* which had also survived the raid on Bari, Italy. On December 23, six of the S.S. *Tilden's* crew stayed on the *Abbott* so as to give them a full gun crew as they had lost men.

"The *Abbott* went back to Bari to unload. They then returned to the States. All of the other men were transferred to the S.S. *George Shires* as passengers which I was one of, and they landed us in Oran, North Africa on December 31. From Oran we were put on a freight train to Casablanca. Our accommodations were on the floor of a boxcar and it took us three days and two nights to get there. It was hot during the daytime and freezing during the night as the train bounced into Casablanca. This train did not have a caboose. The conductor sat on a small box (cupola) which was attached to the top and at one end of the box car. This train was powered by steam to Rabat, Morocco. From here, we got an electric train to Casablanca.

"We departed Casablanca on the USS *General W.A. Mann* (APA-112), landing in Norfolk, Virginia on January 17, 1944."[10]

After having the bottom of his lifeboat blown out, gunner William Walter Waters was taken to the end of the jetty and placed in an ambulance with others and taken to the hospital. "The hospital was so very crowded that as soon as I could, I slipped away and "bummed" a ride to the water front in the same ambulance that was going back for another load. The rest of the night, I along with my Captain and the Gunny officer and three or four other sailors stayed in an open shed and watched our ship and the entire harbor burn.

"The SS *Tilden* was torpedoed by the British because it had drifted too near to the entrance of the harbor. This happened about 2 A.M. on December 3.

"We stayed in Bari for two days in an empty building (the windows had all been blown out) and the British shared what little food they had with us. I had not had time to put on my shoes when I ran to my duty station, so I was still barefooted. One of the British seamen told me if I would help him load up the bodies and parts of bodies on the beaches, he would give me a pair of shoes. So I helped him pick up the bodies and he gave me a nice pair of English boots. I stole a pair of wool socks off the clothes line on the English ship and two days later the English gave me two wool uniforms.

"Two or three days later the Air Force gathered all the ships crew that could travel and trucked us to Taranto, Italy, where we all stayed for five days.Then we got on an LST and went to Bizerte, North Africa. We stayed one week and got a plane to Catania, Sicily."[11]

This group eventually ended up on the S.S. *Lyman Abbott* and included Whitley and Waters. William Waters continues: "The *Abbott* needed only seven men to replace those that were lost; so us twenty men were told to draw numbers and those drawing the seven lowest numbers would stay on the ship and the balance would return to the U.S. for further orders. I drew #13, but I swapped with a married man who had drawn #6. He wanted to return to the States and I wanted to stay!"[12]

"Both the *Tilden* and the *Abbott* had a deck load of mustard gas. This gas was in metal canisters and very plainly printed, 'Mustard Gas,' on the sides of the containers."[13] Waters went on to serve twenty-three years in the Navy and twenty-two years as a deck officer in the merchant marine.

SS *Lyman Abbott*

George Southern was an able-seaman manning a four-inch gun on the forecastle of the British destroyer HMS *Zetland*. The *Zetland* was severely damaged in the raid and was performing rescue operations. Southern wrote a book titled *They Need Never Know* concerning his Bari experience. "The attack began at 1930 and twenty minutes later the master ordered the ship abandoned. Practically all the members of the crew were either injured from shrapnel or burned from mustard gas in the water while rowing to safety. It was remarkable that out of a complement of forty-two merchant crew, twenty-nine Armed Guards, and one passenger, only "One Merchant crewman, one officer, one Armed Guard, and the passenger died, three from shrapnel wounds and the fourth from inhaling mustard gas."[14] The passenger was an Army Cargo Security Officer.

"A boat was lowered from the HMS *Zetland* and a group of five sailors including myself were ordered to help and assist in any way we could. During rescue operations we boarded an American Liberty ship [*Lyman Abbott*] at anchor in the middle of the harbor. We did not know it at the time, but she was carrying mustard gas. There were fires all along her upper decks and our little group decided to give the crew a hand. When we boarded the vessel we were amazed to find her completely deserted. It appears after the explosion the whole crew had abandoned ship and rowed ashore. Nevertheless, we set to and fought the flames and during that period I broke off to make a search of the ship to see if anyone had been left behind; luckily not. After two hours we extinguished the fires."[15]

In the meantime, the master of the *Abbott* was ordered to re-board her and begin clean-up operations. According to his report, Captain Dahlstrom got a small party of four men together for this detail which commenced the next morning at 0200. George Southern continues, "Sometime later, just as we had the flames under control, a party of sailors from the Bari shore base boarded the ship and the senior officer complimented us and said he had been in touch with the master of the ship, who was ashore."[16]

After the "abandon ship" order was given, Second Assistant Engineer George Maury found himself in a lifeboat riddled with holes and water up to the thwarts. Maury stated, "Afterwards I discovered that I had a beautiful brown bottom ... and that the oiler who swam with a line to another raft was badly burned. When we left Bari, Chason the oiler, was still in the hospital laying under a cage, nude, with his body covered with big blisters. I heard afterwards that he recovered. When we finally got ashore, we went to a shelter. I really don't remember much about it or getting any sleep. The next morning we were at the hospital being examined. At that time no one knew about the gas being in the water, although it was beginning to show on people. I had brown lines across my forehead and down the sides of my face, where the straps of my helmet touched my skin. The straps got soaked when my helmet was used to help bail the lifeboat out. When we got to the pier I put the helmet back on. My buttocks were tanned from where I was sitting in the water. My right forearm was the worst. I was wearing a heavy woolen sweater and somehow my arm got soaked and the wool held the water prolonging the exposure to my arm giving the gas time to work on a nice piece of meat and did it ever. The gas burned a hole about the size of a half-dollar on my forearm and when it started to hurt I thought it would never let up. I started to be aware of it when we got back on board the *Lyman Abbott*."[17]

As for the *Lyman Abbott,* she survived to sail again. Later that same morning another work party was brought out to the vessel. George Maury wrote: "We had gone down to the pier, the captain, chief, and the rest of the engineers. We could see the ship was still afloat and we had a British patrol boat take us out to her. What a mess; pieces of ship's steel and parts all over the deck. There were pieces one or two inches to pieces that weighed a ton or more. More of the crew were brought on board to clean up the mess and the engineers went below …

"We received orders that there was going to be a convoy leaving Bari that afternoon and, if possible, we were ordered to join it. No one wanted to stay there so we worked at making the ship seaworthy. We were ready and left with the convoy. The ship had taken a near miss off the port stern quarter. We didn't know it at the time, but the concussion had twisted the rudder post 17 degrees to starboard. It was quite exciting for a while trying to maneuver among other ships. They had to steer with the emergency wheel aft … They found that if they steered with a 17 degree to port that they could handle the ship. After some difficulty we arrived in Augusta, Sicily.

After arriving in Augusta, some of the crew still required medical attention. My eyes were examined frequently to make sure they would not be a problem. We got orders to leave for Bari to unload the cargo. The doctor agreed to discharge us if we would sign a release form absolving him of any blame for anything that might happen to us because our burns were not healing as fast as they thought they should … My arm was still giving me a lot of pain as the doctors had been treating it with something called Venetian Violet. It was painted on like you paint iodine on, but it wasn't helping. The gunnery officer was treating some of his crew with sulfur drugs and we tried it and it improved the healing process. The pain was down in a couple of days and the hole in my arm scabbed over and started to heal. I still have an indentation where it was on my arm."[18]

After getting ashore, a British Navy sailor said to Donald Meissner, "We had a bit of a bloody time, didn't we sailor?" Meissner wrote, "They drove me to British Army hospital and helped me get into a bed. A British nurse came to help me and was wrapping my feet in a blanket when a bomb hit close. She looked at me and said, 'That was a bit close, wasn't it sailor?' The bombs were still screaming down and she said, 'I never worry about that screaming because you never hear the one that gets you.' She brought me a small dish of porridge and a wee spot of tea. The British live on tea. She brought me a new set of British Army issue clothes and a pair of size 12 combat boots. I wear size 9. The nurse said my feet were so swollen she thought size 12 would be best. The doctor ordered my Navy clothes discarded because of the mustard gas.

"The next day the doctor told me that I had a fractured jaw, a ruptured spleen, and a slight fracture of the left leg. They wired my jaw and put a brace on my leg. He said with luck, my spleen would heal. (It later had to be removed.) He also said to watch my lungs because the harbor was full of mustard gas. He was amazed that I got out of the harbor alive.

"A British soldier came with an army truck and took me to a location the British army had taken over. They had control of an area that had some residential homes in it. About eight of my shipmates from the gun crew were there, and the British turned over one of the homes to us. It was a nice home but with no heat or lights. They issued a blanket to each of us, but there were no beds or mattresses. There was an Italian cemetery next to our house. The Germans had bombed it and there were corpses everywhere.

"The British did not fight on their stomachs as bread, jam, and tea was about all they had to eat. On special days, they had spam. They shared everything with us but they had little to begin with. Trying to sleep on a cold concrete floor wasn't easy. Putting my head on it was the hardest part of all. It was so cold that some nights, we would go out on the edge of the cemetery and build a fire. One night some Italians must have been watching and took pity on us. They brought us some "home-brewed vino." At two A.M. we all sat there drinking vino, trying to get warm. We stayed there about two weeks when a British soldier said he had orders to 'take us out of here.'

"He picked us up in an army truck and we headed for the hills. Most of the roads we travelled were like pastures, and a good share of the time we were travelling up a mountain. It took a good four hours before we began to level off at the 'top of the world.' We travelled another four hours and came to a U.S. Army Air base. The base's quarters had been strafed and the field bombed. At one end of the air strip was a German dive-bomber that had been shot down. It did my heart good to see one of those bombers on the ground. We stayed there about two weeks. Every time the pilots came back from a mission, it seemed like they were minus at least one plane. They sure had a rough time of it. I visited quite often with some of the pilots and they had heard about Bari and didn't understand why they were not requested to fly some cover for us. I requested if they were flying over the Adriatic and saw a merchant ship to keep their eye on it because the Germans would certainly try to sink it. They promised me they would.

"One morning a pilot came to us and said he had orders to fly us out. The plane vibrated worse than my 1929 Chevy did. We landed in Catania, Sicily. A U.S. Army soldier met us and we were off for another truck ride. He took us to Augusta, Sicily. Augusta was at the base of Mt. Etna, a large volcano. On the other side of the town was Augusta Harbor. Anchored in that harbor was our ship, the S.S. *Lyman Abbott*! None of us had any idea that our ship was still afloat.

"A small boat met us at the harbor and took us out to our ship. After all the time that had passed, I felt I had found a place where I belonged. We all knew what had to be done. The cargo would have to go back to Bari. The ship was a mess. The decks were blanketed with shrapnel of all kinds. There were complete cases of small-arms ammunition all over the ship. One plate of steel weighing over four tons hit amidships. One Army truck that was secured to the deck had a large cannon shell for a passenger. The nose of the shell projected out of the window and the base was against the front seat. There were very few merchant seamen aboard the ship and only about ten of us to man the guns. The food had deteriorated badly. The flour was full of weevils and large ants. Every time I ate bread or pancakes, I would hope those critters had good nutrients in them. Most of the meat was spoiled, but we had lots of coffee for which I was grateful.

"Guns deteriorate in the salt air when not cleaned every day. It had been a long time and they were neglected and my gun was in bad shape. One part had crystalized from all the heat of the firing. I cleaned it and coated all the parts with a mixture of powdered graphite and kerosene. I put it together and hoped for the best. Our cannon on the stern would fire automatically when a shell was put in and the breach closed. That night in Bari, Leo Krause was the pointer on it and he took a bad hit to his left hip. We cleaned all the debris from our gun areas and also our runways so we could get to our guns quickly.

"Every night British Destroyers would drop depth charges around our ship and the harbor. They would do this all night until dawn. This was done to discourage anyone from attaching a bomb to the ship.

"We finally left Augusta Harbor and headed for Bari. Going back to Bari was the hardest thing I've ever done. We had just left Augusta Harbor when a British heavy cruiser pulled alongside and communicated with the bridge. I think they gave the captain a specific route to take. I watched the cruiser leave and was quite impressed with her 'fire power'..."[19]

The *Lyman Abbott* returned to Bari on December 24. Donald Meissner recalled, "Bari harbor was a graveyard of ships. We had to negotiate very carefully going between the ships and securing to the docks. They started to unload us immediately. We were all relieved when our ship had all of its cargo removed.[20]

"My jaw and spleen were giving me a lot of pain. I would go below deck to the engine room and wrap towels around a steam pipe. I would hold them alternately on my jaw and spleen. There were no aspirins available."[21]

When the *Lyman Abbott* arrived in New York, Donald Meissner immediately went to sick bay at the Armed Guard Center in Brooklyn. "The pain in my jaw was from a bad wisdom tooth which they removed. They removed the braces from my jaw and left leg as x-rays showed them to be ok. My spleen was another story as it had to be removed."[22]

Gunner's Mate Leo Krause, with his shattered leg, was eased onto the pier by sliding him up on a plank. "Then about ten minutes later two British soldiers came by and put me in an ambulance and took me to the hospital. There were wounded all over and they looked at me and put me on a cot on the floor with a lot of the other wounded. They gave me a shot of morphine and that is about all I remembered until the next day when I awoke in a bed. They hadn't done much to me except bandaged me and put my leg in a Thomas splint. By then I also wondered what happened to all the fellows on the ship. Lt. Walker finally found me and brought me up to date. He told me about the fellows that were killed, the wounded, the condition of the ship and the plans to take her to Sicily and make temporary repairs. I felt bad because I knew I was going to be left behind. I stayed there until a few days before Christmas when they flew a planeload of wounded to Palermo, Sicily to a U.S. Navy hospital. There they cleaned me up and operated on me and put me in a Spiker cast. I was in a cast that way for four months and I stayed in Palermo until the end of April. I was still in bad shape as I weighed only 126 lbs., and my regular weight was 190 lbs. Then one day they flew me to Algiers where I stayed overnight in an Army hospital. The next day I flew to Oran where on the 9th of May I left for the States on the U.S.S. *Refuge* hospital ship. We arrived in Charleston on 24 May and I stayed there because I still couldn't walk. My leg was still draining. I stayed there until the end of August and I was then given a furlough of 30 days. I went by train to Philadelphia and finally to home where I got to see Pine Grove again ... I am a Pennsylvania Dutchman — So the guys called me 'Dutch.' I suffered a lot with the burns and my leg was just about blown off, but I made it and I thank God for that."[23]

Naval Sight Setter Stanley Wisniewski: "After the attack I was taken to the English hospital with some of my other wounded mates. I was put to bed in what seemed like a tent area. I was there for about a week and then moved into the main part of the hospital. Because of the raids that were coming every other day we, the Navy wounded, were flown to Palermo, Sicily to recuperate.

"The extent of my injuries consisted of burns of both arms and right side of my face. I had shrapnel wounds in the buttocks, a wound above my right eye and in my right foot above my ankle. The burns on my arms and right side of my face were treated as if they were oil burns.

"Two that I will never forget are the shipmates that were killed the night of the raid. Alfred Lustri, Gunners Mate, and the Merchant Marine Boatswain Mate, Stanley Adamowicz. Alfred, we called him Blackie, was killed at his gun position and taken ashore by the crew. The Boatswain jumped into the water to secure two lifeboats together. He was burned over 90 % of his body. He went into a coma at the hospital and never recovered."[24]

James Roark, who recently passed away, wrote the following regarding the aftermath. "I, myself, had burns on my buttocks, legs, feet that really blistered. We reached the docks and we set out for the English hospital. On the way, while running from the docks, one of our men, Russ Wells, fell into a live electrical wire. We tried to get him out, but because we were all wet we couldn't reach him. An English Army man came along and pulled him out. He showed us the way to the hospital. We were there for a couple of weeks and every night at 7:00 PM the Germans would fly over and we would have to run to the bomb shelter in the basement. One of our men's feet was burned so bad he couldn't walk. But he was scared enough to run all the way to the bomb shelter. Afterwards, he wondered how he had gotten there.

"They didn't know what else to do for us so they sent us on to an American hospital in Palermo, Sicily. On the plane we were followed by a German plane. I told the nurse about it and she said not to say anything, but keep an eye on it. She started telling jokes and stories to keep the men from noticing the German. He soon flew off and I motioned to the nurse to let her know.

"When we got to the American Army hospital in Sicily, the doctor gave us all a bar of brown soap and told us to shower and leave the soap on until it dried. Then, when we started itching again we were to do it all over again. In a week's time we were pretty well healed and most of the blisters were dried up."[25]

Cadet-Midshipman George H. Baist, after assisting the wounded into the lifeboats, was severely burned on the ankles, buttocks, elbows and hips. "The writer and some of his shipmates were taken from the dock to the British Hospital where the doctors removed shrapnel from the writer's hip. After five days in this hospital, the writer was transferred to the American General Hospital, where, on 7 December 1943, General Erickson awarded the writer and several other survivors the Purple Heart with his congratulations."[26]

Author's note: Because of valor displayed by the crew, twenty other crewmen of the S.S. Lyman Abbott *received the Military Order of the Purple Heart which was rarely given out to Merchant Seamen in WW II.*[27]

SS *Grace Abbott*

Ensign Charles Lippert: "So far as I can gather, recalling my talk with the D.E.M.S. Officer at Bari and from re-reading their instructions, the entire defense of the port was based upon the idea that there would be advanced warning of the approach of enemy planes. The surprise nature of the attack appeared to have left the port defense disorganized and completely confused. As stated, I feel that our own fire power was completely lost to the defense of the port. We fired approximately 1500 rounds from our 20mm guns but the enemy planes were never within the range of these guns and, indeed, the gunners were unable to see the attacking planes and fired at flares or at random. Because of the D.E.M.S. instructions I did not open fire with our larger guns, but I feel that these guns were the only ones that could have been of any use in this attack.[28]

"There had been a request to test fire our guns but had been declined by the commodore. And that we encountered a delay of a day or two before being given a berth at one of the unloading piers apparently due to lack of unloading facilities at this port. Most of the ships lost as a result of this attack were waiting for berths. The port facilities appeared to be considerably over-taxed at the time ..."[29]

Bernard Anderson of the *Louis Hennepin* wrote in his diary on December 11:

> We were moved to another pier where we took guns and torpedo tubes off an English destroyer that hit a mine. They are stripping everything off it ... I don't know whether I should write this or not. Yesterday and today the bodies of the fellows that died during the air raid we had here are coming up. A fellow who drowns comes up about a week later. They pulled up about 30. It sure is awful to see the water here in the harbor full of debris and oil and you can't help but see a body when you look. I found out a few days ago one of our ships had mustard gas on it and a lot of the fellows are dying from it. Gee, are we ever lucky the wind was blowing out to sea.[30]

Vince Patterson was on watch in the engine room aboard the S.S. *Thomas B. Robertson* when they entered Bari harbor in January 1944. They were delivering a full load of bombs. At the outset the ship had carried "a portion of the famed 'Tuskegee Airmen' [the Red Tails] all Black fighter group. Sometime in January 1944 we transported and disembarked the Airmen in the boot of Italy and then headed for our cargo unloading point which was Bari, Italy. For two days we spent running up and down outside the harbor because the weather was so bad that we could not get into the harbor ...

"Once we entered the harbor of Bari, it looked like 'LeRoy's junk yard.' Rusted and burnt superstructures and parts of ships sticking out of the water seemed to be littered in each direction. There were no docks for us to tie to. I was on watch in the engine room when we entered the harbor and it had taken a good forty-five (45) minutes of maneuvering with the main engine in order to get tied up to what was left of the docks. At this time we had no idea what had happened. Even when we went ashore we only knew that the Germans had bombed the harbor and nothing of the mustard gas that was spread, as that was top secret and seemed to remain that way while our people were dying ashore in the hospitals."[31]

Bernard Anderson's diary entry of December 7, 1943 to his wife succinctly describes the results of attack, "... today is 2 years since Pearl Harbor and we just about had another Pearl Harbor here. This raid was the worst major disaster since Pearl Harbor. More ships were sunk here in one raid than any other since Pearl Harbor ..."[32]

S.S. *Louis Hennepin*

James Smith: "Some of us were beginning to suffer from eye and nose irritation. We had no idea what the cause was and there was no medical advice available. Our casualties, to the best of my recollection, were the two trying to leave or get back on board, one on the bridge deck hit by 'junk' and some injured either from being hit by debris or knocked down as a result of concussions from the explosions. Personally, my left finger was sliced open from a metal fragment and I went 'fanny over tea kettle' down the ladder from the flying bridge deck to the bridge deck during a roll caused by the explosions. I thought I had broken my left knee or leg. I found out later that the cartilage between the 'ball and socket' in the knee joint had been damaged. We heard that there was a first aid station at the end of the dock so some of us went to find out what could be done for the eye irritation. I went to see what could be done about my left hand. It had become swollen because of the slice on my finger. The aid station was manned by medical personnel from one of the Dominions, New Zealand or India I believe. They drained the pus from my hand and cleaned up the cut on my finger, dusted some powder on the cut and said,

'Don't do any heavy lifting with the hand.' They did not know what caused the eye irritation and told me to 'just keep washing the eyes.' After we left port and got back to sea, the eye problems began to disappear. They couldn't do anything about the leg except to suggest maybe I should go to Taranto for an examination ..."[33]

Bernard Anderson wrote in his diary,

> December 4th — Ed Leahy, the fellow that got hit or thrown against his gun by the concussion of the bombs during the raid, is supposed to have a broken back, but they haven't taken x-rays yet. I sure hope he will be ok. We are the only ship left in the harbor that hasn't been hit.
>
> December 6th — Poor Ed Leahy — we packed his sea bag today and I guess we are going to leave him here.
>
> December 10th — I went ashore this afternoon ... Boy this is a dirty town. The buildings are made of chalk and they are still digging out bodies from the air raid last week.
>
> December 12th — We are now on our way to Augusta, Sicily. We left two fellows behind. Leahy has a bad back, but it isn't busted. They flew him to Africa. He will probably beat us home. The other guy got his nose busted and was at the hospital getting it set when we sailed unexpectedly because of the raid last night ...[34]

James Smith wrote,

> Damage to the *Hennepin* was not major. The engine room sustained most of the damage due to broken steam lines, dents and gashes from flying junk and the life rafts and lifeboats were battered. After leaving Bari, the *Louis Hennepin* sailed to Sicily, Augusta, Malta and Philadelphia. The captain suffered a heart attack, died and was buried at sea in January 1944.[35]

The day after the attack, Bernard L. Anderson wrote in his diary,

We are getting all ready for them tonight, but most of the ships that weren't hit are pulling out. All together 18 ships were burning and sinking, the ammunition in them going off and shrinking you out of your shoes. The air raid was about 1 hour and we kept shooting. The ships are still burning this morning and the air is covered with smoke. Two of the fellows on our ship were blown into the water by the bomb concussions. They are unloading us today ... It is 230 and honey I will close for now and write later ... Darling 530 and everyone is sure nervous. I ate chow but didn't have much of an appetite. We are ready for them planes tonight. Gee I sure hope they don't come. I can't put in words how terrible it was last night. There's things darling I couldn't possibly write or ever explain. It's awful. We have the ammo greased and ready to load in the magazines when they run out. There are only three ships here now. The rest have left. Last night about 5 planes were shot down of about 45. They dropped about 130 bombs, some over 500 lbs.. And some 250. They sure done what they what they set out to do. 18 ships were sunk all over the harbor and the fires are still burning. There is shrapnel all over and there are pieces on deck as big as an apple box side and as jagged as hell. There was a German plane that flew over today probably to see how much damage they had done. I sure wish we were out of here. They are trying to get us unloaded first so we can go.[36]

Concerning the two men in the water after the attack, Anderson wrote:

After we (Anderson and Mannie) shot all the ammo we went to the bow gun and tried to find the two guys up there, but they were gone. Later we found out that the two fellows had jumped to the dock. They thought someone said the ship was sinking. The force of the bombs was so great it threw the ship against the dock and on the way from the dock it broke every line. 8 lines in all were broken. The rope they tie the ship with is 3 to 4 inches in diameter.[37]

SS *John Schofield*

Cadet-Midshipman Theodore Schober: "For some time we heard explosions, many very severe. The ships that were moored at the East jetty were ablaze with flames shooting hundreds of feet into the air. Dense smoke also appeared and was blown to where we were tied up...

"The following day, under orders, we left Bari and proceeded to Augusta, Sicily, where we unloaded the balance of our cargo, and where temporary repairs were made. After we left Bari it was necessary to shift our liquid ballast to the after part of our ship to minimize taking water through the damaged bow."[38]

The American Tankers

From Capt. Hays' Summary report:

> There were no casualties, other than concussion and partial deafness, sustained by personnel, which fact is considered nothing short of miraculous in view of the great amount of shrapnel and metal debris was collected from the decks and various parts of the ship, some of the pieces weighing from six (6) to eight and one-half (8 1/2) pounds.[39]

After the attack, a crew from *Pumper* rescued several men stranded on the East Jetty. They made several trips in their lifeboat, maneuvering in the hazardous burning water now saturated with mustard gas.

The British Ships

George Southern continues with the berthing plan that he sent this author. "I can track the journey we made in the boat from the *Zetland* at berth 25 which took us in front of the line of shipping moored stern-first to the mole. All were on fire. At that moment as we were searching for survivors we saw standing on the mole silhouetted between two blazing ships — a man. I say standing but in fact he was dancing up and down, vigorously waving his arms when he spotted us. He was in a terrible predicament. Fires were raging either side of him and in front of him looking towards us, the surface was a light burning aviation spirit which the wind was driving towards him. The two ships were glowing red with the intense heat. Behind him was the wall of the mole and beyond that the open sea. The poor man must have been roasting alive for we in the boat were soaked with sweat. As we made towards him, the boat pulled up, the propeller clogged with rubbish. The water was covered with debris from the exploded ships and as we could not move we shouted to the man to swim for it. Whether he could hear us above the tremendous din or whether he could even swim, I will never know for black dense smoke obliterated him and when it briefly cleared he was no longer there. Over all these years that nightmarish scene is still as vivid as ever, something I will never forget. Years afterward when I obtained the copy of the berthing plan I was able to judge that the wretched man was trapped between the *Fort Athabaska* and *Joseph Wheeler.*

"Our position was also perilous, in an open boat with no protection from shrapnel which was constantly falling, in the middle of the fairway, helpless, unable to move and only yards away from blazing ammunition ships. Luckily after a short time we managed to free the propeller and move away from the blazing ships. We came upon the *Lyman Abbott* at anchor. As I have explained previously, fires were raging along her upper deck but when we boarded her we found her completely abandoned."[40]

"After two hours we extinguished the fires. Immediately and without a break, in the course of that night another man and I boarded four drifting, deserted and sinking merchantmen. We used explosives to sink one, blast out fires and restrain another from drifting. On that last vessel I saved my companion from serious injury when he made a move from behind the bulkhead where we had retired for safety in order to see why the charge had not gone off. Just as he did so I grabbed him and dragged him back, at that instant the charge exploded. It was almost daybreak when we finally came ashore."[41]

"Lieutenant-Commander Giles, Senior Naval Officer British Coastal Naval Forces based in Bari, carried out salvage operations. After I had departed the *Lyman Abbott*, the drifting deserted Italian ship *Barletta* fouled her own anchor and *Lyman Abbott's*. Lt. Cdr. Giles blasted them apart by using a charge. The next morning *Barletta* turned turtle and sank where she had been berthed.

"Practically all rescue, salvage and fire-fighting was carried out by Royal Navy personnel. Motor-torpedo boats and launches pulled hundreds of men from the water at great risk to life and limb, many finished up in the hospital with contamination and burns. Not only were they in danger from contamination but at the same time ships and dumps were exploding and great chunks of metal were showering them. I personally know five men who carried out rescue work. One of them, Peter Bickmore, rescued a man on a sinking ship who was trapped by the ankle. He was cut free in time with the aid of a hacksaw; the alternative meant amputating his foot. Peter was decorated with the B.E.M. (British Empire Medal), the decoration with which I was awarded. Over twenty decorations were earned that night by Royal Navy men alone."[42]

In correspondence with this author, Southern described British actions that weren't previously recorded. "Not mentioned in Infield's book was the crucial part played by the Coastal Forces Depot Ship H.M.S. *Vienna*, moored on Molo Ridoso. She was near missed by a bomb during the raid and afterwards became the main emergency first-aid station in the harbour. Hundreds of survivors, injured, burned and dying were taken aboard for treatment and part of the ship became a mortuary. The two destroyers *Bicester* and *Zetland*, though badly damaged and contaminated, as was the *Vienna*, carried out first-aid work during and after the raid. The *Zetland* rigged hoses in the wash areas to hose down the survivors — a scene which I witnessed."[43]

HMS *Bicester*'s actions were cited in the Chichester-Constables Report, a British "Most Secret" document inquiring into the Bari disaster. At one point, "a naval officer took instructions to HMS *Bicester* to sink the *John Harvey*, but the *Bicester* was herself heavily damaged and was unable to carry out this instruction."[44]

George Southern continues, "Bob Davies himself had an eventful story. He was on duty on the *Zetland*'s bridge as a signalman from the time the destroyer entered the harbour, all through the raid, then when an explosion knocked all the bridge personnel off their feet, the captain, Lt-Cdr. John Wilkinson received a serious facial injury when hit by a flying chunk of steel. He still carried on for several hours with his face swathed in bandages. Later during repairs it was discovered that the bridge had been forced back two feet by the blast. Bob was sent to the Navy House to collect orders as all the aerials were down and visibility down to zero. He describes hurrying along the mole littered with injured and dying men lying where the explosion had flung them. On his return he was again on duty on the bridge continuously until the vessel reached Taranto two days later. By that time he could barely see out of his blistered eyes.[45]

The HMS *Bisteria* was undamaged in the raid. Journalist and editor Karel Margry described her actions in the aftermath, "After picking up 30 survivors from the slime-covered water, the Port Director ordered her to clear the harbour; she headed to Taranto. Four to six hours later, the entire crew began having eye trouble — a gritty sensation followed by a burning pain. The captain ordered all hands to use an eyewash, but the pain continued. By the time the ship reached Taranto, 18 hours after the raid, the crew was almost completely blind and had great difficulty mooring her. The mustard poison was taking its effect, but as yet nobody understood what had happened to the sailors."[46]

According to an article in the *New Scientist*, Bertram Stevens was two ships away on the HMS *Vulcan* which was also contaminated with mustard gas. The *Vulcan* was ordered to

Taranto, but then received a signal to go to Brandisi, where it arrived some four days later. As soon as the ship dropped anchor, a tug arrived and towed it to the bay where it was instructed to drop anchor away from all the other shipping.

Within five minutes, a motorboat arrived packed with army medical personnel in overalls and gas masks. By that time, Stevens recalls, most of the crew were unable to see and many, including him, were covered with blisters.

The ship was closed for "fumigation" and the crew was sent ashore where the sailors underwent strict decontamination. Their clothes were taken and destroyed.[47]

Thomas Basick was a member of the 12th Troop Carrier Squadron — 60th Troop Carrier Group. He had spent the last week of November at the Bari airfield. One of the American C-47's had a defective engine and he was sent there to repair the engine. It was special time for him because it was Thanksgiving. "It was a treat to go to Bari as it was untouched by the war. It was a treat to go there after Africa and Sicily. While working on the plane we noticed a German reconnaissance plane on at least two separate days uncontested at high altitude."

"We completed our work on the 2nd of December. On that day we made a test flight of the plane to confirm its performance. One of our crew members met a chief steward on a Liberty ship near our quarters in town and invited him on our test flight. We had a nice flight around the middle of the day. The steward then invited us to dine on his ship. What a treat that was for us. After dinner some of us decided to leave for a night on the town. It was just before dusk. Our two pilots decided to stay aboard and take a nice shower that evening.

"On leaving the docks I remember strings of lights and stevedores unloading the ships including many bombs. The place looked like an arsenal. We walked into town a short distance away and decided to see a show. Just as we stepped into the lobby of the theater, we heard the first bomb. This was right after dark. The streets were full of native people who became hysterical as some of the bombs landed in town.

"The first bomb started a fire which illuminated the area. Those dive bombers had easy pickin' after that except for the antiaircraft fire. The shrapnel was coming down like rain. The British MP's did a good job of herding civilians under cover to keep them from getting hurt. I remember seeing some with wounds from shrapnel.

"Even though we had a room in town we decided it was too close to the dock. We got out about five miles away and then we saw one of the biggest explosions I've ever seen. The ammo ship blew up.

"The following morning we headed for the airport to fly and deliver our plane to Sicily. After waiting for a few hours for the pilots to show up we began to have concern for the pilots that stayed aboard the ship the evening before. Did they survive the bombing? It was on our minds. Just before giving up hope for them, we saw two persons walking toward our plane. One had his head bandaged. The two pilots had survived! One pilot had a door blown off slamming into him and he received a purple heart for his injury.

After taking off for Sicily we flew over the harbor. We saw many masts sticking out of the water. It reminded me of Pearl Harbor. We were glad to leave after that experience. The people of Bari finally got a taste of the war."[48]

11

THE
COVER-UP

Bari was a victory beyond all expectation for Germany, somberly echoing the conditions at Pearl Harbor almost exactly two years earlier.

The captain of the *Louis Hennepin* stated after the attack, "Scarcely a bomb was wasted and [I] attributed the success to the combined factors of the crowded condition of the harbor, the careful scouting and observation prior to the attack, and the extreme accuracy of the bombers, plus the failure to receive any advance warning of the approach of bombers and the confusion in defense measures."[1]

Captain Hays gave a stinging, yet wholly accurate account of the British unpreparedness concerning the harbor defense and management in his summation.

In the opinion of the Commanding Officer, the barrage put up by the entire port and ships, as a whole, was very poor. Some ships and

165

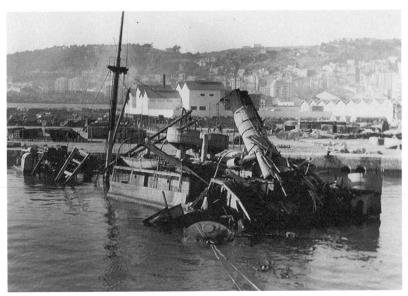

September 1944 and sunken ships were still part of the Bari harbor scene. Russell Krenciprock.

shore guns were firing directly across other ships at low level. Some damage and even casualties to personnel might have occurred from this cause. (*Author's note: Which is exactly what happened*) Fire discipline and control was very poor. This might have been in part, due to the complete surprise with which the attack came and due to the fact that many of the guns on the ships were put out of action as a result of direct hits, even before they were manned, although the entire harbor was lighted at the time of the attack, and subsequent fires from the burning ships and gasoline lit up the entire port.

The Commanding Officer has, in the past, expressed disapproval of lying at anchor fully loaded with 100 octane gasoline, for as many as three (3) to five (5) days, in a port so crowded that ships frequently touch each other whenever the wind shifts. Of all the ships lost in action, most of them were either awaiting berths to discharge their cargoes, or had already discharged and were moored or anchored in the crowded outer harbor, no apparent effort having been made to segregate loaded tankers, ammunition carriers, or other highly dangerous and vulnerable cargoes form the concentration of other shipping.[2]

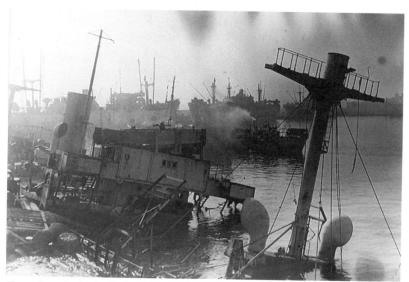

Even though the harbor was still littered with sunken ships nine months after the attack, the vessels unloading in the background bear witness to the fact that it was again an active port. Russell Krenciprock.

It took three weeks to reopen the harbor. Salvage and clean-up at Bari set the Allied land offensive back by three to four months. It also severely reduced the availability of supplies for the newly formed American Fifteenth Air Force and delayed their objective of weakening Germany before the Normandy invasion.

A year later damage was still prominent in the harbor. John Goodhue, Jr., who eventually became the second mate aboard the S.S. *Charles M. Hall,* was in Bari about thirteen months later. "I do remember the sight of my ship's dock, if you could call it that. It was the remains of one of the Liberty ships destroyed in the bombing. The entire midship section of the ship had been blown away and the bow and stern parts with mooring bits were our "dock." The Port of Bari itself had taken a terrific beating and Army personnel, British I believe, had cleared enough of the rubble to keep things going for the port operations."[3]

A lid of secrecy was imposed by the Allies on anything concerning damages, casualties, and the presence of mustard gas. Although indirectly admitting gas being carried on the *John*

Harvey, the British would not directly admit there was mustard gas in the harbor of Bari. The North African Theater Of Operations United States Army (NATOUSA) sent out a communique on December 4. It stated, "... damage was done. There were a number of casualties."[4]

SS *John Harvey*

It is important to understand that the British were in command of Bari harbor and that they knew what kind of cargo the *Harvey* was carrying. This is significant because the British consistently denied knowledge of the *Harvey*'s cargo and the lack of action in expediting the unloading of the deadly gas from that ship. Even after the war, Prime Minister Winston Churchill denied that mustard gas was present in Bari.

In their *Most Secret Report* the British state:

> The *John Harvey* sailed from Oran on 20 Nov in KMS32. Her manifest copies of which were sent by air to Transportation Officer, Bari, showed the following among other types of ammunition and explosives:

Qty.	Pkgs	Description	Weight
722	C/S	Bomb, Gas-HS, M47 A2	1,840,250
1852	C/S	Bomb, Gas-HS M57 A2	981,500

> On 24 Nov, the Ordinance Officer HQ XII AFSC sent the following: "SUBJECT: Ship Manifest TO: Ordinance Officer XII ASAC (SP APO 528 US Army
>
> Ordinance Officer XII AFAC (ADV) APO 528, US Army
>
> Commanding Officer AFOD # 8, APO 528, US Army
>
> 1. Attached is a breakdown of USAAF bombs and amm on the *John Harvey*, now on route to Bari.
>
> 2. Request Acknowledgment of receipt by endorsement hereon.
>
> For Ordinance Officer
>
> The breakdown enclosed showed (*inter alia*) :
>
> 24430 Bomb Chem, HS, 100-lb., M47A2[5]

It was unrealistic for the Allies to think they could keep the attack and mustard gas leak secret, yet this was agreed on by both the American and British leaders. Meanwhile, the people of Bari streamed out of their city spreading the news as did the Allied servicemen who were treated in hospitals outside Bari.

The first security breaks occurred almost immediately, when the British ordered the harbor cleared at 0300 on December 3. Each departing ship carried with it the news that something other than fire had burned the disaster victims at Bari. Soon the word spread to Augusta, Brindisi, and Taranto.

Two weeks later, the *Washington Post* broke the story of the devastating attack and the casualty rate. Calling it the "costliest 'sneak attack' since Pearl Harbor," *Time* further elaborated on the attack by stating:

> Secretary of War Simpson apparently had intended to release a few details at his weekly press conference. But after the *Post* story, newsmen found him sizzling. His anger seemed greater than was justified by a mere premature news "leak." He was brusque, stiff, and cut the conference short. When a reporter wanted to know if the Allies had actually been caught napping, Stimson snapped: "No! I will not comment on this thing!"
>
> The news from Bari was bad. What was even worse was the skittishness in Washington (or London) about telling the facts. If, after four years of World War II, the people of the U.S. should come finally to believe that their leaders are unwilling to trust them to "take" bad news, that disaster would be greater than any in Bari.[6]

Adding to the outrage was the fact that the Germans were able to use the secrecy to gain a psychological advantage. Axis Sally broadcast the news to the world on her nightly program. "I see you boys are getting gassed by your own poison gas," she announced sarcastically over the radio.[7]

The *Army And Navy Register* of April 8, 1944, printed a letter to the managing editor of *The Kansas City Star* and president of the American Society of Newspaper Editors concerning the U.S.

Army's news policy. In the letter, Major General A.D. Surles, U.S. Army Director of Army Public Relations, discussed what he deemed was the public sentiment:

> I can sense the growing idea that we are endeavoring to cover up mistakes under the guise of military security, and yet it is difficult to counteract this impression in view of the fact that the problem complicated by the need for the theater commander to use information as a psychological weapon against the enemy, and because of the necessity for the theater commander to maintain high morale among troops whom are in physical contact with the enemy. I must confess that we, here at home, are in poor position to judge the national interest in terms of these ramifications …[8]

And against the enemy, General Surles uses several examples, one of them Bari. There was still no mention of mustard gas.

> In the Bari incident the Germans tried a new method of attack to invade Radar, struck successfully and, in addition, blew up two ships filled with ammunition, causing great damage.
>
> The harbor is 60 feet deep, and the ships sank completely, with the result that German reconnaissance the next day had no idea of the extent of the damage. They claimed, with what they thought exaggeration, only one half of the loss to us in that harbor. There was an immediate job to be done in harbor clearance, reorganization of Radar and fighter coverage before ordinary security would allow them to know the extent of their operation. In addition, it was a British supply point, and they should have had something to say about the matter …
>
> Frankly, I would like every citizen to be informed concerning circumstances of the incidents described above immediately upon their occurrence. However, I believe that you will agree with me that the explanations, if made too soon, contain information of value to the enemy …[9]

The British, meanwhile, were writing up recommendations for handling, storage, and communication involving the future shipping of toxic ammunition. Brigadier Chicester-Constable in his Report wrote:

Conclusions and Recommendations:

I. Notification of Despatch
… In the particular case under consideration, XII AFSC did in fact notify the addressees … but the message was not received until 28 Nov, the day on which the convoy arrived. The ship's manifest arrived in good time but does not appear to have been circulated. It does not always happen that the manifest arrives before the ship and in any event it does not give any prominence to the fact that a toxic cargo is carried.

We consider that toxic ammunition is of such a nature that it calls for special notification, and that a cable should be sent from the port of dispatch as soon as the ship sails to the Area HQ and the appropriate Port and Ordinance Authorities at the port of discharge, setting out the name of the ship, details of the toxic cargo carried, and expected date of arrival. Ports of call should also be notified, and in every case an acknowledgment required.

II. Stowage
We recommend that stowage of toxic ammunition and explosives on the same ship should, whenever possible, be avoided. It was the explosion on the *John Harvey* of the ammunition she was carrying which was the principal cause of mustard being scattered over the harbour with such unfortunate results. The explosion of such a mixed cargo in port is bound to have most serious and somewhat incalculable consequences.

III. Ports to [*sic*]
It is [*sic*] to recommend that toxic ammunition be not sent to large, busy ports in forward areas. Many factors however, outside the scope of this inquiry, affect the question. Operational and shipping requirements must come first: the number of ports likely to be available in any theatre of war in the early stages of operations is

limited, and we do not consider that the danger from toxic ammunition, provided operation precautions are taken justifies recommendation which might dislocate normal shipping arrangements.

We should point out, however, first that if toxic ammunition were loaded and discharged only at certain ports, the necessary anti-gas stores and equipment and the personnel required to use it could be much more easily prepared. Moreover, adequate equipment and training at least in personal decontamination, might be given to the civil population ...

IV. Discretion and Quick Unloading

It is not the practice in an operational port like Bari to treat a ship carrying toxic ammunition as an abnormal risk. In view of the particular danger this raid illustrated however, we consider that such a cargo should be given high priority of discharge and that while the ship is visiting in port she should be isolated from other ships, particularly ammunition ships, so far as circumstances permit.

Similar considerations apply at a port of loading, if the area is subject to air raids.

V. Warning

The outstanding fact which emerges from our inquiry is that a number of persons suffered from mustard gas burns which might have been allayed and possibly prevented if the true nature of their injuries had been appreciated from the beginning.

The risk present to the minds of the persons who considered the matter after the raid was that there might be splashes of mustard on the moles and on the other ships with possible strong concentrations of vapour. It was not to be expected that the particular, insidious danger which in fact caused so many casualties would occur to them. So far as we are aware, this phenomena of mustard dissolved in oil has never occurred before in anything approaching similar circumstances or on a similar scale.

It is probable that had the appropriate medical authorities received definite information that a ship carrying mustard had exploded in the harbour they would have been able to make a true diagnosis a good deal earlier. As it was they were confronted with patients exhibiting the ordinary symptoms of shock, exposure, burns etc., who therefore received initial treatment actually favourable to the absorption of the mustard. The particular clinical picture was unusual. The burns were not typical of mustard because they had been brought on by long exposure to a solution of mustard in oil, aggravated by resuscitation treatment involving in some cases a long period in blankets.

We recommend that, following the signal notifying the shipment of toxic ammunition, the Port Authorities should notify the Area HQ when and at what berth the ship will discharge. If there is a reason to believe that gas has escaped the ship, through an air raid or otherwise, the Port Authorities should immediately warn the Area HQ and the Commanding Officers and Masters of ships, giving the fullest information available. It must be the responsibility of the naval and military commanders concerned to pass on the warning for the information of hospitals, first aid posts, etc., and definite arrangements for the speedy dissemination of this information should be made beforehand.

A situation may well arise, as it did in Bari, where all who have risked contamination should be warned to decontaminate themselves. The normal Gas Alarms, intended to indicate a choking gas attack, can rarely be appropriate in such circumstances, and would probably only add to the confusion. The essential thing is to state what the precise danger is, e.g., from a particular contact. Such information can probably only be passed by word of mouth, loudspeakers, etc.

VI. Secrecy

There appears to be nothing secret about the Allies' policy with regard to chemical warfare; it has been proclaimed that we intend to retaliate if the enemy begins.

The movement of toxic ammunition is subject to the same rules of secrecy as the movement of any other ammunition. The Security Officer and the special attachment of men who accompany toxic ammunition are there to supervise stowage and handling.

Normally the principles of secrecy and safety work together; but if they come in conflict, the former should give way where toxic ammunition is concerned to the needs of the latter, in exactly the same way as we would be in the case with other kinds of ammunition. Obviously the enemy should be kept in ignorance so far as possible of the presence of toxic ammunition in any particular place; but warning must be given when any danger arises, whether the ammunition concerned is our own or the enemy's.

We recommend that this relationship between secrecy and safety be made clear to those who might possibly have to give a decision in the matter ...[10]

Brigadier Chicester-Constables's Report continued, but seemingly the British had recognized their mistakes and were correcting them accordingly. The final conclusion was that whatever is necessary is done to defeat the enemy. Some tactics will always remain confidential to avoid compromising the objective.

In 1976, George Southern organized a reunion in London for the surviving crew of the HMS *Zetland*. Fifty ex-shipmates attended and heard, for the first time, of the presence of mustard gas in Bari. Southern states, "Though Bob Davis and I and the rest of our shipmates were there in the harbor, none of us knew anything about the existence of mustard gas until we all met at a reunion I organized in London in 1976. As you can imagine it came as a complete surprise to us all."[11]

On December 2, 1993, George Southern attended a reunion at the Imperial War Museum in London. "I received the Official U.S. and U.K. accounts that very morning, exactly fifty years to the day later ... According to the U.S. Report, after the raid someone aboard the *Lyman Abbott* shouted 'Gas' and the crew donned gas masks. Why they should have done that is a mystery for nobody in the harbor on board other ships donned masks for there was no reason to. The conclusion I draw is that the *Lyman Abbott* was also carrying gas, the crew were aware and made a hasty abandonment. The ship sailed from Baltimore, the same port that the SS *John Harvey,* which had mustard gas on board, also sailed from. According to the Official British Report, the Senior Officer in his statement said that when he boarded the *Lyman Abbott* he found her to be deserted which is absolutely untrue as I have previously described ...[12]

Was this another American and British attempt to cover up the fact that there was mustard gas present in Bari Harbor? Stanley Wisniewski wrote this author on the day before Thanksgiving in 1998. His feelings show the bitter aftertaste of this raid. "Till this day I harbor feelings of anger. Where were the English lights and shore batteries? Where were the air raid sirens? They knew that a recon plane had flown over at noon the day of the raid. Why weren't they on alert? Our ships carried no radar. I will feel to the day I leave this earth that the coverup by Churchill and Eisenhower should not have been hushed up. They are dead, but I still carry the scars from that raid. There was absolutely no reason why we were carrying mustard gas. I can only conclude that the War Department and the commanders knew what was on the ships when we left the States. I know General Eisenhower was a great commander but to order mustard gas is beyond my comprehension. We were winning the war and for Churchill to act as if he did not know this was going on is also beyond my belief. So, to all those that died from this raid maybe the truth will come out and will ease the pain of the relatives of those who lost their lives at Bari."[13]

Stanley Wisniewski, an American hero, no longer has to carry those scars because he passed away in April of 1999.

> ... when British Prime Minister Winston Churchill heard of it, he refused to believe that there were any mustard gas casualties at Bari. He simply would not accept that any of the casualties were caused by mustard. The argument continued for several days, with messages being relayed back and forth between Algiers and London at a furious pace, but Churchill refused to be convinced. Eisenhower, assured that Alexander's diagnosis was correct, approved the report and it was entered into the official records. Churchill, on the other hand, directed that all British records be purged of any mention of mustard and refer to the burns as "due to enemy action".[14]

Even after the war, Churchill denied gas was present. Eisenhower in his book, *Crusade in Europe*, written in 1948, never mentioned the fact that mustard gas caused deaths in Bari harbor. He blamed the catastrophe on a fire spreading to the other ships in the harbor. "Fortunately the wind was offshore and the escaping gas caused no casualties."[15]

Churchill sent a telegram to Allied Headquarters Mediterranean which contained the order that all mustard gas symptoms were to be described as *dermatitis*.[16]

"No records or follow-up routines were instituted at the time or since. As the 30 year censorship applied, very few people knew about the involvement of mustard gas and the survivors were scattered far and wide. Many survivors who spent time in the hospital never knew that they had been exposed to the poison until many years later, if at all. Many, many more will have died since of related illnesses such as cancer, leukemia, and bronchial and chest and throat trouble. Their relatives, doctors, and surgeons who attended and treated these men would be ignorant of the fact that he had been exposed to mustard gas."

In conducting research for his book, George Southern inquired from the Royal Army Medical Corps about the part the 98th General Hospital played at Bari. "The reply was, 'We have no knowledge of the incident.'" He received the same reply from the British army units involved in the aftermath of the Bari raid.

British medical records (presumably of the patients dealt with by the Royal Army Medical Corps in the 98th British General Hospital in Bari) are not due to be released until the year 2018.[17]

12

OPERATION DAVEY JONES' LOCKER

A s the American, British, and French forces moved into Germany, the necessity of capturing toxic ammunition became essential. It was feared that Germans still in hiding might use it, in desperation, against the Allies. To prevent this, Britain, France, Russia and the United States formed a committee to decide how to dispose of the toxic weapons, called the Continental Committee on Dumping.

In 1946, Major General Alden H. Waitt wrote the following in a *Saturday Evening Post* article:

> We in the Chemical Warfare Service were satisfied that Germany was well prepared for a gas offensive. We knew that she had begun large-scale production in 1938, more than a year before she started war ...
>
> Yet, when our forces moved into France, we were surprised to find no indications of enemy gas. As we pushed forward, German

177

preparations still failed to appear, and when we reached the Rhine, no gas stocks had been uncovered. A few of us who were responsible for our Army's gas preparations began to worry whether the folks back home might feel we had misled them in spending money to protect ourselves from something that did not exist.

As soon as we crossed the Rhine, however, these apprehensions were allayed. From then on, it became increasingly clear that all our planning and priming had been more than justified. Once we got into Central Germany, Nazi chemical-warfare installations and gas-storage depots appeared in increasing numbers, and vast supplies of offensive gas munitions were uncovered.[1]

The easiest way to get rid of the toxic munitions was to dump them at sea. "The group also decided that the occupying powers in each zone could destroy the chemical weapons on their territory in a manner that was most convenient to them. Captured German chemical weapons totaled 296,103 tons. The American zone contained 93,995 tons; the British 122,508; the Russian 70,500; and the French 9,250."[2]

Five German ammunition depots already containing toxics were selected for the collection of chemical ammunition in the American zone. They were located at Frankenberg, Grafenwohr, Schierling, Wildflecken and St. Georgen. Between May 1945 and June 1947 captured chemical munitions were either burned, shipped to the U.S., or scuttled in surrounding waters aboard U.S. or German ships. Some material was kept and used in the re-building of Germany's industry and some shipped back to Italy.

In 1947, the European Chemical Corps Chief, Colonel H.M. Woodward, Jr., compiled a report concerning the captured toxic ammunition in the German and Austrian sector that came under United States control. The report entitled, *The History of Captured Enemy Toxic Munitions in The American Zone*, was a narrative, statistical and photographic account of the action taken to rid the sector of chemical munitions.

As to toxics scuttled at sea, the St. Georgen Depot dumped by far the most tonnage: 15,553 long tons. This disposal effort became known as "Operation Davey Jones Locker," an odd name for an operation that would ultimately result in many environmental tragedies.

The St. Georgen Depot was surrendered to the invading American forces 3 May 1945 with all facilities in relatively good condition … Depot is not far from the Austrian border, is approximately 50 kilometers from Salzburg, Austria …

The depot was concealed in a heavily wooded area. Buildings and bunkers were built in the woods with a minimum change in the surrounding terrain. This natural camouflage included wire netting threaded with ribbons of plastic paper in greens and browns. Doorways, entrances, and sides of buildings were cleverly concealed so that detection from the air was all but impossible. The effectiveness of their efforts is evidenced by the fact that the depot was not subjected to any major bombing raids.

No efforts were made by the Germans to blow up any of the facilities before surrendering, so that the entire installation was turned over to the Americans intact.

The depot comprises an irregularly shaped, heavily wooded area about 2 1/4 miles long by 1 1/4 miles wide. At one end of the depot is the regular munitions area, which contains administrative buildings, barracks, mess halls, motor pool, munitions bunkers, munitions houses and hangars used for assembling, storing and shipping of 105 mm and 150 mm artillery shells. This area is oval in shape with a diameter of approximately 1 1/4 miles.

Beyond the munitions area at the other end of the depot, is the "N" or toxic area, which contains huge tanks for the storage of bulk mustard, also buildings containing modern and elaborate machinery for the filling, storage and shipping of toxic artillery shells and land mines …

In the late Autumn 1944 work was again started in "N" Section. For several months production was at its peak and the laborers were working twenty-four hours a day … employees, laborers and soldiers numbered around 1500 …

Approximately 40,000 tons of Class V captured enemy material were found at St. Georgen as well as approximately 10,000 tons of

Class II and IV items.* The Class V items included hundreds of thousands of 105 mm toxic German artillery shells, also 150 mm artillery shells, 150 mm rockets, toxic land mines, fuses, bursting charges, cartridge cases, propellant charges, French and Italian artillery shells. In addition there were the tremendous storage tanks of bulk mustard also drums of Hungarian and Italian bulk mustard and smaller quantities of various chemicals. Work carried on at the depot during 1946 included the following:

1. Filling and shipping of mustard bombs to the United States.
2. The destruction of liquid mustard by burning.
3. The receipt and storing of Class II, IV, and V CEM (Captured Enemy Material) shipped into the depot from other installations.
4. Segregation and classification of CEM found at the depot.
5. Shipment of toxic munitions to Bremerhaven for sea dumping.[3]

Accompanying the official report were photographs that included captions revealing the extent of the large supplies Germany had stocked in St. Georgen. The Germans had constructed an effective railroad line into the depot.

> … The railroad network throughout the depot could accommodate 1,000 freight cars at a time … As the German armies met reverses in Italy and to the East in the Russian Zone, thousands of rounds of toxic artillery shells and quantities of liquid toxics were shipped into St. Georgen for storage. Much of this was hurriedly unloaded and left in open storage evidencing the fact that there was insufficient time or possibly as a result of insufficient labor for proper storage.[4]

---

* The material classifications are:
  I   = Nerve agents
  II = Blood agents
  III = Irritants
  IV = Lung agents
  V   = Blister agents

The Germans also received their own munitions back from the Eastern front as the Russians advanced. Photographs indicated the haste in which they had to store the incoming toxics.

> With rapid advance of the Russian armies in the East, various artillery and gas dumps were ordered evacuated and contents shipped to what was considered a safer area in St. Georgen. After the capitulation, thousands of artillery shells ... were found at the St. Georgen Depot. The hap-hazard and hasty arrangement of field stacks ... is evidence of the tremendous strain under which the Germans were working in effort to hold their lines.[5]

Much of the toxic munition was being shipped back to Germany from Italy. Stackloads of Italian 75 and 105mm artillery shells were found. Whether these munitions were made before the War by the Italian government is questionable. They may have been made by Germany and shipped to Italy.

> ... photograph shows a field stack of Italian 105 mm artillery shells, white phosphorus filled. Shells were shipped into the depot from the Italian front after the German armies had started their retreat. One of the German supervisors, currently engaged by Military Government in the work of converting these munitions, was a German artillery captain in Italy and personally directed the shipment of toxics from Italy into southern Germany.[6]

German workmen indicated that much of the toxics had been manufactured in 1937.

> In the foreground [of the photograph] are shown some 305 mm and in the background additional quantities of 210 mm White Cross Italian artillery shells. According to information secured from German workmen who were previously employed at the depot, the majority of these shells came into the depot from the Italian front in 1943 and 1944. Markings indicate that many of these shells were manufactured in 1937. The metal of the shell contains cadmium which tends to prevent the metal from rusting thus making it possible

to store this type of shell in the open for long periods of time without serious deterioration.[7]

Other field stacks consisted of 210 mm Italian artillery shells. Large quantities of bulk toxics were found in well-camouflaged bunkers.

> Bulk toxics found in drums at St. Georgen after the capitulation included:
> Italian mustard in 55 gallon drums, 4500 gallons
> Italian chlorpicrine in 55 gallon drums, 6000 gallons
> Hungarian mustard in 16 gallon drums, 87,500 gallons
> Hungarian mustard in 55 gallon drums, 215,000 gallons.[8]

A total of "19,000 drums found on hand at St. Georgen contained approximately 400,000 gallons of liquid toxics."[9]

Approximately twenty percent of the toxics not burned or shipped elsewhere were dumped at sea in "Operation Davey Jones Locker." Shipping the toxics to Bremerhaven, they were then loaded on hulks and transported to the Skagerrak Sea. The Skagerrak is extremely deep and is the portion of the North Sea which touches the shores of Denmark, Norway, and Sweden.

Transport of the chemicals to the hulks commanded the utmost attention as they were shipped in German railway wagons.

> Prior to shipment, at the depots, the wagons were sealed and placards placed on the sides stating the contents. These shipments were given high priority on the railroad and rail transportation officers along the entire route were notified to expedite the shipment of the toxic agents to the Port. The rail transportation officer at Bremerhaven promptly notified the Port Chemical Officer upon the arrival of each shipment. The Port Chemical Officer was responsible for the inspection of all wagons and for the supervision of unloading the wagons and loading the hulks.[10]

Toxics were loaded into the hulks and hatch covers bolted and sealed over with cement. Three of the first five ships scuttled were:

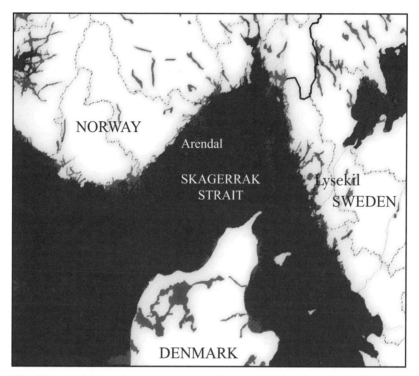

The Skagerrak Sea, also known as the Norwegian Trench, was used by both Britain and the United States as a dump site for chemical munitions.

Sperrbrecher (German minesweeper) — 1349 tons

T-65 (German flak ship) — 1526 tons

U-J 305 (German trawler) — 671 tons

These ships were scuttled on July 1 and 2, 1946 in water 650 meters deep. Another mission saw the *Alco Banner* (American Hog-Islander) with 2,765 tons scuttled on July 14, 1946 in the same area. Finally on August 30 this part of the mission was ended as the Liberty Ship *James Otis* was sunk with 3,653 tons of toxic munitions aboard.[11]

"Operation Davey Jones Locker" was over.

However, the disposal operation wasn't complete and a concluding phase was initiated because "as of June 1, 1947, approximately 50,500 long tons of toxic material awaited disposition."[12] A total of 13,000 tons was burned and another 36,000 long tons was shipped to Italy for scrap metal. "However, toxic shipments to Italy were halted from time to time due to the Italian railway labor difficulties. A total of approximately 10,500 long tons were eventually delivered in Italy."[13]

Because of the continued labor problems in Italy, it was decided to scuttle the remaining toxics in the Skagerrak waters. From June 1947 to August 1948, six ships were scuttled in waters between 665 and 1180 meters in depth. "The ships were the American Liberty ships; *James Sewell, James Harrod, George Hawley, Nesbitt,* and the German freighters *Philip Heiniken,* and *Marcy.*"[14]

The American dumping didn't end in 1948. The U.S. continued to ship back German toxics to America. Eventually the U.S. had to contend with its own supplies of chemical munitions. "The last U.S. dumpings of captured German weapons are believed to have taken place in 1958."[15]

> Between 1945 and 1949, the British dumped 34 shiploads carrying 127,000 tons of chemical and conventional weapons in the Norwegian Trench, much of it 25 miles east of the town of Arendal in a 2,300-foot (700 meters) deep site. The British also dumped more chemical weapons at a site 20 miles west of the Irish coast.[16]

According to Mitretek Systems (an organization involved with scientific research, engineering, and development in the public interest.)

> The British dumped approximately 175,000 tons of chemical weapons at sea, with 100,000 tons coming from Scotland and the balance from the captured German stockpile. During 1955-56, the British dumped a further 17,000 tons of captured German munitons. During 1956-1957, the British disposed of the remainder of their stockpile of chemical weapons, 8000 tons of World War II vintage mustard and phosgene munitions.[17]

Gotland Island, a Swedish possession and Bornholm Island, belonging to Denmark, were near the locations of Russian chemical weapons dumps.

The Baltic was also used as a dumping ground. Unlike the North Sea area, this body of water is very shallow. The average depth is only fifty meters.

As soon as World War II ended, 46,000 tons of chemical weapons were dumped in the Baltic areas known as the Gotland Deep, Bornholm Deep, and the Little Belt, according to information submitted to the 1994 Helsinki Commission. The Russians alone are reported to have dumped 30,000 tons in an area 2,000 square kilometers in size near Gotland and Bornholm Islands.[18]

According to other estimates, "between 1946-1947, an estimated 50,000 — 150,000 tons of chemical munitions were dumped in the Baltic Sea."[19]

Dumping also occurred off the coast of Italy. In unpublished reports, "The United States dumped unspecified quantities of phosgene, hydrogen cyanide, and cyanogen chloride bombs in the

Adriatic Sea … near Bari from 12 October to 5 November 1945 and from 1- 15 December 1945. Unspecified quantities of mustard and/or Lewisite bombs were dumped at the same site from 1-23 April 1946.[20]

Although not the focus of this book, it should also be noted that tons of chemical munitions were also dumped in the ocean in the Far East and off the coast of Japan.

13

FIFTY YEARS LATER

The Allies made every attempt to safely remove the chemical munitions and prevent leakage and accidents. However, many leakers developed enroute to the ships, in ships to be scuttled and in transport to the United States. Worse yet, there seemed to be no consideration given to the possibility that the scuttled ships containing munitions might leak, or that ocean dumping of toxics would someday become hazardous to the environment.

Bomb shells containing mustard still lie at the bottom of Bari harbor. It has also come to light that the Allies dumped mustard in the Adriatic Sea off Bari. "Unpublished U.S. government records indicate that unspecified quantities of mustard and/or Lewisite bombs were dumped at the same site ..."[1] There have been many reports of fishermen being burned by mustard from bombs caught in their fishing nets in the waters between Molfetto, Giovinazzio and Bari.

The mustard is dragged to the surface in fishing nets after the containers holding it are broken or have corroded. It consists of a lumpy mass that hardens upon exposure to sea water enabling it to be brought to the surface. The unsuspecting fishermen subsequently handle the tackle and the mustard, inhaling fumes and getting vapor in their eyes.

Doctors Georgio Assennato and Donato Sivo of the Department of Internal and Occupational Medicine at Bari University, Italy, have studied those fisherman. In one of their papers they state,

> From 1946 to 1997 hundreds of fishermen from the town of Molfetta, a town located in Apulia, 38 km north of Bari on the Adriatic Sea, have experienced exposure to sulfur mustard. This experience is common also in other Apulian fishermen communities, but complete information is available for the Molfetta fishermen ... we used data from Molfetta hospital ... From 1946 to 1997 (last case in June) we identified a sample of 236 cases of Sulfur mustard intoxification. All subjects were males and were working as fishermen at the time of exposure ...[2]*

The Central Institute for Scientific and Technological Research Applied to the Sea (ICRAM) studies included the number of fishermen burned, how many and the types of bombs remain, where the bombs are located, the type of mustard and containers used, and the effects on the ecosystem. ICRAM has had difficulty getting information from the U.S. Edgewood Research facility and other U.S. agencies.

An article in the *Bulletin of the Atomic Scientists,* states, "It is known that at least twenty-one — possibly as many as fifty — ships loaded with chemical weapons were scuttled in the Skagerrack seabed between Norway, Sweden, and Demark at the end of WW II."[3] A new dumpsite was found "just twenty nautical

---

* *Since this article was written, three more cases have been reported according to a 12 October 1999 email message from Dr. Sivo.*

miles offshore from the Swedish town of Lysekil. It is possibly the largest dumping ground in Scandinavia.[4]

The problem of what to do with the remaining undersea chemicals remains. One thing is certain: "their containers are deteriorating. Ship hulls constructed early in this century were 20-25 millimeters thick. Skagerrak seawater, with its high salt content, can break through such metal in forty or fifty years. Leaking shells have already been retrieved."[5] But, more seriously, "no study has been done on the possible environmental effects of the 300,000 tons of chemical ammunition lying at the bottom of Scandinavian seas."[6]

In the Baltic, "Swedish and Danish fishermen frequently suffer injuries from mustard gas dragged up in the nets. Both countries have built special hospitals and decontamination facilities along their coasts to treat mustard-gas wounds — the legacy of ocean dumping after World War II."[7]

The fishermen of these areas call the scuttled ships "Gas Ships," and wisely avoid the dumping areas.

Personnel responsible for removing and shipping the chemical toxics back to the U.S. were also injured. Edward H. Aho was in the U.S. Merchant Marine and helped ship toxics back to America. For over fifty years his health, especially his nervous system, has been problematic. The following was submitted and published by Ed in the July 22, 1998 *Journal of Commerce*:

Fifty Years Later, still no recognition

In April of 1946, I served as a mariner on a War Shipping Administration Liberty Ship, S.S. *Isaac Mayer Wise,* loading cargo at Antwerp, Belgium. After unloading our cargo of nitrate, a crew of carpenters came aboard ship and built collision bulkheads in each hold about six or eight feet from the sides of the ship. The bulkheads were made of wood and extended from the bottom of the holds to the underside of the deck.

The Army and Belgium stevedores then started to load German poison gas bombs in the holds. We were issued gas masks and given some training on their use. We were taking on a cargo of 3,908 long tons of German poison gas bombs, which consisted of mustard gas and phosgene. The bombs were in army green boxes and crates. Each bomb was in an individual box.

After a few days of loading they stopped because there were some "leakers" in No. 4 hold. How well I remember as three of us were ordered to go down into No.4 hold and find a leaking German poison gas bomb. This happened more than once, which caused the stevedores to strike for several days. As documented by Army gas warfare specialists from Aberdeen Proving Grounds, we had 20 "incidents" of leaking German poison gas. The covers of the forepeak tanks were removed and the tanks were loaded with detonators ... maybe the fuses were removed?

While at Antwerp, the S.S. *Edward Richardson*, moored next to us, also took on German poison gas bombs, which included Sarin. She had 16 "incidents" of leaking German poison gas. While crossing the Atlantic bound for San Jacinto Army Ordinance Depot, Texas, we had phosgene leaking out of the forward holds. It smells like fresh cut corn. While unloading, five men suffered mustard gas burns. We couldn't sign off because a crew was required should the ship have to be moved due to an emergency. There was another ship behind us that carried poison gas bombs. Our cargo was destined for Arkansas ... On five Liberty Ships that carried German poison gas bombs to the United States and elsewhere, there were 96 documented incidents of leaking poison Gas ...[8]

Edward Aho has spent countless hours on the phone with U.S. government authorities relating his medical symptoms, akin to those exhibited by Gulf War veterans, but to no avail. He has yet to receive any assistance.

The shipments brought back to the U.S. were dumped at sea in various sites on the eastern seaboard, the Gulf of Mexico, and off California. The toxics were also stored in eight mainland sites. Those scuttled in ships at sea were part of Operation CHASE. CHASE meant Cut Holes And Sink 'Em. These operations continued until 1972.

14

EPILOGUE

Bari recovered slowly after the attack. No one who was there will ever forget the horror unleashed on December 2, 1943.

The American and British governments tried to cover-up the episode. Even today, the British have sealed surveys and medical information until 2015 and 2018 respectively in the Public Record Office. The U.S. has countless unpublished documents relating to Bari and the subsequent dumping of chemical toxins.

After the war, most civilized nations focused on nuclear disarmament. Chemical and biological warfare disarmament were forgotten. The U.S. finally stopped production of chemical weapons in 1968. In 1971 a disarmament conference was held in Geneva, the Conference of the Committee on Disarmament (CCD). They issued a document on Chemical and Biological warfare known as the "Convention on the Prohibition of the Development, Production and Stockpiling of Bacteriological and

Toxin Weapons." After nineteen years of negotiations, another conference was held in Geneva in 1992. A final document was created embracing both the Geneva Protocol of 1925 (which prohibited the use of biological and chemical toxins) and the 1972 agreement which called for the elimination of production, and destruction of stockpiled supplies.

Meanwhile, the U.S. had been stockpiling chemical toxics in eight mainland facilities: Aberdeen, Maryland; Richmond, Kentucky; Anniston, Alabama; Pine Bluff, Arkansas; Pueblo, Colorado; Newport, Indiana; Tooele, Utah; Umatilla, Oregon and on Okinawa. The U.S. had been dumping some of these toxics along with those captured from Germany in scuttled ships at sea in the previously cited Operation CHASE (Cut Holes And Sink 'Em). This came to an end with the passage of the Marine Protection Act of 1972. The army subsequently made the decision to incinerate its stores of toxics. The incineration commenced in 1990.

In the 1980's, a previously unknown aspect of poison gas warfare surfaced. U.S. Veterans of World War II asked the Veterans' Administration for compensation resulting from injuries and/or experiments with mustard gas. The VA, ignorant of the background or details, rejected the claims. The VA finally agreed to have a study conducted by the Institute of Medicine (IOM). The information was not forthcoming. The VA had to invoke the Freedom of Information Act repeatedly to get data from the Department of Defense.

The study was a document published in 1993 entitled *Veterans at Risk: The Health Effects of Mustard Gas and Lewisite*. Letters were sent out to service personnel who had participated in experiments, worked with toxics, transported them, or were injured by them.

What the IOM found regarding the experiments is shocking:

> By the time the war ended, over 60,000 U.S. servicemen had been used as subjects in this chemical defense research program. At

INSTITUTE OF MEDICINE
NATIONAL ACADEMY OF SCIENCES
2101 CONSTITUTION AVENUE   WASHINGTON, D.C. 20418

DIVISION OF HEALTH PROMOTION
AND DISEASE PREVENTION

May 26, 1992

FAX: 202/334-2939

Mr. Warren A. Brandenstein
Rt. 1 Box 768
Banner Elk, NC 28604

Dear Mr. Brandenstein,

On behalf of the Institute of Medicine's Committee to Survey the Health Effects of Mustard Gas and Lewisite I would like to thank you for writing to me about your exposure to mustard gas. We have read a good deal about the disaster at Bari, but have heard from only a few veterans who were present. It would be helpful to our committee if you could provide a little bit more information on your immediate health problems and injuries at the time and information on any health problems you currently have. If you prefer, you may telephone me with this additional information by calling collect to 202/334-3387. If I am not available, my assistant Jennifer Streit, or my research assistant, Cathy Liverman, will be able to help you.

The information you provide, along with that provided by others, will help the committee to identify gaps in the formal medical literature regarding the possible relationships between exposure to these gases and certain diseases. We hope to complete the report of this committee by December and will send you a copy of the report at that time. It is expected that this report will contain a summary of what is known about the health effects of exposure to these gases and recommendations about how gaps in our present understanding of these health effects can be resolved. It is important to us that you understand that this committee is not part of the Department of Veterans Affairs (DVA) and, as such, the committee is not able to make decisions or recommendations regarding individual compensation decisions. However, the report, which will be released to the DVA, the public, and the press, will also include a summary of all the information we received from you and your fellow veterans.

I have enclosed a list of the members of the committee for your information. Once again, thank you for your help.

With best wishes,

Sincerely,

Constance M. Pechura, Ph.D.
Study Director

Letter sent to Warren A. Brandenstein, a Naval Armed Guard injured by mustard gas aboard the S.S. John Bascom *on the night of December 1943. Warren Brandenstein*

least 4,000 of these subjects had participated in tests conducted with high concentrations of mustard agents or Lewisite in gas chambers or in field exercises over contaminated ground areas. The human subjects had experienced a wide range of exposures to mustard agents or Lewisite, from a mild (a drop of agent on the arm in "patch" tests) to quite severe (repeated gas chamber trials, sometimes without protective clothing). All of the men in the chamber and field tests, and some of the men in the patch tests, were told at the time that they should never reveal the nature of the experiments. Almost to a man, they kept this secret for the next 40 or more years.[1]

The IOM recommended that the Department of Defense identify and contact all the people who had ever come in contact with chemical toxics so they could obtain the medical care and benefits to which they were entitled.

APPENDICES
ENDNOTES
ABOUT THE AUTHOR
BIBLIOGRAPHY
INDEX

APPENDIX A

CHEMICAL WARFARE BEFORE WORLD WAR II

The first use of a toxic chemical substance in warfare was in the Peloponnesian Wars of 431 to 404 B.C. between the Greek city-states of Athens and Sparta. The Spartan armies burned a concoction of sulfur and pitch, creating a deadly cloud of sulfur dioxide. This later evolved into a missile or fireball containing burning oil and arsenic which was hurled at enemy forces both on land and at sea. For the next several hundred years toxic warfare consisted of similar incendiaries, all of which emitted incapacitating smoke which, in many cases, caused blindness.

In 1871 an international arbitration resolving a shipping dispute that occurred between Great Britain and the United States during the U.S. Civil War was held in neutral Switzerland. It marked the first time an international dispute was decided by a neutral country and accepted by the parties involved. This settlement became known as the Geneva Tribunal and had a significant impact in keeping peace in Europe during the late nineteenth century. Tsar Nicholas II saw it as a way to de-escalate the growing arms race between between Germany, Britain and Russia and of continuing the existing peace.

Therefore, in 1898 Tsar Nicholas II convened what became known as the Hague Court which led to the first Hague Conference in 1899, attended by representatives of twenty-six nations, and a second in 1907 attended by representatives of forty-six nations. The goals were to settle international disputes, codify international law, and promote disarmament.

Although the conference reached consensus on the conduct of land and naval warfare, mine laying, dropping bombs from balloons, the use of dumdum bullets in rifles, and the treatment of prisoners of war, total disarmament was never achieved. In fact, the United States refused to sign the disarmament pact in the 1899 Conference which renounced the use of chemical warfare, although twenty-five other nations did so. American reasoning was that the pact covered chemical agents delivered by projecile only, leaving other means of chemical warfare permissible.[*]

Germany first used tear gas against Russia in January of 1915 during World War I enabling them to drive several miles through Russian lines. A new, effective, and deadly form of warfare had been unleashed. Then, on April 22, 1915, they used chlorine gas against Allied troops at Ypres, Belgium. "At 1700 hours the Germans released a 5 mile wide cloud of chlorine gas from some 520 cylinders (168 tons of the chemical)."[1]

As the gas drifted over them the troops saw:

> ... the vast cloud of greenish-yellow gas spring out of the ground and slowly move down wind towards them, the vapor clinging to the earth, seeking out every hole and hollow filling the trenches and shell holes as it came. First wonder, then fear; then as the first fringes of the cloud enveloped them and left them choking and agonized in the fight

---

[*] Germany took advantage of this "loophole" in World War I by placing its poisonous gases in cylinders rather than projectiles.

for breath — panic. Those who could move broke and ran, trying, generally in vain, to outstrip the cloud which followed inexorably after them.[2]

This surprise attack and the fact that gas was used for the first time on the Western Front, were psychologically devastating to the Allies.

Later that year, the U.S. War Department sent observers to see firsthand this new form of warfare. One result of this visit was that the responsibility of designing a breathing apparatus in the form of a gas mask was assigned to the U.S. Surgeon General's Department. Development was slow and it was not until 1917 that

---

MUSTARD GAS

Named because of the so-called smell of mustard and garlic, mustard gas is a caustic chemical that penetrates anything it comes in contact with, including masks. It was easily packaged in projectiles and shot at the enemy, eliminating the need to release it downwind from the aggressor's trenches.

Upon first contact, mustard gas reddens the skin, even turning it a coppery color. Large blisters develop, especially in the sweat gland areas of the under arms and groin. The blisters eventually burst.

The eyes begin to react within hours, feeling as if they are being scratched by sand. Pain and extreme discomfort are followed by swelling, closing and extreme sensitivity to light. In severe cases blindness may result.

If the gas is inhaled it causes the throat to burn followed by difficulty in swallowing and breathing. Eventually, the lining of the lungs becomes inflamed and blisters. Throat and lung tissue becomes infected, diseased, and, if enough quantity of gas was inhaled, death follows in a few hours or days.

If the victim survives inhalation, he suffers chronic shortness of breath, cough, and pain. Mustard gas is a carcinogen, and can lead to birth defects and leukemia. Contact also has severe effects with the digestive system and the elimination of bodily waste.

the first masks were ready. Prior to this, research was a low priority because it was believed that the U.S. had effective measures to counter the chlorine gas used by the Germans.

Because the U.S. Bureau of Mines had conducted experiments on poisonous gases in mines they offered their expertise to the National Research Council (NRC). In April 1917, the NRC began to study poisonous gas, the development of varieties of gas, and the defenses required to survive an attack. Thus began sustained chemical warfare research in the United States.

Then, when the Germans used mustard gas concealed in projectiles in July 1917, the "War Department began to give serious consideration to preparations for gas warfare. Mustard gas was persistent; it proved to be a high casualty producer and it considerably widened the scope of chemical warfare."[3] The use of mustard gas was particularly effective because it adhered to and penetrated anything it touched.

In 1917 General John Joseph (Blackjack) Pershing was appointed the first American Expeditionary Force (AEF) commander. He assigned Lt. Col. Amos A. Fries as Chief of the Office of Gas Service charged with overseeing the entire gas warfare operation.

Lt. Col. Fries' first priority was the production of an adequate gas mask. Early American masks were tested by the British and proved totally unsuccessful. The design of a new gas mask became the responsibility of the Medical Department.

A second but equally important priority became the production of gas-filled ordnance. This was assigned to a new arsenal built in the Fall of 1917 in Edgewater, Maryland. Edgewater Arsenal grew to become an impressive manufacturing and research facility. In the brief time of its operation before the 1918 armistice, the Edgewater Arsenal, "… manufactured over 6,000 tons of chemicals in 1918, and filled over 1,500,000 shells and grenades."[4]

The Office of Gas Service became an important operation because of General Pershing's insistence on developing offensive and defensive gas warfare programs and equipment. Eventually this effort lead to the formation of the Army's Chemical Warfare Service (CWS). Major General William Sibert was the Chemical Warfare Service's first chief.

Before the end of the war, the Allies retaliated in kind to the German use of gas warfare. "125,000 tons of chlorine, mustard gas, and other poisons had been released, killing 91,000 and disabling 1.2 million more ..."[5]

The toll of gas casualties in the First World War was appalling.

A total of 1,296,853 military personnel were casualties; 91,198 died. The Russians suffered far worse than any of the countries involved. They had a casualty total of 475,340 of which 56,000 died. Almost two-thirds of all the deaths caused by gas warfare in WW I was suffered by the Russians. In comparison, the U.S. had only 72,807 casualties of which only 1,462 died.[6]

GAS CASUALTIES IN THE FIRST WORLD WAR			
Country	Non-Fatal	Deaths	Total
Russia	419,340	56,000	475,340
Germany	191,000	9,000	200,000
France	182,000	8,000	190,000
British Empire	180,597	8,109	188,706
Austria-Hungary	97,000	3,000	100,000
United States	71,345	1,462	72,807
Italy	55,373	4,627	60,000
Others	9,000	1,000	10,000
Total	1,205,655	91,198	1,296,853

At the end of the war, the future of the Edgewater Arsenal was in doubt. In March of 1919, General Sibert wrote:

> There is, perhaps, no act perpetrated by the Germans in the Great War that has attracted more universal condemnation than that of the introduction of toxic gas as an agent of warfare. Our papers and magazines have vied with each other in describing the terrible effects of gas upon the troops, while pictures and cartoons have set forth in a still more effective way the horrors of this new agent. As a result, there is a general opinion prevalent that the Peace Congress, now in session at Paris, will put an end to the use of toxic gas, and actions already taken seem to indicate that the Chemical Warfare Service of the United States Army will be abolished.[7]

However, the CWS was ordered by Congress to continue its research activities, training of Army personnel, and production of chemical warfare weapons. General Sibert said, "Would it not be well for the authorities to think long and earnestly before deciding to abolish the Chemical Warfare Service?"[8]

An intensified revulsion toward gas warfare came out of World War I. It was deemed a heinous, cowardly way to wage war. In 1921, the Conference on the Limitation of Armaments was convened in Washington, D.C. America's position — and worldwide opinion — was that gas warfare should be banned. For the most part, gas warfare had already been condemned by existing treaties. Article 5, drawn up at the Conference, prohibited gas warfare via the uses of noxious gases and submarine action. The U.S. ratified this treaty, although the French never signed the agreement because they felt it restricted their submarine development.

In 1925, a second conference was held in Geneva. The major outcome, known as the Geneva Gas Protocol, banned the use of toxic agents in wartime. This agreement also covered the use of biological toxins:

> A protocol to prohibit the use of poisonous gasses and bacteriological methods of warfare was signed by forty-four

Countries. While it prohibited the use of gasses in war and bacteriological warfare, the protocol did not forbid the manufacture, possession, testing, or domestic use of chemical and bacteriological agents. Although the United States helped negotiate the treaty and signed it, the Senate refused to approve ratification.[9]

The U.S. Secretary of State, Frank Kellogg, contended in 1926 that the U.S. must continue to research and be defensively prepared to use gas warfare tactics, regardless of existing treaties. The U.S. military supported his position. A joint Army-Navy policy on chemical warfare in 1934 stated:

> The United States will make all necessary preparations for the use of chemical warfare from the outbreak of war. The use of chemical warfare, including the use of toxic agents, from the inception of hostilities, is authorized, subject to such restrictions or prohibitions as may be contained in any duly ratified international convention or conventions, which at the time may be binding upon the United States and the enemy's state or states.[10]

In October of 1935, Italy invaded Ethiopia with more than 100,000 troops. Emperor Haile Selassie petitioned the League of Nations to impose economic sanctions against Italy. The attempt was unsuccessful and the ensuing war a travesty. The Italian army was well-trained and equipped with heavy armor and air support. The Ethiopian army, largely equipped with spears, was outnumbered three to one.

At the outset however, the Ethiopian army proved difficult to overcome because of their use of guerilla tactics. Furious at the lack of immediate success, Benito Mussolini replaced the army leader with General Pietro Badoglio. General Badoglio, in direct violation of the 1926 Geneva Convention, which Italy signed, used mustard gas against the Ethiopian army and citizens, killing or wounding approximately 15,000 Ethiopian soldiers.[11]

Why was mustard gas used against such a weak foe? Col. Stanley D. Fair (Ret.), worked for the Chemical Corps and was a consultant at the U.S. Army War College. He maintains that there were two probable reasons, both stemming from World War I.

> In at least two major battles the Italians suffered heavy losses from the enemy's use of chemical weapons: on the plateau of Doberdo in June 1916, and at Caporetto in October 1917. The Austro-Hungarian use of a chlorine-phosphene mixture at Doberdo has been rated as one of the most effective gas-cylinder attacks of World War I. The Italians suffered approximately 6,000 casualties, about 5,000 of them fatal ...[12]

> The retreat of the Italian forces from Caporetto, described vividly by Ernest Hemingway in *A Farewell to Arms*, continued for 100 miles to the Piave River where the Italian front finally held. This major defeat was a severe blow to the national morale of Italy, but Marshal Badoglio took over as chief of the general staff and organized a new army.[13]

> ... the past was not the only influence on Marshal Badoglio's decision to use chemical weapons against Ethiopia. He was interested in the potential of aero-chemical warfare (the delivery of gas weapons from airplanes), a subject that had concerned the military of all nations since World War I.[14]

Against Ethiopia, Marshal Badoglio first used tear gas, then mustard gas bombs and spray from airplanes. He bombed the flanks and rear of the Ethiopian army. "Marshal Badoglio used these tactics from late January until the end of organized resistance in early April 1936, and they were effective in producing heavy casualties among the Ethiopians as well as panic and lowered morale."[15]

Benito Mussolini spoke to the League of Nations in May, 1936. His reason for using gas warfare against the thoroughly out-manned and inferior Ethiopian armies was that the Ethiopians committed "abominable atrocities ... which would be inconceivable in civilized countries." Haile Selassie, who would become *Time* magazine's Man of the Year in 1936, appealed to the League of Nations. Part of his appeal read:

I pray to Almighty God that he may spare nations the terrible sufferings that have just been inflicted on my people, and of which chiefs who accompany me here have been the horrified witnesses.

It is my duty to inform the Governments assembled in Geneva, responsible as they are for the millions of men, women, and children, of the deadly peril which threatens them, by describing to them the fate which has been suffered by Ethiopia. It is not only upon the warriors that the Italian Government has made war. It has above all attacked populations far removed from hostilities, in order to terrorize and exterminate them. At the beginning, towards the end of 1935, Italian aircraft hurled upon my armies bombs of tear-gas. Their effects were but slight. The soldiers learned to scatter, waiting until the wind had rapidly dispersed the poisonous gases. The Italian aircraft then resorted to mustard gas. Barrels of liquid were hurled upon armed groups. But this means also was not effective; the liquid affected only a few soldiers, and barrels upon the ground were themselves a warning to troops and to the population of danger.

It was at the time when the operations for the encircling of Makalle were taking place that the Italian command, fearing a rout, followed the procedure which is now my duty to denounce to the world. Special sprayers were installed on board aircraft so that they could vaporize, over vast areas of territory, a fine, death-dealing rain. Groups of nine, fifteen, eighteen aircraft followed one another so that the Fog issuing from them formed a continuous sheet. It was thus that, as from the end of January, 1936, soldiers, women, children, cattle, rivers, lakes and pastures were drenched continually with this deadly rain. In order to kill off systematically all living creatures, in order to more surely poison waters and pastures, the Italian command made its aircraft pass over and over again. That was its chief method of warfare ...

These fearful tactics succeeded. Men and animals succumbed. The deadly rain that fell from the aircraft made all those whom it touched fly shrieking with pain. All those who drank the poisoned water or ate the infected food also succumbed in dreadful suffering. In tens of thousands, the victims of Italian mustard gas fell. It is in order to denounce to the civilized world the tortures inflicted upon the Ethiopian people that I resolved to come to Geneva. None other than myself and my brave companions in arms could bring the League of

Nations the undeniable proof. The appeals of my delegates addressed to the League of Nations had remained without any answer; my delegates had not been witnesses. That is why I decided to come myself to bear witness against the crime perpetuated against my people and give Europe a warning of the doom that awaits it, if it should bow before the accomplished fact.[16]

The U.S. reaction to Selassie's speech was indifferent. The country was bogged down in an economic depression, a presidential election was around the corner, and the Olympics were being held that summer in Berlin. The U.S. looked to its own interests, underlain by the desire to remain neutral.

Italy was not alone in defying world opinion. During the 1930s, Japan used chemical weapons against China.

The Japanese discovered that gas was a superb weapon when used against poorly trained and largely ignorant opponents. They made extensive use of chemical, and possibly biological, weapons against the Chinese ... Operations in China became textbook examples of chemical warfare tactics. Accounts of the attacks were printed in a series of lessons distributed among students at the Japanese Chemical Warfare School in Narashino.[17]

Compared to intelligence reports on Germany, the United States reports on the Japanese development of gas warfare were sketchy, at best. It was thought that the Japanese,

... would probably supplement their gas attacks from planes and use them as long-range artillery. Little is known of their plans with regard to the use of gas spray tanks, beyond the fact that they have such apparatus. With respect to gas bombs the position is clearer. They are reported to have made small scale experiments with gas bombs in China. A 110-pound bomb filled with a mixture of mustard gas and Lewisite has been captured. A bomb the same size, filled with phosphene and a 33-pound bomb, filled with a combination of HE (mustard) and toxic smoke also has been reported. An earlier report also mentions gas bombs up to 440 pounds filled with mustard, Lewisite, phosphene, and diphosgene.[18]

Captured documents indicated that the Japanese had developed defensive as well as offensive strategies using gas warfare. Both were used against the Chinese. These plans had

> been employed in cases in which the Chinese were applying pressure and the Japanese wished to conserve manpower. In general, large amounts were used on small fronts, to support Japanese counter attacks. The chemical operations were never widespread but rather concentrated in certain areas and repeatedly used... Efforts were made to achieve surprise by firing chemical shells immediately after bombardment with HE (mustard), as well as by sudden gas attacks. Gas fire was delivered at dawn or evening, with the maximum wind velocity at 11 miles per hour. Smoke was used to hide gas clouds or to precede them.[19]

In October of 1941, the Chinese mounted an attack to retake Ichang. The Japanese counterattacked by using tear gas. The Chinese were able to take the city, but Japanese troops were arrayed in a defensive position surrounding the city. "When the Chinese pressed the attack to take this ridge, the Japanese launched counterattacks from both flanks, and great quantities of a persistent war gas were placed on the attackers and low areas behind them. From 10 to 12 October, planes dropped gas bombs all over the area.[20] "... Chinese military spokesmen charged that Japanese planes blasting at Chinese troops outside Ichang dropped 300 gas bombs, killing nearly 2000 Chinese soldiers."[21]
The Military Intelligence report stated:

> The Chinese troops were either barefoot or wearing straw sandals, without gas masks or protective clothing, and they were severely gassed and burned. Their reserves also were gassed heavily and received many casualties, most of which proved fatal. Forced to abandon their attack the Chinese had to proceed through low areas to

avoid machine gun fire and thus crossed heavily concentrated gas barriers. Laboratory tests of samples of the gas and parts of shells and bombs showed the agent used to be a mixture of mustard and Lewisite. Use of gas by the Japanese in China in another action to prevent a Chinese crossing of a river is also reported.[22]

It was discovered that the Japanese also used spray devices containing mustard and/or Lewisite to contaminate the ground.

A Chinese report states that the Japanese have used mustard gas in defense of one of their positions to contaminate an area of 2,735 yards by 55 yards ... Where Japanese forces are weak, or it is necessary to economize on their commitment, a large amount of ground contamination is used as a barrier against the attacking enemy ...[23]

The Japanese were also prepared to use gas defensively at home. A document referring to the protection of the seacoast against enemy invasion stated,

Make the available landing points for the enemy ineffective, or when the wind direction is favorable, utilize poison gas and lay gas clouds on a sea surface where the landing is in course of preparation... the use of gas must be vigorously stressed.[24]

As early as February 1937, the Japanese government had published the *Gas Defense Handbook (Gas Bogo Kyohan)*:

In familiar terms, and with few deviations from the U.S. practice, it discusses the principles of gas warfare, the tactical use of gas, and the duties of officers and men in defense against chemical attack. It lays down procedures for individual and collective protection, first aid for men and animals, and the care and decontamination of equipment. It also provides measures for control and decontamination of gassed areas, as well as for gas reconnaissance, gas security, and meteorological observation.[25]

Gas as a mode of warfare was opposed by American government leaders.

Beginning in 1921 and continuing until 1941, the mission of the Chemical Warfare Service was the subject of almost continuous debate by the War Department Staff (WDS). During these years there was scarcely a time when the CWS felt that it enjoyed undisputed membership on the War Department team. Hence a great deal of energy was continually expended by the CWS in defending its statutory position. This fact had considerable bearing on the development of the new service.[26]

The questions most frequently raised by the War Department were: Could the Chemical Warfare Service be eliminated and its duties distributed among the other services? Could the Chemical Warfare Service be relieved of combat functions and its activities limited to technical and supply duties and to defensive training?[26]

President Roosevelt vetoed the name changing of the Chemical Warfare Service to that of the Chemical Corps in 1937.

It has been the policy of this Government to do everything in its power to outlaw the use of chemicals in warfare. Such use is unhuman and contrary to what modern civilization should stand for.

I am doing everything in my power to discourage the use of gases and other chemicals in any war between nations. While, unfortunately, the defensive necessities of the United States call for the study of the use of chemicals in warfare, I do not want the Government of the United States to do anything to aggrandize or make permanent any special bureau of the Army or Navy engaged in these studies. I hope the time will come when the Chemical Warfare Service can be entirely abolished. To dignify this Service by calling it the "Chemical Corps" is, in my judgement, contrary to a sound public policy.[27]

APPENDIX B

CHEMICAL WARFARE DURING WORLD WAR II

Despite the Geneva Gas Protocol which outlawed chemical warfare in 1925, military strategists considered its use a strong possibility in any future war. Essentially, each side was more fearful of the other side using it. Britain, Russia, Germany and Italy all signed the Geneva Protocol calling for no first use. The only countries that did not sign the accord were Japan and the United States. Meanwhile, all the future participants in World War II made it clear that they would not hesitate using gas warfare if provoked by another country.

The subtitle of a *Collier's* magazine article read, "If the Axis turns on the gas, our chemical warfare experts think it will spell Fascist suicide."[1] Both the Allies and Axis had plentiful supplies of chemical warfare gases. Britain and the United States had large domestic reserves. Germany had supplies stored in Russia and were using French factories to produce chemical weapons.

United States

At the outset of World War II, the U.S. was ready to use the many types of gas warfare it had developed. These consisted of two basic classifications: harassing and casualty. Harassing gasses were either the familiar tear gas or those that induced vomiting. Casualty gases included those such as mustard gas which caused choking and blistering, and systemic gases which affected the blood and nervous system.

Despite the ban on chemical warfare, most American planners believed its use was relatively humane. They reasoned that

> In the last war ninety-five percent of all bayonet wounds proved fatal. Twenty-four percent of those hit by bullets and shell fragments died. But only two percent of the gas casualties failed to recover. There were only thirty-eight cases of blindness caused by gas in the 1918 A.E.F.[2]

The necessity for developing a chemical warfare program required vast amounts of manpower to produce, maintain, and train personnel in the offensive and defensive use of equipment and armament. These resources and materials could then be used in other areas of the offensive program. For example, the U.S. set up the Office of Civilian Defense which consisted of 10,000 volunteers in Decontamination Units. "This gas defense organization is made up primarily of the chemically trained men of the communities and, in case of gas attacks, will form a large nucleus for the expansion of gas protection services as required."[3]

The chemical warfare program developed and used by the U.S. concentrated mostly on: Smoke (white phosphorus being the most effective), Sprays, and Incendiaries such as napalm (jellied oil which, upon exploding, covered everything with a sticky, viscous, burning liquid). However, the use of airborne gas was always considered a possibility and part of the planning. An Edgewater spokesman explained,

Gas could be laid wherever artillery can fire or planes fly. Our Mitchells and Bostons can carry 1,000 pounds in spray tanks. Mortars, 48 to a battalion, can lay down five tons of gas in two minutes. After two minutes such fire is useless, because the enemy is either a gas casualty or has put on his mask.[4]

The Chemical Warfare Service was very busy.

In the European and Pacific theaters of war, the enemy has taken some of his most bitter punishment from a group of weapons developed by the Chemical Warfare Service of the U.S. Army. To the U.S. and Allied air forces, the Chemical Warfare Service supplies the incendiary bombs which constitute more than 40 % of the heavy bomber cargoes that have been unloaded on Fortress Europe. Through general conflagrations in Berlin, Hamburg and other cities, incendiaries have vastly extended the acreage of devastation beyond the areas destroyed by direct hits ...[5]

Incendiary bombs at this point in the war constituted fifty percent of the Chemical Warfare Service's budget.

Flame throwers were also important weapons. They "reduced pillboxes and strong points that resisted high-explosive fire. Smokescreens blanketing the beaches of France and blinding enemy gunners gave important support to the Allied invasion of Europe."[6]

Perhaps the most effective chemical weapon developed was delivered by mortar. The U.S. developed the 4.2 inch mortar called the "Goon Gun."

An unsung hero of nearly every U.S. campaign in World War II was the rifled 4.2 inch chemical mortar. German and Japanese defenders often faced American attackers from positions in rough terrain, chosen to block the flat trajectory, high velocity of artillery ... Even so, the defenders fell in thousands to 4.2 inch shells, which dropped high explosives and searing white phosphorus nearly straight down into their midst."[7]

The "goon gun" was easily maneuvered because it weighed only about 300 pounds including the cart it was transported on. This unit could be carried in the back of a Jeep. A well trained crew could have it in place and firing in about four minutes. A German prisoner of war exclaimed after a mortar attack, "What the hell was that new weapon which blew us out of our fox holes and burned off our tails at the same time?"[8] This weapon lobbed 25-pound shells that, on exploding, sent blazing phosphorus over a forty-square-yard area.

Mortars were extremely effective in the D-day invasion.

> … the mortars would completely blanket a hedgerow corner by dropping high explosive and white phosphorus on both sides of the hedgerow and into the ditches, leaving no place for the enemy to hide. The artillery, on the other hand, to attack such a target with its flat trajectory, would have to blast the hedgerow hummock and the ditches flat before they could drive the enemy from such cover.[9]

Smoke weapons were developed and used as screens. They were delivered from generators, grenades, pots, or shells. Further evidence to the effectiveness of these weapons was that

> Sheets of white phosphorus hid the American Fifth Army when it spanned the Volturno River one cold midnight under a frosty moon. Smoke saved the day at Anzio. Natural morning mists rising from the Lorraine meadows mingled with the artificial fog when the American Third Army crossed the Moselle River in France. Thanks to a huge smoke screen the 90th Infantry Division stayed invisible for two weeks in December 1944 when it ferried across the Saar, wiped out 260 German pillboxes, took 1,200 prisoners, and returned without being seen.[10]

Years after the war, John White (whose father was the Chief Engineer killed aboard the mustard gas ship *John Harvey* at Bari) was awaiting orders with three other airmen and drinking coffee in a snack bar at Westover Air Force base. An argument ensued about the U.S. using gas weapons. White mentioned that the U.S.

had poison gas at Bari. Two of the other fellows said we never used gas in World War II. The fourth fellow said, "Hold it! I was in the Chemical Mortar Battalion and we trained in Chemical Warfare."[11]

There is no doubt that the U.S. and its allies would have used mustard gas and/or other gas laden bombs to inflict casualties if Germany had resorted to first use.

Britain

In early 1942, Britain received espionage reports that Germany was about to use gas weapons against the Russians. They offered gas supplies to Russia, but Stalin refused. Further intelligence reports indicated that Germany had issued a new type of gas mask which was being rushed to the Eastern front. Churchill broadcast his response on May 5, 1942:

> The Soviet Government have expressed to us the view that the Germans in desperation of their assault may make use of poison gas against the Armies and people of Russia. We are ourselves firmly resolved not to use this odious weapon unless it is first used by the Germans. Knowing our Hun, however, we have not neglected to make preparations on a formidable scale. I wish to make it plain that we shall treat the unprovoked use of poison gas against our Russian ally exactly as if it were used against ourselves, and if we are satisfied that this new outrage had been committed by Hitler, we will use our great and growing Air superiority in the West to carry gas warfare on the largest possible scale far and wide upon the towns and cities of Germany... Of one thing I am sure — that the British people, who have entered into the full comradeship of war with our Russian Ally, will not shrink from any sacrifice or trial which that comradeship may require.[12]

Subsequently, however, German railroad cars filled with chemical weapons and gas were captured on the way to the Eastern front, finally prompting Stalin into accepting gas supplies from the Allies in 1943. Both offensive and defensive preparation for gas warfare was increased in Russia.

Britain feared using chemical weapons as much as Russia. But, because they could never trust Germany *not* to use poison gas, it was necessary to be prepared defensively for gas attacks, in the event Germany invaded England. In this, England excelled.

> In Britain, only the defensive preparations for gas warfare were fairly complete. A War Office memorandum compiled shortly before the war began regarded British gas protection, detection and decontamination equipment as 'among the best in the world.' On the other hand, it regarded Britain's offensive capability as woefully inadequate.[13]

When France surrendered, the likelihood of Germany invading Britain was a distinct possibility. Invasion of the homeland was not Britain's only concern. They had to protect their interests and territories in the Mediterranean and North Africa.

> Later in 1940, mustard gas was dispatched for use in the Middle East for it was felt that the Italians might well use gas, as they had in Ethiopia, therefore Britain's potential to retaliate by spraying was stepped up and trials were carried out in the Sahara. The problem of refilling in the field had to be considered again as it was not practical to return empty containers to the United Kingdom for refilling.[14]

Prime Minister Winston Churchill seriously considered using mustard gas to defend Britain. Churchill stated:

> Supposing lodgements were effected on our coast, there could be no better points for the application of mustard than these beaches and lodgments. In my view there would be no need to wait for the enemy to adopt such methods. He will certainly adopt them if he thinks it will pay. Home Defence should be consulted as to whether the prompt drenching of lodgments would not be great help. Everything should be brought to the highest pitch of readiness, but the question of actual employment must be settled by the Cabinet.[15]

To this end, Churchill authorized the increased production of mustard gas and made 1,000 pound mustard gas bombs available for the RAF.

> In August when the possibility of invasion was very real, the use of gas was again considered … Lysanders, Blenheims, and Battles of the RAF were adapted to carry 250 lb. or 500 lb. bombs or containers for spraying gas onto the beaches if the enemy landed.[16]

The British built "chemical lorries," tanks that could be transported by rail or pulled by truck.

> Hundreds of them would be taken to the area where the enemy had landed to spray the mustard gas on the roads and railways to inhibit his movement inland — a 'scorched earth' policy if ever there was one. Presumably, the civilian population would have been evacuated but what happened afterwards can only be conjecture. It sounds a most extraordinary story but the filling of these containers has been officially recorded and Winston Churchill noted his own feelings of 1940: 'The possible use and counter use of poison gas, if invasion should come in the New Year, weighs heavily upon me.'[17]

By the end of the war, Britain had produced large quantities of mustard gas. Much of it was stored underground in a ninety acre site in the hillside at Rhydymwyn. They also developed an extensive and sophisticated system of Forward Filling Depots (FFDs).

> … bombs and liquid mustard were also stockpiled nearer to the airfields which would need the supplies. … filling depots were constructed at sites selected by the Air Ministry. In all there were five: Nos. 1 and 2 controlled by the US Army Eighth Air Force Service Command and the remainder by the RAF.[18]

Italy

Germany never stockpiled gas munitions in North Africa. The high temperatures in the desert made such storage inpractical. The type of tank warfare there also precluded its use. However, a real possibility would have been for the Italians to use it during the Sicily landings. But the Italian government never followed up against the Allies with gas weapons as it had against Ethiopia. "Small stores of enemy toxics were found, but their placement and manner of storage indicated that there was no intention of using them.[19]

Italy developed

> gas equipment, such as gas hand grenades, smoke munitions (including smoke candles) and small mustard gas spray cylinders ... suitable from a technical point of view, but available in altogether insufficient quantities. The training of troops was particularly inadequate ... Very thorough and able work was done in the Centro Chimico Militare. Large scale smoke screen tests carried out in Northern Italy with big tanker trucks shortly before the outbreak of the war proved successful. Special chemical battalions and companies had been constituted for this purpose.[20]

> The Italian chemical force was yet in its infancy when the war broke out. Various organizational set-ups and various weapons had been tested out, but no final decisions had been reached, probably because no definite opinion had yet been formed as to the weapons with which it would be best to equip the units ...[21]

As a result, the "Italian chemical forces did not come into evidence during the past war."[22]

When the Allies landed on the Italian mainland, it was feared that the Germans might use gas to defend against the invasion. This was one of the reasons the U.S. shipped mustard gas to Bari. Again, small Axis reserves were found, but

> no clear signs of German intent were found when troops broke through into the Italian mainland. The prolonged struggle along the Rapido and the Winter Line would have given the Germans an excellent tactical opportunity to use gas, but again no evidence turned up that they considered the employment of toxics.[23]

France

The French army suffered greatly from gas attacks in the First World War. Although fearing Germany would again resort to gas warfare, France did little to develop her chemical weapons before World War II. However, the Germans knew

> that together with the British, the French had carried out extensive experiments with gas in North Africa, using airplanes. In these tests the effect of gases on various animals was studied. Obviously, the gases used affected not only the eyes and respiratory organs, but also, and particularly, the skin.[24]

The French also developed a new weapon called the *Gas Candle* which greatly interested the Germans. "They could be ignited by a single ignition system and then for a few minutes produced a gas that very seriously irritated the eyes and the respiratory organs."[25] The gas was yellow in color and required the immediate donning of masks when encountered. The Germans considered the

> possibility of using it together with other gases, above all with skin affecting gases, and to conceal other gases such as mustard gas; and the possibility of exhausting and weakening the enemy by a simple means requiring little manpower, and by depleting his supply of gas filters, namely by releasing gas at frequent intervals and, if necessary over a period of several hours.[26]

The French could have used gas against the Germans when they were broaching the Maginot Line in World War II. According to former Generalleutnant Herman Ochsner,

> Once the German attack had reached the Somme without the French having used gas, the responsible German authorities heaved a sigh of relief. If the French did not use gas in the Weygand line, then it was assumed, the danger we had so much feared would have definitely have passed so far as the west front was concerned. In anxious suspense reports were awaited from the front. Once again no

signs of gas were reported. The German advance raced on into Southern France. Even at this stage the use of gas could have proved a serious obstacle to us. However, by now the French army was probably too badly battered and too urgently pressed for time to be able to handle so complicated and difficult a matter as a systematic gas attack on a large scale ...[27]

Russia

Russia signed the Geneva Protocol prohibiting the use of gas. They upheld this policy, but, like Britain and the United States, warned the Axis that they would not hesitate to use gas. They were well aware of Germany's capabilities.

It is in this context that the country's considerable preparations in the chemical weapons sphere should be understood. Chemicals were not the weapons with which the USSR would choose to wage a future war — strategies based on tanks and aircraft were far more attractive — but if chemicals were used, then the USSR had to be ready to respond in kind in a convincing manner. Nor did this position change with time: if anything, it grew stronger as Soviet commanders and politicians alike stood by and watched the use of these weapons in the Italo-Abyssinian conflict in 1936 and the first skirmishes in 1937 of what was to be part of — if not the beginning of — the Second World War: the Sino-Japanese conflict.[28]

As early as 1927 German specialists using German aeroplanes carried out tests twenty miles from Moscow under an agreement with the Red Army, continuing tests conducted in Germany in 1925 under the cover of 'pest control.' The training area was called Ukhtomskaja, from which the name of the new joint project was also derived.[29]

However, gas warfare development suffered tremendously in Russia when Stalin purged the Russian army in 1937. Caught in the purge were many chemical warfare engineers and scientists. Because of this, at the outset of the war, Russia lacked the technological expertise to defend against, or launch, a chemical warfare offensive. Furthermore, Soviet gas warfare protective equipment was inferior. Ineffective capes were used to shield soldiers from mustard gas. Heavy and cumbersome, their use eventually led to exhaustion. Soviet gas masks were of inferior quality and ineffective in sub-freezing temperatures.

Russia's development of gas warfare equipment improved as the war progressed.

> From 1942 on the Russians also dropped phosphorus incendiary bombs … the main objectives attacked with these phosphorus incendiary bombs were German ammunition and equipment dumps, provision dumps, airfields, shelters and railway installations.[30]

The Russians also developed "the so-called *Stalin Organ*, a motor truck capable of cross country travel and equipped with rocket launchers …[31] It was believed the launchers could be charged with chemicals if needed. Rocket propelled mines were captured after the summer of 1942. These too

> could have been used with a chemical charge in gas warfare … The Russian chemical projector was an excellent weapon … It would also have proved a very useful weapon in gas warfare. The Russians had also developed spray tanker trucks as well as spray cylinders for airplanes. The intention was to use these in laying mustard gas barriers to delay the enemy in favorable terrain sectors, in order to seal the enemy off in the flanks or in the rear.[32]

Russian participation in World War II consisted of two phases: defending against the German offensive into Eastern Russia followed by the counter-offensive on the heels of the German retreat. Germany's rapid movement toward and away from Moscow prevented their using gas. It would have slowed them down too much.

Germany

Germany always thought of itself as lagging in chemical warfare development because of the disarmament constraints placed on it by the 1919 Treaty of Versailles. It was not until 1935 that, under Hitler, she seriously began rearming. Germany always feared the Allies' chemical warfare capabilities despite the fact that she was one of the world's leading military chemical producers.

> As a long-term solution it was decided to build a new, large plant for the production of phosgene and mustard gas at Grafenhainichen, near Halle in central Germany. The plant was to be a chlorine factory equipped for the secret production of mustard gas and with the loading facilities for a capacity of 7,000 tons per year, more than Germany had produced during the First World War. In addition, contacts were made with the Soviet government in order to have additional production, beyond the reach of the Entente, in case of war ...[33]

In 1938, Hermann Goering suggested a plan that would expand mustard gas production from

> 700 tons per month ... to 9,300 tons per month ... to be carried out within four years ... that further plans aimed at a maximum production capacity of 19,300 tons per month by 1945. A ratio of 1:2 between poison gas and conventional explosives was to be achieved.[34]

The Germans were prepared defensively against chemical warfare attack. "Long before D-day the Germans had intensified all chemical protective measures. They had run special gas schools, issued a special FE-42 gas mask filter, and held numerous practice alerts throughout all organizations ...[35]

On two occasions Germany considered using gas against Russia.

> The Soviets were never forced to subject their flawed chemical defense posture to the hard test of reality since the Germans were not particularly eager to use chemical weapons against them. In the course of the German occupation of the USSR, only twice was the use of chemicals seriously considered. Logistical and political constraints prevented such attacks from being carried out.[36]

One occasion was at Stalingrad. Gas was considered when Germany's attack stalled. Plans were drawn up to gas the Russians with artillery fire. However, German military leaders realized that too many artillery pieces were needed, not enough ammunition was on hand, and more importantly, too many train cars were necessary to transport the components to the war front.

According to German and Soviet authorities, Germany did use incendiaries, another type of chemical warfare, on the Kerch Peninsula to move the enemy out of caves.

> Soviet sources and a former GDR author give the number of deaths which ensued as lying in the thousands and also allege that chemical weapons were used by the Germans in this instance. Closer examination suggests that an incendiary mixture was actually employed in this operation. The reason why Soviet writers allege that chemical weapons were used may be that incendiary weapons belong to the domain of the Chemical troops of the Soviet ministry of Defence and were sometimes classified as chemical weapons in the USSR.[37]

Eventually, the German advance was halted and a full scale retreat ensued. Russia was still worried they might use gas to protect their retreat. The Soviets sought and received training and assistance from both the U.S. and Britain in this regard.

An additional factor in Germany not using gas against Russia was the strength of the German Air Force. Use of chemical warfare effectively requires air superiority. The Germans had air superiority for only a short time at the beginning of the war. When they lost the air battle over Britain and eventually France, their capability to drop gas was effectively lost. The same was true in Russia. Germany simply ran out of planes to bomb and deliver chemical weapons. By the time of the Normandy invasion all the Luftwaffe "could put in the air was 198 bombers and 125 fighters, against an Allied force of 3,467 bombers and 5,409 fighters."[38]

At one point, Germany planned to use mustard gas on London.

Uninterrupted large-scale attacks were, according to these plans, to be carried out not only against enemy armies but also against the civilian population ... With an eye to the approaching struggle with Britain, (Colonel) Ochsner suggested planned daily attacks using every kind of poison gas: 'There can be no doubt that a city such as London could be terrorized in this way that enormous pressure would be extended on the enemy government'. The 'material destruction and psychological effect' of poison gas made 'its regular use as part of an overall plan and not only as deterrent or retaliation absolutely essential ...[39]

However, the Germans never followed through on this plan. Another opportunity where Germany could have used gas (and probably very effectively) was during the D-day invasion. After the war, Major General Alden Waitt, Chief of the Chemical Warfare Service said,

... as a student of chemical warfare for nearly thirty years, I believe that subjecting our forces to the heavy gas attacks that were possible at Normandy might have delayed our invasion for six months and made later landings at new points necessary. Such a delay could have given the Germans sufficient time to complete new V weapons, which would have made the Allies' task all the harder and England's long range bombardment considerably worse.[40]

But we were ready. Had it not been for loaded gas munitions available at our airfields, and reserves at our depots in England for speedy use in place of high explosives and incendiaries, I believe the Germans would have turned loose a powerful and effective gas offensive on us in Normandy. But because we had so much, and on time, they did not dare start the gas war here. They feared the retribution that was certain to fall upon their armies and centers of industry.[41]

By the end of the war, German chemical warfare depots were well-stocked.

Thousands of tons of aircraft bombs, artillery shells and mines loaded with effective chemical-warfare agents were found in German storage depots.... Waitt further stated, "Once we got into Central Germany, Nazi chemical-warfare depots appeared in increasing numbers, and vast supplies of gas munitions were uncovered.[42]

The German gas installations at Raubkammer

had been unknown until the Allied troops actually moved in, although it covered an area of fifty square miles. It more than equaled the combined facilities of our own installation at Edgewater Arsenal, Maryland, and Dugway Proving Ground, Utah....[43]

After the war, former German Army Generalleutnant, Herman Ochsner, stated the German attitude that,

We had no doubts whatever that even if the war should last very long, the US would have immense stockpiles of material for gas warfare, just as they had for other methods of warfare, and those stockpiles would be available once the supply system across the Atlantic had been established. All German experts concurred in the opinion that the US held a strong trump card in their chemical arm and that, as their air supremacy grew progressively with the duration of the war, they alone would decide whether this card should be played out or not.[44]

Perhaps one reason Germany did not use gas in World War II was that Adolph Hitler had experienced its effects. He was gassed during a British attack while a soldier in World War I. In his book, *Mein Kampf,* he described the experience:

During the night of October 13th-14th, the British opened an attack with gas on the front south of Ypres. They used the yellow gas whose effect was unknown to us, at least from personal experience. I was destined to experience it that very night. On a hill south of Werwick, in the evening of October 13th, we were subjected for several hours to a heavy bombardment with gas bombs, which continued throughout the night with more or less intensity. About midnight a number of us were put out of action, some for ever. Toward morning I also began to feel pain. It increased with every quarter of an hour; and about seven o'clock my eyes were scorching as I staggered back and delivered the last dispatch I was destined to carry in this war. A few hours later my eyes were like glowing coals and all was darkness around me.

Endnotes

Chapter 2 — The Attack

1. Franklin D. Roosevelt, "Roosevelt Warns Axis on Gas Warfare," *Current History* August 1943: 405.
2. R.C.T. Chichester-Constable, *Report On The Circumstances In Which Gas Casualties Were Incurred At Bari On 2/3 December 1943.* 1.
3. Ibid.
4. Glenn B. Infield, *Disaster At Bari* (New York: Macmillan Company, 1971) 16-17.
5. Chichester-Constable, *Ibid.* 2.
6. Karel Margry, "Mustard Disaster At Bari," *After The Battle* No. 79 (1993): 36.
7. Glenn B. Infield, "America's Secret Poison Gas Tragedy," *True* July 1961: 98.
8. Infield, *Disaster,* 29.
9. Infield, "America's Secret," 98.
10. Margry, 42.
11. Infield, Ibid, 99.
12. George Southern, Letter to author, 11 January 1999.
13. U.S.S. *Aroostock. Report of Anti-Aircraft Action Against The Enemy,* 5 December 1943.
14. "Bari Facts," *Time* 27 December 1943: 19.

Chapter 3 — The Mediterranean Theater and North Africa 1941-1943

1. Werner Baumbach, *The Life and Death of the Luftwaffe* (New York: Coward-McCann, Inc., 1960) 133.
2. Cajus Bekker, *The Luftwaffe War Diaries* (Garden City, N.Y.: Doubleday & Company, Inc., 1968) 357.
3. W.G. I. Jackson, *The Battle For Italy* (New York: Harper & Row Publishers, 1967) 12.
4. Ibid.

227

5.   Louis Snyder. "World War II: U.S. War Effort." *Academic American Encyclopedia*, 1990 ed.

Chapter 4 — The Mediterranean Theater: Sicily and Italy, 1943.

1.   Walter Karig, *Battle Report: The Atlantic War* (New York: Rinehart & Company, Inc., 1946) 264.
2.   F.H. Hinsley, *British Intelligence In The Second World War* (New York: Cambridge Univ. Press, 1988) 573.
3.   Ibid, 577.
4.   Ibid.
5.   Ibid, 581.
6.   H.M. Woodward, Jr., *The History of Captured Enemy Toxic Munitions in the American Zone European Theater... Section I St. Georgen Chemical Corps Captured Enemy Material ...* (Office Of The Chief Chemical Corps Headquarters European Command, 1946) Picture No. 17.
7.   Ibid, Picture No. 20.
8.   Ibid, Picture No. 21.
9.   Ibid, Picture No. 23.
10.   Brooks Kleber, *The United States Army The Technical Services. The Chemical Warfare Service: Chemicals in Combat* (Washington, D.C.: Office Of The Chief Of Military History, 1966) 122.
11.   Hinsley, 577.
12.   United States. Air Force. Office of Air Force History, *The Army Air Forces In World War II. Volume Two. Europe: Torch To Point Blank ...* (Washington D.C.: Office of Air Force History, 1948) 544.
13.   Ibid.
14.   Ibid, 574.
15.   Ibid.
16.   Ibid, 579.
17.   Ibid, 582.
18.   James Doolittle, *I Could Never Be So Lucky Again: an autobiography* (New York: Bantam Books, 1991) 369.
19.   United States. Air Force, *The Army Air Forces In World War II. Volume Three. Europe: Argument To V-E Day ...* (Washington D.C.: Office of Air Force History, 1983) 331.
20.   Ibid, 332.
21.   United States. Air Force, *The Army Air Forces In World War II. Volume Two,* 587.

Chapter 5 — The U.S. Merchant Marine

1.   John Slader, *The Fourth Service: Merchantmen at War 1939-1945* (London: Robert Hale Limited, 1994) 246.

2.   Samuel J. Pitittieri, "How My Trip To Bari, Italy Started," 21 June 1998.

3.   Justin F Gleichauf, *Unsung Sailors: The Naval Armed Guard in World War II* (Annapolis, MD: Naval Institute Pr., 1990) 271.

4.   Felix Riesenberg Jr., *Sea War: The Story Of The U.S. Merchant Marine In World War II* (New York: Rinehart & Company, Inc., 1956) 197.

5.   Ibid. 198.

6.   Don Quesinberry, "Battle of the Atlantic," *The Pointer* April-June 1998: 11.

7.   U.S. Department Of Commerce Maritime Administration, *The United States Merchant Marine : A Brief History* (Washington, D.C., 1972) 3.

8.   Charles A. Lloyd, *The Liberty Ships Of World War Two* (Raleigh, N.C.: U.S.N. Armed Guard WW II Veterans, 1988) 3.

9.   Dan and Toni Horodysky, "U.S. Merchant Marine in World War II: Casualties." <http://usmm.org/ww2.html>, 5 March 2001.

10. Emory S. Land, *The United States Merchant Marine At War:* (Washington, D.C.: War Shipping Administration, 1946) 31.

11. Ibid, 3.

12. Justin F. Gleichauf, "Navy Armed Guard: Unsung Heroes," *American Legion Magazine* April 1986: 24.

13. Charles A. Lloyd, "U.S. Navy Armed Guard WWI And WW II," *USN Armed guard WW II Veterans Newsletter* [n.d.].

14. Ibid.

Chapter 6 — Bari Harbor, 2 December 1943

1.   Donald H. Gritton, Jr., Email to author, 21 October 1998.

2.   Ibid.

3.   Ibid

4.   Ibid.

5.   Arthur R. Moore, *A Careless Word ... A Needless Sinking* (Kings Point, NY: American Merchant Marine Museum at the U.S. Merchant Marine Academy, 1990) 161.

6.   Ibid. 155

7.   Joseph Oliver, Letter to author, 4 February 1998.

8.   John J. White, Jr., *The Last Two Years 1942-1943 John J. White, Commander, United States Maritime Service 7 December 1941 - 2 December 1943* (1993) 5.

9.   Melissa Catania and Tiffany Soriente, *John J. White and the Disaster at Bari* (Deer Park, NY: Sand Cyril and Saint Methodius School, 1997).

10. James L. Cahill, *S.S. John Harvey - Loss of.* 10 January 1944.

11. R.C.T. Chichester-Constable, *Report On The Circumstances In Which Gas Casualties Were Incurred at Bari on 2/3 December 1943*: 2-3.

12. "The Merchant Marine Pearl Harbor," *American Merchant Marine Veterans Emerald Sea Chapter Newsletter* Vol. 4, February 1993.

13. Chichester-Constable, 3.

14. Ibid.

15. Warren Brandenstein, Letter to author, 6 February 1999.

16. Gerald Reminick, *Patriots and Heroes: True Stories of the U.S. Merchant Marine in World War II* (Palo Alto, Ca.: The Glencannon Press, 2000) 146-147.

17. John F. Whitley, "Our Trip to Bari, Italy," 20 November 1998.

18. B.A. Conrad, *Summary of Statements by Survivors S.S. Samuel J. Tilden, U.S. Cargo Ship* (Wash., D.C.: Navy Department Office Of The Chief Of Naval Operations, 18 January 1944).

19. William Waters, Letter to author, 10 November 1998.

20. Donald Meissner, "The Disaster At Bari," Ed. Thomas Bowerman. WWII Navy Armed-Guard Veterans Association 13 March 1999 <http://www.armed-guard.com>.

21. Stanley Wisniewski, Letter to author, 25 November 1998.

22. Meissner.

23. Theodore Schober, Letter to Arthur R. Moore, 7 July 1988.

24. Bill Collett, Letter to author, 9 July 1999.

25. Bernard L. Anderson, *Diary*, 22 November 1943.

26. D.E. Upson, *Recommendations For Commendation Of Enlisted Personnel*, 25 November 1943.

Chapter 7 — "Little Pearl Harbor"

1. R.C.T. Chichester-Constable, *Report On The Circumstances In Which Gas Casualties Were Incurred at Bari on 2/3 December 1943*: 3-4.

2. Robert M. Browning, Jr., *U.S. Merchant Vessel War Casualties Of World War II* (Annapolis, Md., Naval Institute Press, 1996) 380.

3. Eugene J. Kuhn, *Report of Bombing Attack at Bari, Italy, on 2 December 1943*. 6 December 1943.

4. Thomas Edward Harper, *S.S.* John L. Motley - *Disaster Report of.* 29 March 1944: 1.

5. Glenn B. Infield, *Disaster At Bari* (New York: The MacMillan Company, 1971) 55.

5. Harper, 2.

7. Arthur R. Moore, *A Careless Word ... A Needless Sinking* (Kings Point, NY: American Merchant Marine Museum at the U.S. Merchant Marine Academy, 1990) 155.

8. Infield, 61.

9. Moore.

10. Myron Boluch, Letters to author, 2 and 22 April 1998.

11. Infield, 77.

12. Moore.

13. Ibid.

14. Browning, 281.

15. James L. Cahill, *S.S. John Harvey - Loss of.* 10 January 1944.

16. *Summary of Statements by Survivors of the S.S.* John Bascom (Wash., D.C.: Navy Department Office Of The Chief Of Naval Operations, 28 February 1944).

17. William A. Kreimer, *S.S.* John Bascom - *Disaster Report of* (New Orleans: Amred Guard Center, 22 March 1944) 1.

18. Ibid.

19. *Summary of Statements.*

20. Gerald Reminick, *Patriots and Heroes: True Stories of the U.S. Merchant Marine in World War II* (Palo Alto, Ca.: The Glencannon Press, 2000) 148.

21. Leroy C. Heinse, *S.S.* John Bascom - *Loss of.* 17 March 1944.

22. Warren A. Brandenstein, Letter to author, 6 February 1999.

23. "Gunner Lauds Ensign's Courage At Bari, Italy, 'Pearl harbor.'" *Associated Press* 29 January 1944.

24. Kreimer.

25. Ibid, 2.

26. Ibid.

27. *Summary of Statements.*

28. *Kreimer.*

29. *Navy Department Intelligence Report Enemy Attacks On Merchant Ships*) Wash., D.C.: Office Of Navy Intelligence, 8 February 1944) 2.

30. "Gunner Lauds Ensign's Courage."

31. Brandenstein.

32. Infield, 58.

33. Ibid, 59.

34. Reminick, 150.

35. O. Heitmann, *Statement of Master of S.S.* John Bascom [n.d.]

36. *Commendatory Conduct of Armed Guard Unit Assigned to S.S.* Samuel J. Tilden, *U.S. Cargo Ship* (Wash., D.C.: Navy Department Office Of The Chief Of Naval Operations, 18 January 1944).

37. Ibid, 3.

38. "Gunner Lauds Ensign's Courage."

39. B.A. Conrad, *Summary of Statements by Survivors S.S.* Samuel J. Tilden, *U.S. Cargo Ship* (Wash., D.C.: Navy Department Office Of The Chief Of Naval Operations, 18 January 1944).

40. Ibid.

41. Robert F. Donnelly, *S.S.* Samuel J. Tilden - *Loss of* (Wash., D.C.: War Shipping Administration Training Organization, 2 February 1944).

42. Conrad, 2.

43. John F. Whitley, "Our Trip to Bari, Italy," 20 November 1998.

44. William Waters, Letter to author, 10 November 1998.

45. D.B. Queen, Letter to author, 15 November 1998.

46. Conrad.

47. Waters.

48. Conrad.

49. Queen.

50. Conrad.

51. Edward J. Mowery, "Yank Tells How Nazi Caught Bari Like A Duck." *World Telegram* [n.d.]

52. George W. Maury, Letter to author, 4 October 1998.

53. Leo L. Krause, Letter to author, 11 November 1998.

54. Donald Meissner, "The Disaster At Bari," Ed. Thomas Bowerman. WWII Navy Armed-Guard Veterans Association 13 March 1999 <http://www.armed-guard.com>.

55. Frank Nicholls, Letter to author, 4 October, 1998.

56. James Roark, Letter to author, 27 March 1999.

57. Stanley Wisniewski, Letter to author, 25 November 1998.

58. Maury.

59. George Baist, *Enemy Action: Report on.* 14 March 1944.

60. Nicholls.

61. Charles P. Lippert, Jr., *Voyage Report - S.S.* Grace Abbott. 3 January 1944.

62. Maury.

63. Lippert.

64. Theodore Schober, Letter to Arthur Moore, 7 July 1988.

65. Browning, 379.

66. Schober.

67. Bette McAnulty, Letter to author, 7 June 1999.

68. Bernard L. Anderson, *Diary,* 2 December 1943.

69. James E. Smith, *Remembrances 1942-1946,* 26 June 1991.

70. W.R. Hays, *Summary of Anti-Aircraft action against the enemy and recommendations for suitable rewards to officer and men for outstanding performance of duty during such actions. AOG 14/A16 - 2/P15 (Serial:88)* 5 December 1943.

71. W.R. Hays, *Anti-Aircraft action against the enemy - Report of. AOG 14/A16 - 3 (Serial:87)* 5 December 1943.

72. Ibid.

73. Ibid (Serial:88).

74. Ibid (Serial:87)

75. Infield, 70.

76. Ibid, 71.

77. George Southern, Letter to author, 11 January 1999.

78. Robert J. Fulton, *Summary of Statements by Survivors of the M.V. Devon Coast, British Tanker, 646 G.T., Ministry of Transport* (Wash., D.C.: Navy Department Office Of The Chief Of Naval Operations, 28 February 1944).

79. Ibid, *Summary of Statements by Survivors of the* Fort Athabaska, *British Freighter, 7132 G.T.* (Ibid, 28 February 1944).

80. George Southern, Letter to author, 4 December 1998.

81. Fulton, *Summary of Statements by Survivors of the S.S.* Testbank, *British Freighter, 5,083 B.T.* (Ibid, 28 February 1944).

82. Southern, Ibid.

83. B.A. Conrad, *Summary of Statements by Survivors of the S.S.* Fort Lajoie, *7,134 G.T., British Ministry of War Transport* (Wash., D.C.: Navy Department Office Of The Chief Of Naval Operations, 26 April 1944).

84. George Glenton, *No Safe Haven* (Ringwood, Hampshire: Navigator Books, 1995) 187.

85. Ibid, 192.

86. Ibid, 193.

87. Infield, 124.

88. George S. Bergh, ed., *A History of the Twenty-Sixth General Hospital* (Minneapolis, Minn.; Bureau of Engraving, Inc., 1946) 132.

89. Ibid.

90. Robert J. Casey, "Eyewitness Story of Disastrous 'Hush-Hush' Raid On Bari, Italy," *Chicago Daily News* 15 February 1944.

91. Ibid.

92. Anderson, *Diary,* 4 December 1943.

93. Ibid, 6 December 1943.

Chapter 8 — Nightmare In Bari

1. George S. Bergh, ed., *A History of the Twenty-Sixth General Hospital* (Minneapolis, Minn.; Bureau of Engraving, Inc., 1946) 130.

2. Ibid, 129.

3. Ibid, 131.

4. Ibid, 132.

5. Gwladys M. Rees Aikens, *Nurses in Battledress: The World War II story of a member of the Q.A. Reserves* (Halifax, Nova Scotia: Cymru Press, 1998) 88-92.

6. George Southern, Letter to author, 11 January 1999.

7. E.M. Somers Cocks, *Kia Kaha: Life at 3 New Zealand General Hospital 1940-1946* (Christchurch, N.Z.: Caxton Press, 1958) 242-45.

8. R.C.T. Chichester-Constable, *Report On The Circumstances In Which Gas Casualties Were Incurred at Bari on 2/3 December 1943*: 4.

9. Ibid.
10. Ibid.
11. Ibid, 5.
12. Gene Dorsey, Letter to Author, 5 October 1998.
13. James E. Smith, *Remembrances 1942-1946,* 26 June 1991.

Chapter 9 - The Truth
1. Stewart F. Alexander, "Medical Report of the Bari Harbor Mustard Gas Casualties," *The Military Surgeon* 101, No. 1 (1947): 2.
2. Ibid.
3. Glenn B. Infield, *Disaster At Bari* (New York: The MacMillan Company, 1971) 199.
4. Karel Margry, "Mustard Disaster At Bari," *After The Battle* No. 79 (1993): 45.
5. R.C.T. Chichester-Constable, *Report On The Circumstances In Which Gas Casualties Were Incurred at Bari on 2/3 December 1943*: 7.

Chapter 10 — ...But For The Grace Of God ...

1. John Willig, Letter to author, 3 October 1998.
2. Juel Hansen, Jr., *My Life Story Volume I* (Bowie, MD) W-24.
3. Anthony Pellegrini, Letter to John H. White, Jr., 9 May 1993.
4. John H. Brown, Letter to John White Jr., [n.d.].
5. Harry O. Lehrnan, Letter to John White, Jr., 24 March 1993.
6. John White Jr., *The Last Two Years 1942-1943, John J. White, Commander, United States Maritime Service 7 December 1941- 2 December 1943* (District Heights, MD: 1993) 1.
7. Ibid, 2.
8. Gerald Reminick, *Patriots and Heroes: True Stories of the U.S. Merchant Marine in World War II* (Palo Alto, CA.: The Glencannon Press, 2000) 151-53.
9. Warren Brandenstein, Letter to author, 6 February 1999.
10. John F. Whitley, "Our Trip To Bari, Italy." 20 November 1998.
11. William Waters, Letter to author, 10 November 1998.
12. Ibid.
13. Ibid.
14. Robert Browning, Jr., *US. Merchant War Casualties Of World War II* (Annapolis, MD: Naval Institute Press, 1996) 380.
15. George Southern, Letter to author, 11 January 1999.
16. Ibid, 4 December 1998.
17. George Maury, Letter to author, 4 October 1998.
18. Ibid.
19. Donald K. Meissner, "The Disaster At Bari," Thomas Bowerman, Ed. W.W.II Navy Armed Guard Veterans Association. 13 March 1999 <http://www.armed-guard.com>.

20. Ibid.

21. Ibid.

22. Ibid.

23. Leo Krause, Letter to author, 12 November 1998.

24. Stanley Wisniewski, Letter to author, 25 November 1998.

25. James Roark, Letter to author, 27 March 1998.

26. George H. Baist, *Enemy Action. Report on.* 14 March 1944.

27. Floyd V. Kilgore, *Letter Order To Mdspmn George H. Baist. Headquarters 26th General Hospital US. Army.* 14 January 1944.

28. Charles P. Lippert, Jr., *Voyage Report - S.S.* Grace Abbott. 3 January 1944.

29. Ibid.

30. Bernard L. Anderson, Diary, 11 December 1943.

31. Vince Patterson, Letter to author, 7 January 1998.

32. Anderson, 7 December 1943.

33. James E. Smith, *Remembrances,* 26 June 1991.

34. Anderson, 4,6,10,12 December 1943.

35. Smith.

36. Anderson, 3 December 1943.

37. Ibid, 4 December 1943.

38. Theodore Schober, Letter to Arthur R. Moore, 7 July 1988.

39. W.R. Hays, *Summary of Anti-Aircraft action against the enemy and recommendations for suitable rewards ... AOG 14/ A 16-3/P1S* (Serial: 88) 5 December 1943.

40. George Southern, Letter to author, 20 January 1999.

41. Ibid, 11 January 1999.

42. Ibid.

43. Ibid.

44. R.C.T. Chichester-Constable, *Report On The Circumstances In Which Gas Casualties Were Incurred At Bari On 2/3 December 1943.*

45. Southern, Letter to author, 11 January 1999.

46. Karel Margry, "Mustard Disaster At Bari," After The Battle No.79 (1993): 43.

47. Judith Perera and Andy Thomas, "Britain's victims of mustard-gas disaster," *New Scientist* 30 January 1988: 26-7.

48. Thomas Basick, "It Was A Treat To Go To Bari," 25 January 1999.

Chapter 11 — The Cover-up

1. Glenn B. Infield, *Disaster At Bari* (New York: The Macmillan Com-pany, 1971) 277.

2. W.R. Hays, *Anti-Aircraft action against the enemy -Report of AOG 14/A16-3* (Serial:87) 5 December 1943.

3. John M. Goodhue, Jr., Letter to author, 18 January 1999.
4. "Bari Facts," *Time* 27 December 1943: 19.
5. R.C.T. Chichester-Constable, *Report On The Circumstances In Which Gas Casualties Were Incurred At Bari On 2/3 December 1943*: 2.
6. "Bari Facts."
7. Infield, 207.
8. "Army News Policy,"*Army And Navy Register* 8 April 1944: 9.
9. Ibid.
10. Chichester-Constable, 6-8.
11. George Southern, Letter to author, 4 December 1943.
12. Ibid.
13. Stanley Wisniewski, Letter to author, 25 November 1998.
14. Karel Margry , "Mustard Disaster At Bari," *After The Battle* No.79 (1993): 46.
15. Dwight D. Eisenhower, *Crusade In Europe* (New York: Doubleday and Company, 1948) 204.
16. Southern.
17. Ibid. Letter to author, 20 January 1999.

Chapter 12 — Operation Davey Jones' Locker

1. Alden H. Waitt, "Why Germany Didn't Try Gas," *The Saturday Evening* Post 9 March 1946: 137.
2. E.J. Hogendoom, " A Chemical Weapons Atlas," *The Bulletin of the Atomic Scientists* September/October 1997. 9 March 1999 <http://www.bullatomsci.org/issues/1997/so97/5o97hogendoom.html>.
3. H.M. Woodward, Jr., *The History of Captured Enemy Toxic Munitions in the American Zone European Theater, May 1945 to June 1947* (Office Of The Chief Chemical Corps Headquarters European Command, 1947) Section I. St. Georgen Chemical Corps, May 1946: 1-3.
4. Ibid, Picture no.17 .
5. Ibid, No.18.
6. Ibid, No.20.
7. Ibid, No.21.
8. Ibid, No.23.
9. Ibid, No.24.
10. Ibid, Section IV. Operation Davey Jones Locker Chemical Corps, June 1946: Picture No.1.
11. Ibid, Picture Nos. 20, 25-27.
12. Charles F. Loucks, *Addendum to The History of Captured Enemy Toxic Munitions in the American Zone European Command June 1947 to August 1948* (Concluding Phase) Part I: 1.
13. Ibid, 2.

14. Ibid. I,.
15. Hogendoom.
16. Ibid.
17. Mitretek Systems, "Ocean Dumping of Chemical Weapons: Bari Harbor and the Adriatic," 6 October 1999<http:www.mitretek.or mission/ envene/chemical/histoy/UNDERWTR.html>.
18. Hogendoom.
19. Mitretek, 2.
20. Ibid, 1.

Chapter 13 — Fifty Years Later

1. Mitretek Systems, "Ocean Dumping of Chemical Weapons: Bari Harbor and the Adriatic," 6 October 1999 <http://www.mitretek.org/mission/ envene/chemical/history/UNDERWTR.html.>.
2. G. Assennato and D. Sivo, "Health Implications Of The Ocean Dumping Of Chemical Weapons In A Fishermen Community In South Italy," (Paper) 1998.
3. Fredrik Laurin, "Scandinavia's Underwater Time Bomb," *The Bulletin of the Atomic Scientists* March 1991: 11.
4. Ibid, 13.
5. Ibid, 15.
6. Ibid.
7. "A Deadly Catch,"1 July 1998 < http://archive.abcnews.com/ sections/us/gulfwartimeline2/index.html>.
8. Edward H. Aho, "Fifty Years Later, Still No Recognition," *Journal of Commerce* 22 July 1998, 22 April 1999 <http;//www.usmm.org/ fifty_years.html>.

Chapter 14 — Epilogue

1. Constance M.Pechura and David P. Rall, eds., *Veterans at Risk: The Health Effects of Mustard Gas and Lewsite* (Washington, D.C.: National Academy Press, 1993) 1.

Appendix A — Chemical Warfare Before World War II.

1. Mike Iavarone, *Trenches on the Web-Amory: Gas Warfare*, 28 October 1998 <http://worldwar1.com/arm006.htm>.
2. Amos A. Fries and Clarence J.West, *Chemical Warfare* (New York: McGraw-Hill, 1921) 11.
3. Leo P.Brophy and George B. Fisher, *United States Army in World War II. The Technical Services: The Chemical Warfare Service: Organizing For War* (Washington, D.C.: Office Of The Chief Of Military History, 1959) 4.

4.   Jeffrey K. Smart, *From Plowshare to Sword: Armistice,* 1 July 1998 <http://www.cbdcom.apgea.army.mil/RDA/enterprise/history.armistic.html>.

5.   *Coming Clean,* 28 October 1998 <http://www.ornl.gov/orn194/coming_clean.html>.

6.   "Gas Casualties in the First World War." *The Sparticus International Internet Encyclopedia of the First World War.* 1 July 1998 <http://www.sparticus.schoolnet.co.uk/FWWgasdeaths.htm>.

7.   Smart.

8.   Ibid.

9.   Russell Robb and Paul V. Graham, *Section Three: Between the Great Wars,* 20 February 1998 <http://www.sanctum.com/realty/remax/hd/between.html>.

10.   Leo P. Brophy, *The United States Army ...,* 21.

11.   Robb. Ibid.

12.   Stanley D. Fair, "Mussolini's Chemical War," *Army* January 1985: 46.

13.   Ibid.

14.   Ibid, 48.

15.   Ibid.

16.   Haile Selassie, *Appeal To The League Of Nations, 30 June 1936.* 11 November 1998 <http://www.boomshaka.com/HIM/league.html>.

17.   Robb, 2.

18.   Military Intelligence Division, *Enemy Tactics in Chemical Warfare: Special Series No. 24* (Washington, D.C.: War Department, September 1944) 82.

19.   Ibid.

20.   Ibid, 83.

21.   Robb, 2.

22.   Military Intelligence Division, 83.

23.   Ibid.

24.   Ibid, 84.

25.   Ibid.

26.   Leo P. Brophy, 22.

27.   Ibid.

Appendix B — Chemical Warfare During World War II

1.   Jim Marshall, "We Are Ready With Gas." *Colliers* 7 August 1943: 21.

2.   Ibid, 59.

3.   Eugene W. Scott, "Role of the Public Health Laboratory in Gas Defense." *American Journal Of Public Health* 34 (1944): 276.

4.   James Colvin, "If the Axis Uses Gas." *Popular Mechanics* December 1943: 30.

5. "Chemical Warfare: Its Terrible Fire, Flame And Smoke Have Confused, Seared And Suffocated Enemy Armies." *Life* 16 June 1944: 70.

6. Ibid.

7. Walter J. Eldridge, "Firing smoke and conventional shells, the 4.2 - inch chemical mortar earned respect on the battlefield." *World War II* February 1999: 8.

8. "By Fire and Fog: Now Chemical War Secrets of Death-and-Life Can Be Told." *Newsweek* 15 October 1945: 84.

9. Adrian St. John, "Chemical Warfare in the European Theater of Operations." *Military Review* 24 (1944): 60.

10. "By Fire and Fog...," 85.

11. John White, Jr., Letter to author, 4 January 1999.

12. Robert Harris and Jeremy Paxman, *A Higher Form of Killing* (New York: Hill and Wang, 1982) 252.

13. Edward M. Spiers, *Chemical Warfare* (Chicago: U.of Illinois Pr., 1986) 63.

14. T.I.J. Toler, "Poison Gas manufacture in the UK." *After The Battle* No. 79 (1993): 15.

15. Spiers, 68.

16. Toler, 15.

17. Ibid, 18.

18. Ibid, 24.

19. Brooks E. Kleber and Dale Birdsell, *The United States Army In World War II The Technical Services:* (Washington, D.C.: Office Of The Chief Of Military History United States Army, 1966) 122.

20. Herman Ochsner, *History of German Chemical Warfare in World War II :* (USAREUR Foreign Military Study P-004, 1948) 26.

21. Ibid.

22. Ibid.

23. Kleber and Birdsell.

24. Ochsner, 26.

25. Ibid, 25.

26. Ibid, 26.

27. Ibid, 18.

28. Joachim Krause and Charles K. Mallory, *Chemical Weapons In Soviet Military Doctrine:* (Boulder, CO.: Westview Pr., 1992) 84.

29. Wilhelm Deist, ed., *The German Military in the Age of Total War* (Warwickshire, UK: Berg Publishers, 1985) 177.

30. Ochsner, 28.

31. Ibid.

32. Ibid, 28-29.

33. Deist, 174.

34. Ibid, 186.

35. St. John, 57

36. Krause and Mallory, 91-92.

37. Ibid, 92-93.

38. Bekker, Cajus. *The Luftwaffe War Diaries* (Garden City, NY: Doubleday & Company, 1968) 355.

39. Deist, 188-189.

40. Alden H. Waitt, "Why Germany Didn't Try Gas," *Saturday Evening Post* 9 March 1946: 137.

41. Ibid.

42. Ibid.

43. Ibid.

44. Ochsner, 28.

ABOUT THE AUTHOR

Gerald Reminick is a Professor of Library Services at the Western Campus Library, Suffolk County Community College, Brentwood, New York. He was educated in the New York area, receiving his Bachelor of Science degree from Adelphi University in 1967, a Master of Arts from SUNY [State University of New York] at Stonybrook in 1975 and a Master of Science in Library and Information Science at Long Island University in 1979.

Formerly an avid sailor, he gave that up to research and write about maritime history. His published works include poetry and the book *Patriots and Heroes, True Stories of the U.S. Merchant Marine in World War II.* He is an associate member of the North Atlantic, Kings Point and Edwin J. O'Hara chapters of the American Merchant Marine Veterans. He is also a member of the U.S. Merchant Marine Veterans of World War II.

He is currently working on the P.O.W. biography of a former U.S. maritime officer. And, encouraged by the enthusiastic reception of *Patriots and Heroes,* he is also collecting for a second volume of World War II merchant marine stories.

He and his wife, Gail, have two children, Danielle and Bradley.

Bibliography

Aho, Edward H. "Fifty years later, still no recognition." *Journal of Commerce* (Letters) 22 July 1998. 22 April 1999 <http://www.usmm.org/fifty_years.htm>.

- - -. Letter to author. 5 March 1999.

Aikens, Gwladys M. Rees. *Nurses In Battledress: The World War II story of a member of the Q.A. Reserves.* Halifax, Nova Scotia: Cymru Pr., 1998.

Alexander, Stewart F. "Medical Report of the Bari Harbor Mustard Gas Casualties." *The Military Surgeon* 101 (1947): 1-17.

Anderson, Bernard L. *Berth Map of Bari Harbor,* 1943.

- - -. *Diary.* 22 November and 2-4, 6-7, 10-12 December 1943.

"Armistice." 1 July 1998 <http://www.cbdcom.apgea.army.mil/ RDA/enterprise/history/armistic.html>.

"Army News Policy." *Army And Navy Register* 8 April 1944: 9.

Assennato, G. and D. Sivo. "Health Implications Of The Ocean Dumping Of Chemical Weapons In A Fisherman Community In South Italy." (Paper) 1998.

Baist, George H. *Enemy Action: Report on.* 14 March 1944.

"Baltic Bombs Become Deadly Catch." *Environment* October 1991.

Bari Berthing Plan. (Copied from Chart # 653 At Time of Explosion)(Courtesy of George Southern).

"Bari Facts." *Time* 27 December 1943: 19.

Basick, Thomas. "It Was A Treat To Go To Bari." 25 January 1999.

Baumbach, Werner. *The Life and Death of the Luftwaffe.* New York: Coward-McCann, Inc., 1960.

Bekker, Cajus. *The Luftwaffe War Diaries.* Garden City, NY: Doubleday & Company, Inc., 1968.

Bennett, Jim. The *Rohna* Survivors Memorial Association. 8 December 1998 <http://www.whidbey.net/rohna/ library.htm>.

Bergh, George S. ed., *A History of The Twenty-Sixth General Hospital. February 1, 1942-September 14, 1945.* Minneapolis, MN: Bureau of Engraving, Inc., 1946.

Beryman, Alfred H. *S.S. John Bascom - Loss of.* 23 February 1944.

Blair, Joseph. *United States Coast Guard Report on U.S. Merchant Vessel War Action Casualty. S/S Samuel J. Tilden.* 30 October 1944.

Boluch, Myron. Letters to author. 2 and 22 April 1998. Photographs of Section P-343, United States Merchant Marine Academy, March 1943. (Courtesy of Lt. Cdr. Myron Boluch, USNR (Ret.)).

Borland, Hal. "Where There's Smoke There's No Fire." *Popular Science* July 1944: 84-91+

Brandenstein, Warren A. Letter to author. 6 February 1999.

- - -. Personal interview. 6 February 1999.

Brooks, Jerry E. "Why Nazi Germany Did Not Use Chemical Warfare In World War two — A New View." MA Thesis, James Madison U., 1990.

Brophy, Leo P. and George J.B. Fisher. *United States Army In World War II. The Technical Services. The Chemical Warfare Service: Organizing For War.* Washington, D.C.: Office of the Chief of Military History, 1959.

- - -. et al. *United States Army In World War II. The Technical Services. The Chemical Warfare Service: From Laboratory To Field.* Washington, D.C.: Office Of The Chief Of Military History, 1959.

Brown, Frederick J. *Chemical Warfare: A Study in Restraints. Princeton: Princeton U. Press, 1968.*

Brown, John R. Letter to John White Jr., [n.d.].

Browning, Robert M. Jr., *U S. Merchant Vessel War Casualties Of World War II.* Annapolis, MD: Naval Institute Pr., 1996.

Bunker, John. *Heroes in Dungarees.* Annapolis, MD: Naval Institute Pr., 1995.

- - -. *Liberty Ships.* Salem, New Hampshire: Ayer Company Publishers, Inc., 1991.

Burdick, Charles B. *Germany's Military Strategy and Spain in World War II.* Syracuse: Syracuse Univ. Pr., 1968.

"By Fire and Fog: Now Chemical War Secrets of Death-and-Life Can Be Told." *Newsweek* 15 October 1945: 82+.

Cahill, James L. *S.S.* John Harvey - *Loss of.* 10 January 1944.

Carnes, Sam Abbott and Paule Watson. "Disposing of the U.S. Chemical Weapons Stockpile." *JAMA* 262 (1989): 653-659.

Casey, Robert J. "Eyewitness Story Of Disastrous 'Hush-Hush Raid On Bari, Italy." *Chicago Daily News, Inc.,* 15 February 1944.

Catania, Melissa and Tiffany Soriente. *John J. White and the Disaster at Bari.* Deer Park, NY: Saint Cyril and Saint Methodius School, 1997.

Charles, Dan. "U.S. admits guilt over mustard gas tests." *New Scientist* 16 January 1993: 8.

"Chemical Warfare: Its Terrible Fire, Flame, And Smoke Have Confused, Seared And Suffocated Enemy Armies." *Life* 16 June 1944: 70-78.

The Chemical Weapons Convention: A Guided Tour of The Convention on the Prohibition of the Development, Production, Stockpiling and Use of Chemical Weapons and Their Destruction. 22 April 1999 <http://www.opcw.nl/ guide.htm>.

"Chemical Weapons dumped off UK coast." *The Environmental Digest* # 1 1995. 28 October 1998 <http://www.reast.demon.co.uk/wr91.htm#TARGET80>.

Chemical Weapons Working Group — Kentucky Environmental Foundation. *Background Info on CW Stockpile Site in Aberdeen, Maryland.* 13 October 1998 <http://www.cwwg.org/Maryland.html>.

- - -. *A Brief History of the U.S. Stockpile of Chemical Weapons.* 9 March 1999 <http://www.cwwg.org/history.html>.

Chepesiuk, Ron. "A Sea of trouble?" *Bulletin of the Atomic Scientists* 53 (1997). 9 March 1999 http://web2.searchbank.com/itw/ses.../939/7999242w5/3.xrn_1_0_A19724413>.

Chichester-Constable, R.C.T. *Report On The Circumstances In Which Gas Casualties Were Incurred At Bari On 2/3 December 1943. Most Secret.* (Courtesy of John White).

China: Chemical Weapons Abandoned in China by a foreign state. 18 February 1992. 22 April 1999 <http://www.trillium.net/norenvironmental/cd1127.htm>.

Cocks, E.M. Somers. *Kia-Kaha: Life At 3 New Zealand General Hospital 1940-1946.* Christchurch, N.Z.: Caxton Press, 1958.

Collett, Bill. Letter to author. 9 July 1999.

"Colored Chemical Smokes Help in Identifying Japs." *Science News Letter* 11 August 1945: 88.

Colvin, James. "If the Axis Uses Gas." *Popular Mechanics* December 1943: 27-31+.

Coming Clean. 28 October 1998 <http://www.ornl.gov/ornl94/coming_clean.html>.

Commendatory Conduct of Armed Guard Unit Assigned to SS John Bascom - Report of. New Orleans: Armed Guard Center, 1 March 1944.

Committee On Veterans Affairs United States Senate. *Is Military Research Hazardous To Veterans Health? Lessons Spanning Half A Century.* Washington, D.C.: U.S. Government Printing Office, 8 December 1994.

Conard, B.A. *Summary of Statements by Survivors SS* Fort Lajoie, *7,134 G.T., British Ministry of War Transport.* Washington, D.C.: Navy Department Office Of The Chief Of Naval Operations, 26 April 1944. (Collection of John White, Jr.).

- - -. *Summary of Statements by Survivors SS* Samuel J. Tilden, *U.S. Cargo Ship.* Washington, D.C.: Navy Department Office Of The Chief Of Naval Operations, 18 January 1944.

Cooke, Robert. "U.S. Goes Far to Destroy Nerve Gas." *Newsday* 22 July 1990.

Cousins, Norman. "The Poison Gas Boys." *The Saturday Review* 22 January 1944: 12.

Dahlstrom, Carl P.R. *United States Coast Guard Report On U.S. Merchant Vessel War Action Casualty.* 30 October 1944.

"A Deadly Catch." 1 July 1998 <http://archive.abcnews.com/sections/us/gulfwartimeline2/index.html>.

Deal, Carl H. *United States Coast Guard Report On U.S. Merchant Vessel War Action Casualty.* 28 October 1944.

Defense Manpower Data Center. *Listing of Personnel Present in Harbor at Bari, Italy on December 2, 1943.* 14 February 1996.

Deist, Wilhelm ed., *The German Military in the Age of Total War.* Leamington Spa, Warwickshire, UK: Berg Publishers, 1985.

"Disaster at Bari." *Time* 27 December 1943: 27.

Donnelly, Robert F. *SS Samuel J. Tilden — Loss of.* Washington, D.C.: War Shipping Administration Training Organization, 2 February 1944.

Doolittle, James H. *I Could Never Be So Lucky Again: an autobiography.* New York, NY: Bantam Books, 1991.

Dorsey, Gene. Letter to author. 5 October 1998.

Eldredge, Walter J. "Firing smoke and conventional shells, the 4.2 inch chemical mortar earned respect on the battlefield." *World War II* February 1999: 8+.

Eisenhower, Dwight D. *Crusade In Europe.* New York: Doubleday & Co., Inc., 1948.

Fair, Stanley D. "Mussolini's Chemical War." *Army* 35 (1985): 44-53.

Fievet, John P. "World War II's Secret Disaster." *American History* August 1994: 24+.

Form M.E. 17 (British Hospital Evacuation Card) For George Baist. 12 December 1943.

Forwood, Jill. "Night nearly 1,000 men died." *South Wales Evening Post* 11 November 1998:12. (Courtesy of George Southern).

Freeman, Karen. "The 'Man-Break' Tests." *Bulletin of the Atomic Scientists* 49 (1993): 39.

Fries, Amos A. and Clarence J. West. *Chemical Warfare.* New York: McGraw Hill, 1921.

Fulton, Robert G., *Summary of Statements by Survivors of the SS Fort Athabasca, British Freighter, 7132 G.T., Ministry of War Transport.* Washington, D.C.: Navy Department Office Of The Chief Of Naval Operations. 28 February 1944. (Courtesy of John White, Jr.).

- - -. *Summary of Statements by Survivors of the M.V.* Devon Coast, *British Tanker, 646 G.T., Ministry of War Transport.* Ibid. (Courtesy of John White, Jr.).

- - -. *Summary of Statements by Survivors of the SS* Testbank, *British Freighter, 5,038 G.T.,* Ibid. (Courtesy of John White, Jr.).

Garnett, Richard A. "Restraint in Warfare: Strategic Bombing and Chemical Warfare During the World Wars." Diss. University of North Carolina, 1993.

"Gas Attacks Anticipated: Soldiers were equipped with the latest type of gas masks, protective coverings. Protective ointment and special eyeshields." *Science News Letter* 6 October 1945: 215.

"Gas Casualties in the First world War." *The Spartacus International Internet Encyclopedia of the First World War.* 1 July 1998 <http://www.spartacus.schoolnet.co.uk/FWWgasdeaths.htm>.

"Gas Tested On Troops." *CP/Toronto Sun* 17 December 1997. 28 October 1998 <http://www.ccnet.com/~suntzu75/news_archives/mil97231.htm>.

"Gas warfare's ominous comeback." *U.S. News & World Report* 19 March 1984: 11.

Gleichauf, Justin F. *Unsung Sailors: The Naval Armed Guard in World War II.* Annapolis, MD: Naval Institute Pr., 1990.

- - -. "Navy Armed Guard: Unsung Heroes." *American Legion Magazine* April 1986.

Glenton, George. *No Safe Haven.* Ringwood, Hampshire: Navigator Books, 1995.

Glinnie, J.S. "Medical History Card - Brandenstein, Warren Adolph." 3 December 1943.

Goodhue, John M. Jr., Letter to author. 18 January 1999.
Gritton, Don Jr., Email letter to author. 21 October 1998.
- - -. Telephone interview. 3 April 1999.
"Gunner Lauds Ensign's Courage At Bari, Italy, 'Pearl Harbor.'"*Associated Press* 29 January 1944.
Hansen, Juel Jr. *My Lifestory Volume I.* Bowie, MD., [n.d.].
- - -. Photographs, 1943. (Courtesy of Juel Hansen, Jr.).
Harper, Thomas Edward. *SS John Motley — Disaster Report of.* 29 March 1944.
Harris, Robert and Jeremy Paxman. *A Higher Form of Killing.* New York: Hill and Wang, 1982.
Hays, W.R. *Anti-Aircraft action against the enemy - Report of.* AOG 14/A16-3, (Serial:87) 5 December 1943.
- - -. *Summary of Anti-Aircraft action against enemy, and recommendation for suitable awards to officer and men for outstanding performance of duty during such actions.* AOG 14/A16-3/P15 (Serial: 88) 5 December 1943.
Heinse, Leroy C. *SS John Bascom — Loss of,* 17 March 1944.
- - -. "Hell and Back." *Patriots and Heroes.* Comp. Gerald Reminick. Palo Alto, California: Glencannon Press, 2000.
Heitmann, O. *Statement Of Master Of SS John Bascom.* [n.d.].
Helberger, Harvey. *Bari.* Videotape.[n.d.].
Hinsley, F.H., et al. *British Intelligence in the Second World War: Its Influence on Strategy and Operations. Vol. 3 Part 2.* New York: Cambridge U., 1988.
Hogendoorn, E.J. "A Chemical Weapons Atlas." *The Bulletin of the Atomic Scientists* 53 (1997). 9 March 1999 <http://www.bullatomsci.org/issues/1997/so97hogendoorn.html>.
Horodysky, Dan and Toni. "U.S. Merchant Marine In World War II: Casualties." 5 March 2001 <http.//usmm.org/ww2.html>.
Iavarone, Mike. *Trenches on the Web - Armory: Gas Warfare.* 28 October 1998 <http://worldwar1.com/arm006.htm>.
Infield, Glenn B. "America's Secret Poison Gas Tragedy." *True* July 1961: 27, 98-101.
- - -. *Disaster At Bari.* New York: The Macmillan Company, 1971.

"IOM Encounters Poison — Gas Curtain." *Science* 258 (1993): 167.

Jackson, W.G.I. *The Battle For Italy.* New York: Harper & Row Publishers, 1967.

James, Jules. *SS Lyman Abbott - Enemy Attack on.* 5 April 1944.

Jenkins, Laura. "My Husband Was A Guinea Pig For The U.S. Government." *Good Housekeeping* April 1994: 105.

Karig, Walter. *Battle Report: The Atlantic War.* New York: Rinehart & Company Inc., 1946.

Kilgore, Floyd V. *Letter Order To Mdspmn George H. Baist. Headquarters 26th General Hospital U.S. Army.* 14 January 1944.

Kindley, Ernest K. "War Tides: Thoughts on the Use of Gas in Warfare." *Newsweek* 20 December 1943:24.

Kleber, Brooks E. and Dale Birdsell. *The United States Army In World War II The Technical Services: The Chemical Warfare Services: Chemicals In Combat.* Washington, D.C.: Office Of The Chief Of Military History United States Army, 1966.

Krause, Joachim and Charles K. Mallory. *Chemical Weapons in Soviet Military doctrine: Military and Historical Experience, 1915-1991.* Boulder, CO: Westview Pr., 1992.

Krause, Leo L. Letter to author. 11 November 1998.

Kreimer, William A. *SS John Bascom — Disaster report of.* New Orleans, Armed Guard Center, 22 March 1944.

Kuhn, Eugene J. *Report of Bombing Attack at Bari, Italy, on 2 December, 1943.* 6 December 1943.

Land, Emory Scott. *The United States Merchant Marine At War: Report of the War Shipping Administration to the President.* Washington, D.C.: 15 January 1946.

Lane, Earl. "Mustard Gas Exposure Panel: Thousands suffer from secret WW II tests." *Newsday* 7 January 1993.

Laurin, Frederik. "Scandinavia's Underwater Time Bomb." *The Bulletin of the Atomic Scientists* March 1991.

Lee, Cynthia. *Bad nerves: Is the Army ready to get rid of its chemical weapons?* 28 October 1998 <http://bsd.mojones.com/MOTHER_JONES/MA96/lee.html>.

Lehman, Harry O. Letter to John White, Jr., 24 March 1993. (Collection of John White, Jr.).

Lienhard, John H. "Engines of Our Ingenuity: Episode No. 1190: Mustard Gas." 7 September 1998 <http://www.uh.edu/ admin/engines/epil1190.htm>.

Life At The Arsenal. http://www.cbdcom.apgea.army.mil/RDA/ enterprise/history/life.html (1 July 1998).

Lindley, Ernest K. "Thoughts on the Use of gas in Warfare." *Newsweek* 20 December 1943: 24.

Lippert, Charles P., Jr., *Voyage Report — SS Grace Abbott.* 3 January 1944.

"Little Pearl Harbor." *Newsweek* 27 December 1943:26.

Lloyd, Charles A. *The Liberty Ships Of World War Two.* Raleigh, NC: USN Armed Guard WW II Veterans, 1988.

- - -. "U.S. Navy Armed Guard WWI and WW II." *USN Armed Guard WW II Veterans Newsletter,* [n.d.].

Loucks, Charles E. *Addendum to the History of Captured Enemy Toxic Munitions in the American Zone European Command June 1947 to August 1948 Inclusive. (Concluding Phase).* Office Of The Chief, Chemical Division Headquarters European Command, January 1949.

Love, Dave. *Trenches on the Web - Special: The Second battle of Ypres, April- 1915.* 28 October 1998 <http://worldwar1.com/ sf2ypres.htm>.

Mahar, Ted. "Bombed U.S. ship scene of WW II's only gas attack." *The Oregonian, 1971.*

Margry, Karel. "Mustard Disaster At Bari." *After The Battle* No.79 1993: 34-47.

Marshall, Jim. "We Are Ready With Gas." *Colliers* 7 August 1943: 21+.

Maury, George W. Letter to author. 4 October 1998.

McAnulty, Bette. Letter to author. 7 June 1999.

Meissner, Donald K. "The Disaster At Bari." Thomas Bowerman. WW II Navy Armed Guard Veterans Association.13 March 1999 <http://www.armed-guard.com/>.

"The Merchant Marine Pearl Harbor." *American Merchant Marine Veterans Emerald Sea Chapter Newsletter.* Vol. 4. February 1993.

Military Intelligence Division. *Enemy Tactics in Chemical Warfare: Special Series No. 24.* Washington, D.C.: War Department, September 1944.

Military Intelligence Service of the U.S. War Dept., General Staff. *Enemy Capabilities For Chemical Warfare.* 15 July 1943.

Mitretek Systems. "Ocean Dumping of Chemical Weapons: Bari Harbor and the Adriatic." 6 October 1999 <http://www.mitretek.org/mission/envene/chemical/history/UNDERWTR.html >.

Moore, Arthur R. *A Careless Word ... A Needless Sinking.* Kings Point, N.Y.: American Merchant Marine Museum at the U.S. Merchant Marine Academy, 1990.

- - -. Telephone interview. 15 June 1999.

"More on Poison Gas." *The Saturday Review* 19 February 1944: 16-17.

Morison, Samuel Eliot. *History Of United States Naval Operations In World War II. Vol. 9. Sicily-Salerno-Anzio.* Boston: Little, Brown And Company, 1968.

"Mother Seeks Identification." (Photograph) *Boston Daily Post* 26 July 1945.

Mowery, Edward J. "Yank Tells How Nazis Caught Bari Like A Duck." *World Telegram* [n.d.]. (Collection of Warren A. Brandenstein).

Muller, Rolf-Dieter. *World Power Status through the Use of Poison Gas? German Preparations for Chemical Warfare 1919-45.* Warwickshire, England: Berg, 1985.

Navy Department Intelligence Report Enemy Attacks On Merchant Ships. Washington D.C.: Office of Naval Intelligence. 8 February 1944.

Nicholls, Frank. Letter to author. 10 October 1998.

Oliver, Joseph. Letter to author. 4 February 1998.

Ochsner, Herman. *History of German Chemical Warfare in World War II. Part I : The Military Aspect.* USAREUR Foreign Military Study P-004, 1948.

Patterson, Vince. Letter to author. 7 January 1998.

Paulding, C.G. "Poison Gas." *Commonweal* 22 June 1945: 229.

Pechura, Constance M. "The Health effects of mustard gas and Lewisite." *JAMA* 269 (1993): 453.

- - -, and David P. Rall, eds. *Veterans at Risk: The Health Effects of Mustard Gas and Lewisite.* Washington, D.C.: National Academy Press, 1993.

Pellegrini, Anthony. Letter to John White, Jr. 9 May 1993. (Collection of John White, Jr.).

Perera, Judith and Andy Thomas. "Britain's victims of mustard-gas disaster." *New Scientist* 30 January 1986: 26-27.

Pitittieri, Samuel J. "How My Trip To Bari, Italy Started." 21 June 1998.

Porter, William N. "Watch Out Smoke." *Saturday Evening Post* 20 November 1943: 24-25+.

Prazenica, Andrew L. Letter to author. 2 October 2000.

Program Executive Officer — Program Manager For Chemical Demilitarization. *Chemical Stockpile Disposal: Chemical Weapons Movement History Compilation.* Aberdeen Proving Ground, MD. 12 June 19[sic]7. (Courtesy of Edward A. Aho).

Queen, D.B. Letter to author. 15 November 1998.

Quesinberry, Don. "Battle of the Atlantic," *The Pointer* April-June 1998: 11.

Reminick, Gerald. *Patriots and Heroes: True Stories of the U.S. Merchant Marine in World War II.* Palo Alto, Ca.: The Glencannon Press, 2000.

Riesenberg, Felix, Jr., *Sea War: The Story Of The U.S. Merchant Marine In World War II.* New York: Rinehart & Co., 1956.

Rich, Norman. *Hitler's War Aims: The Establishment Of The New Order Vol. II.* New York: W.W. Norton & Company, Inc., 1974.

Roark, James. Letter to author. 27 March 1998.

Robb, Russell and Paul V. Graham. *Section Three: Between the Wars*. 18 February 1998 <http://www.sanctum.com/realty/remax/hd/between.html>.

Roosevelt, Franklin D. "Roosevelt Warns Axis on Gas Warfare." (American War Documents) *Current History* August 1943: 405.

Ruberry, William. "Agency's action too late to help area veteran." *Times-Despatch* 14 March 1993. (Courtesy of Warren Brandenstein).

- - -. "Nation races time to right old wrong: Hunt on for veterans exposed to poison gas." *Richmond Times* 14 February 1993: 1. (Courtesy of Warren Brandenstein).

Saunders, D.M. "The Bari Incident." *United States Naval Institute Proceedings* 93:9 (1967): 35-39.

Selassie, Haile. *Appeal To The League of Nations*. 30 June 1936. 11 November 1998 <http://www.boomshaka.com/HIM/league.html>.

Schober, Theodore. Letter to Arthur Moore. 7 July 1988. (Courtesy of Mrs. Rosalie Schober).

Scott, Eugene W. "Role of the Public Health Laboratory in Gas Defense." *American Journal of Public Health* 34 (1944): 275-8.

Shcherbakova, Anna. "Poisonous bomb: 40,000 Tons of Toxins are stored on Russian territory."

Green Cross Russia 20 May 1997. 28 October 1998 <http://www4.gve.ch/gci/GreenCrossPrograns/legacy/articles/poisonous.html>.

"Should the U.S. Use Gas?" *Time* 3 January 1944: 15.

Sivo, Donato. Email to author. 12 October 1999.

Slader, John. *The Fourth Service: Merchantmen at War 1939-1945*. London: Robert Hale, 1994.

Smart, Jeffrey K. *From Plowshare To Sword: Historical Highlights Of Gunpowder Neck And Edgewater Arsenal To The End Of World War I*. 1 July 1998 <http://www.cbdcom.apgea.army.mil/RDA/enterprise/history/intro.html>.

Smith, James E. *Remembrances 1942 - 1946.* 26 June 1991.

Snyder, Louis. "World War II: U.S. War Effort." *Academic American Encyclopedia,* 1990 ed.

Southern, George. Letter to author. 20 January 1999.

- - -. Letter to author. 11 January 1999.

- - -. Letter to author. 4 December 1998.

- - -. "They Need Never Know." 4 December 1998.

Spiers, Edward M. *Chemical Warfare.* Chicago: U. of Illinois Pr., 1986.

St. John, Adrian. "Chemical Warfare in the European Theater of Operations." *Military Review* 24 (December 1944): 57-65.

Summary of Statements by Survivors of the SS John Bascom. Washington, D.C.: Navy Department Office of the Chief of Naval Operations, 28 February 1944.

Swillinger, Ralph. Letter to author. 24 April 1998.

Toler, T.I. "Poison Gas manufacture in the UK." *After the Battle* No. 79 (1993): 12-33.

Toro, Taryn. "Baltic bombs surface in fishing nets." *New Scientist* 3 August 1991.

United States. Air Force. Office of Air Force History. *The Army Air Forces In World War II. Volume Two. Europe: Torch To Point Blank, August 1942 To December 1943.* Washington, D.C. 1948.

- - -. *The Army Air Forces In World War II. Volume Three. Europe: Argument To V-E day, January 1944 To May 1945.* Washington, D.C.: 1983.

United States Coast Guard. *Report On U.S. Merchant Vessel* War *Action Casualties -S/S John L. Motley.* 31 October 1944.

- - -. *S.S. John Harvey.* 28 October 1944.

- - -. *S.S. Joseph Wheeler.* 28 October 1944.

U.S. Department of Commerce. Maritime Administration. *The United States Merchant Marine: A Brief History.* Washington, D.C.: 1972.

U.S. Department of Health and Human Services Public Heath Service Agency for Toxic Substances and Disease Registry. *Mustard Gas.* 28 October 1998 <http:// atsdr1.atsdr.cdc.gov:8080/tfacts49.html>.

U.S. War Department Military Intelligence Service. *Enemy Capabilities for Chemical Warfare.* Special Series No. 16, 15 July 1943.

USS Aroostock: Report of Anti-Aircraft Action Against The Enemy. 5 December 1943.

Upson, D.E. *Recommendations for Commendation of Enlisted Personnel* 25 November 1943. (Courtesy of Bernard L. Anderson).

"The VA's Sorry, The Army's Silent." *Bulletin of the Atomic Scientists* (March-April 1993).

Waitt, Alden H. "Why Germany Didn't Try Gas." *Saturday Evening Post* 9 March 1946: 17+.

War Shipping Administration Training Organization. *File on Loss of S.S. John Harvey.* Report No. 424. (Washington, D.C.: 10 January 1944).

Waters, William Walter. Letter to author. 10 November 1998.

"Weapons: Into the Night." *Time* 14 January 1946.

"Weed-Killing Aids War." *Science News Letter* 21 April 1945: 250.

"What Total War Might Have Been Like." *Science Digest* November 1946: 66.

White, John J. Jr., *The Last Two years 1942-1943, John J. White, Commander, United States Maritime Service 7 December 1941 - 2 December 1943.* District Heights, MD: 1993.

- - -. Letter to author. 4 January 1999.

Whitley, John F. "Our Trip To Bari, Italy." 20 November 1998.

Willig, John. Letter to author. 3 October 1998.

Wilmot, Chester. *The Struggle For Europe.* New York: Harper Publishers, 1952.

Wisniewski, Stanley A. Letter to author. 25 November 1998.

"World War II Navy guinea pig dark secret for nearly 50 years even from wife." *Houston Chronicle* 16 January 1998. 28 October 1998 <http://www.chron.com/cgi-bin/auth/...olitan/98/02/01/guineapig.2-0.html>.

"WW1, 1914-18, Mustard Gas Poisoning." 18 February 1998 <http://www.ourworld.compuserve.com/homepages/kylet1/gas.htm>.

Wood, John R. "Chemical Warfare — A Chemical and Toxicological Review." *American Journal of Public Health* 34 (1944): 455-60.

Woodward, H.M., Jr., *The History of Captured Enemy Toxic Munitions in the American Zone European Theater May 1945 to June 1947.* Office Of The Chief Chemical Corps. Headquarters European Command, 1947.

Ziroli, H.W. *U.S. Naval Personnel Casualties from Action at Bari, Italy, 2 December 1943.* 22 December 1943. (Courtesy of John White, Jr.).

Index